The Graduate Career Guidebook

Macmillan Study Skills

Academic Success
Academic Writing Skills for International Students
The Business Student's Phrase Book
Cite Them Right (11th edn)
Critical Thinking and Persuasive Writing for
    Postgraduates
Critical Thinking Skills (3rd edn)
Dissertations and Project Reports
Doing Projects and Reports in Engineering
The Employability Journal
Essentials of Essay Writing
The Exam Skills Handbook (2nd edn)
Get Sorted
Great Ways to Learn Anatomy and Physiology
    (2nd edn)
How to Begin Studying English Literature (4th edn)
How to Use Your Reading in Your Essays (3rd edn)
How to Write Better Essays (4th edn)
How to Write Your Undergraduate Dissertation
    (3rd edn)
Improve Your Grammar (2nd edn)
The Mature Student's Handbook
Mindfulness for Students
The Macmillan Student Planner
Presentation Skills for Students (3rd edn)
The Principles of Writing in Psychology
Professional Writing (3rd edn)
Skills for Success (3rd edn)
Stand Out from the Crowd
The Student Phrase Book
The Student's Guide to Writing (3rd edn)
Study Skills Connected
The Study Skills Handbook (5th edn)
Study Skills for International Postgraduates
Studying in English
Studying History (4th edn)
Studying Law (4th edn)
Studying Physics
The Study Success Journal
Success in Academic Writing (2nd edn)
Smart Thinking
Teaching Study Skills and Supporting Learning
The Undergraduate Research Handbook (2nd edn)
The Work-Based Learning Student Handbook (2nd edn)
Writing for Engineers (4th edn)
Writing History Essays (2nd edn)
Writing for Law
Writing for Nursing and Midwifery Students (3rd edn)
Write it Right (2nd edn)
Writing for Science Students
Writing Skills for Education Students
You2Uni: Decide, Prepare, Apply

Pocket Study Skills

14 Days to Exam Success (2nd edn)
Analyzing a Case Study
Blogs, Wikis, Podcasts and More
Brilliant Writing Tips for Students
Completing Your PhD
Doing Research (2nd edn)
Getting Critical (2nd edn)
Managing Stress
Planning Your Dissertation (2nd edn)
Planning Your Essay (2nd edn)
Planning Your PhD
Posters and Presentations
Reading and Making Notes (2nd edn)
Referencing and Understanding Plagiarism
    (2nd edn)
Reflective Writing
Report Writing (2nd edn)
Science Study Skills
Studying with Dyslexia (2nd edn)
Success in Groupwork
Successful Applications
Time Management
Where's Your Argument?
Writing for University (2nd edn)

Research Skills

Authoring a PhD
The Foundations of Research (3rd edn)
Getting to Grips with Doctoral Research
Getting Published
The Good Supervisor (2nd edn)
The Lean PhD
PhD by Published Work
The PhD Viva
The PhD Writing Handbook
Planning Your Postgraduate Research
The Postgraduate Research Handbook
    (2nd edn)
The Professional Doctorate
Structuring Your Research Thesis

Career Skills

Excel at Graduate Interviews
Graduate CVs and Covering Letters
Graduate Entrepreneurship
How to Succeed at Assessment Centres
Social Media for Your Student and Graduate
    Job Search
The Graduate Career Guidebook (2nd edn)
Work Experience, Placements and Internships

For a complete listing of all our titles in this area please visit **www.macmillanihe.com/study-skills**

THE GRADUATE CAREER GUIDEBOOK

2ND EDITION

STEVE ROOK

macmillan
international
HIGHER EDUCATION

RED GLOBE
PRESS

This edition published 2019 by
RED GLOBE PRESS

Previous edition published 2013 under the imprint PALGRAVE

Red Globe Press in the UK is an imprint of Springer Nature Limited, registered in England, company number 785998, of 4 Crinan Street, London, N1 9XW.

Red Globe Press® is a registered trademark in the United States, the United Kingdom, Europe and other countries.

ISBN 978–1–352–00516–5 paperback

This book is printed on paper suitable for recycling and made from fully managed and sustained forest sources. Logging, pulping and manufacturing processes are expected to conform to the environmental regulations of the country of origin.

A catalogue record for this book is available from the British Library.

A catalog record for this book is available from the Library of Congress.

Brief contents

Contents

Contents

Contents

Contents

Contents

Preface

I have written this guide because I am passionate about helping people find fulfilling careers. This is because I faced a massive struggle to get my own career going and I want to pass on what I've learned along the way.

I found it almost impossible to get started because I got a third-class degree during a recession and had no idea what career planning involved (or anything else for that matter!). Consequently, I decided to apply for a hundred jobs. I received 50 rejections and the rest didn't even respond!

Therefore, I drifted around the world for many years and only started to appreciate how I could turn my career around in my mid-thirties. A light suddenly went on in my head and I realised that, instead of just looking for jobs, I should focus more on what I wanted to do in life and carefully plan my journey. Since then I have emigrated to Australia, worked as a primary school teacher, run my own recruitment company, counselled numerous students as a university careers adviser and now write books.

In recent years I have come to see life as one big opportunity where anything is possible, and I want to pass on this confidence to my readers. I sincerely hope you are able to successfully navigate your way through my guide and find a successful path in life. Please feel free to contact me on steventhomasrook@yahoo.co.uk for any reason at all.

Steve Rook

Acknowledgements

A great number of people have made it possible for me to write this guide and I want to say thanks.

My mother ensured that I gained a sound education in difficult circumstances and my sister Caroline has recently given me the support and guidance that I have needed to realise my writing ambitions.

The careers advisers in Perth, particularly Marilyn Prestage, helped me get into the careers field and Ann Collins at Southampton gave me my first opportunity. Since then, I have also been lucky enough to have worked with some incredibly dedicated and proficient colleagues in the field, especially Ann Berry and Catherine Gregory who have continued to provide support and encouragement.

My GP, Dr Paul Culliney, and Sharon Brooks at the Sheffield Asperger Syndrome Service have recently given me the wonderful opportunity to find peace and contentment for the first time ever as an autistic person.

However, greatest thanks must go to the two Suzies in my life and the whole team at Red Globe Press. Suzannah Burywood kept an open mind about my proposals, welcomed me into the fold and patiently helped me put the book together, whilst my wife Susan and her family encouraged me, supported me and gave me the confidence to help thousands of students and graduates who currently face such a daunting journey in life.

Publisher acknowledgements

The author and publishers wish to thank the following for permission to reproduce copyright material:

Prospects, for the data in the tables 'What graduates did in 2017' and 'Type of work for those in employment 2013 and 2017', from *What do graduates do? 2018/19*.

The Institute of Student Employers (ISE), for the data in the table 'Regional breakdown of vacancies in 2017', from the organisation's *Recruitment Survey 2018*. Further information about the ISE is available at https://ise.org.uk/.

Taylor and Francis, for permission to adapt the table entitled 'The USEM account of employability' from *Learning, Curriculum & Employability in Higher Education* by Peter Knight and Mantz Yorke (London: Routledge, 2003).

Steve Rook, *Work Experience, Placements and Internships*, 2016, Red Globe Press, reproduced with permission of Springer Nature Ltd.

The Noun Project (www.thenounproject.com) for 'Globe' icon by Thuy Nguyen, p. 120.

Introduction
Help! Where do I start?

> 'Begin at the beginning,' the King said, very gravely, 'and go on till you come to the end: then stop.'
>
> *Lewis Carroll*

So, what now?

Finding a fulfilling and successful graduate career can be daunting because there are so many directions to take and factors to consider. Nevertheless, you shouldn't be overwhelmed. Once you work out a plan and take your first steps, things usually take care of themselves. Sure, from time to time, you'll pick the wrong options and go down a few blind alleys but, if you use every experience as a chance to learn a little more about yourself and the career you want to enter, you should be alright. Above all, stay positive and open to new ideas. Your determination will be rewarded!

What 'career' means to you

Careers encompass so much more than just finding a job and clocking on for the next fifty years, because everyone has their own unique opportunities, attributes and priorities. Therefore, in order to find fulfilment in your own journey in life, you first need to ask yourself what will make you happy?

Explore what will make a career fulfilling for you in the two-minute test shown below, by reflecting on how you personally differentiate 'careers' from 'jobs'.

Two-minute test: The difference between careers and jobs

Take two minutes to list five things that you think differentiate 'careers' from 'jobs'.

Careers are...

-
-
-
-
-

Reflecting on your answers: People usually see careers as being more long-term than jobs and linked to abilities, aspirations and interests. If you struggled to narrow down what it means to you, just close your eyes and envision where you want to be at the highest point in your life journey.

Are you sitting comfortably?

Once you've identified some things that are important to you in your career, you're ready to start making them happen, but first, prepare yourself for the road ahead. Make sure you're in a safe, comfortable environment and ready to face the inevitable challenges. Avoid putting yourself under too much pressure and ...

- Think of a strategy (read through the following pages).
- Research a wide range of roles. You don't want to miss your perfect career just because you've never heard of it!
- Find a role that makes you excited – you will have a much greater chance of success.
- Ensure that you can support yourself financially while you plan your next steps (you may have to get a part-time or temporary job).
- Get support from friends and family.

Then let's begin

This guidebook systematically divides the career planning process into seven discrete sections to help you take control of your next steps in life, as follows:

Part I – Careers in a complex world: An outline of who employs graduates, employability and managing the career planning process.

Part II – Finding your niche: Identifying and assessing all your career options and making a choice.

Part III – Upping your game: Boosting your employability and planning your next steps.

Part IV – Making it happen: Managing each step of your route into work including experience, internships, networking, and time out.

Part V– Finding a job: Finding vacancies and succeeding at every stage of the application process.

Part VI – An introduction to self-employment: A brief outline of self-employment with chapters on becoming an entrepreneur and setting up your own business.

Part VII – Down the line: Moving your career forward, changing direction, keeping your eyes open and answers to some frequently asked questions.

You can either follow these discrete, manageable steps from start to finish or dip into them according to your needs. If you're not sure where to start, just turn to the opening chapter and take it from there. Hopefully, before long you'll feel more positive and in control of your own career journey.

Why a book is best

The book is dead – long live the book!

All new inventions supposedly herald the death of old technologies but this book perfectly dovetails with its younger and newer competitors. The key benefits of this resource are:

- You can rely on its quality, authority and advice.
- It has room for numerous examples and exercises.
- The contents focus on every sector, not just the blue-chip employers.
- It provides practical personal guidance as well as information and advice.
- Its uniform structure easily enables quick reference across a broad range of topics.
- It builds up knowledge in a logical, cumulative way.
- It can be used as a universal directory of useful websites and social networks at a time when the World Wide Web is buckling under the weight of resources of varying quality.

Using this book

You may want to tell the world you're researching your career and bring this book out at every opportunity or just sit with it in silence in your bedroom and take it all in. However, whatever you do, make sure you engage with the self-assessment exercises, as the secret to career planning is to make it personal and get away from all the platitudes and jargon that prevail in this area. Also, don't use the book as your only source of research: speak to your family, friends, contacts, academics and, especially, your careers centre. Some of the services they generally offer are:

- Careers advice and guidance on every chapter of this book, and more.
- Employer events.
- Workshops on topics such as CVs and interviews.
- Networking opportunities.
- Job postings.
- Volunteering opportunities.
- Warm rooms out of the rain.

The companion website

This guide also comes with a companion website, available at www.macmillanihe.com/rook-gcg-2e. On this site, you'll find a wide range of additional material.

Extra resources for students

- A selection of the exercises provided in the book.
- Extra examples, case studies, CVs and much more.
- Video advice.
- Extra links to even more online resources.

Extra resources for academics/careers advisers

- Advice on effective teaching and learning in this area.
- PowerPoint presentations for each topic.
- An outline of engaging class activities.
- Assessment suggestions.
- Marking grids for assessments.

Help from the author

For students/graduates

If you have any questions, please don't hesitate to get in touch (steventhomasrook@yahoo.co.uk). I am more than happy to help you explore any career related issue.

❝ If you need help on any issue, please contact the author at steventhomasrook@yahoo.co.uk. ❞

For academics/careers advisers

I often tour the UK delivering enthusiastic and engaging workshops for students on all employability issues. If you have any questions, or you would like me to come in and speak directly to your students, please feel free to contact me on steventhomasrook@yahoo.co.uk.

All that's left to say now is 'Good luck and enjoy the journey!'

PART I

CAREERS IN A COMPLEX WORLD

This section prepares you for your career journey by outlining what employers are after and how you can make yourself employable and plan a successful career.

CHAPTER 1
Graduate employment and recruitment

A world of opportunity, but you have to grab it!

Contents

New horizons

Each year, the graduate employment market grows from strength to strength. Today, there are more opportunities than ever before, an ever-increasing diversity of roles, more flexible points of entry and fairer access. So, despite the increasing costs of degrees and the massive growth in student numbers, the benefits of a Higher Education qualification still remain undimmed and future prospects look rosy.

Nonetheless, there's a catch. These new freedoms and opportunities also mean that a degree alone is no longer all you need to kick-start your career. You also need to make the most of your time at university by:

(a) Securing the best possible grades.
(b) Planning what to do when you leave.
(c) Developing appropriate skills and contacts.

This chapter explores today's graduate employment and recruitment markets in more depth so you can take control.

A story of growth

Student and graduate numbers

The HE sector has grown beyond all recognition since the early 1960s. Numerous new universities have opened their doors; a vast array of courses has blossomed into almost every possible academic area; and student numbers have risen exponentially. At the dawn of that decade, there were fewer than 50 universities and only 22,400 students graduated per year. Unbelievably, there are now 162 institutions and, wait for it … 1.75 million undergraduates![1] This incredible growth has largely been because vacancies in all sectors have increasingly required an ever-growing range of transferable and technical skills. However, this doesn't mean that jobs are harder to come by.

> **ᏝᏝ** The HE sector has grown beyond all recognition since the early 1960s. **ᎫᎫ**

Graduate vacancies

The good news is that, just as student numbers have massively expanded over recent years, so have graduate vacancies. However, the 'traditional'/ specialist vacancies that have always targeted graduates have hardly grown at all. A whole raft of fresh opportunities has arisen. For example, whereas sixty years ago, law graduates would have almost certainly become solicitors or barristers, they can now move into any number of legal roles such as legal executive, licensed conveyancer, paralegal, barrister's clerk, legal secretary, company secretary, legal publisher, patent attorney, trade mark attorney and CPS caseworker.

> **ᏝᏝ** The good news is that, just as student numbers have massively expanded over recent years, so have graduate vacancies. **ᎫᎫ**

Elias and Purcell[2] categorised these fresh graduate roles into three new categories:

1 **New roles:** Occupations that have:
    (a) Recently become more 'professional' because they require greater technical skills.
    (b) Seen an increasing influx of graduates with relevant skills.

    Examples include marketing and sales positions, management accountants and therapists.
2 **Niche roles:** Jobs that necessitate a high level of expertise and the ability to manage within employment sectors that do not generally require graduates. For example, agricultural consultants, detectives and graphic designers.
3 **Modern roles:** Professions that have increasingly required a degree. For example, managers, software engineers, primary school teachers, journalists and counsellors.

What graduates do

According to the publication 'What Graduates Do', compiled by the Higher Education Careers Services Unit (HECSU), university leavers took the paths shown in the table below in 2017 (six months after graduating). These figures are roughly the same every year, and although they are very broad-brush, it is clear that most people get out there and find something positive. In fact, this document also contends that 71.4% of employed graduates (roughly 50% of the full total) had already found 'professional' roles by the half-yearly point after finishing their studies. However, figures like these are very open to interpretation and, if you're still working down the chip-shop a year down the line, and wondering what on earth to do now, do not fear, your degree can still take you places!

What graduates did in 2017

What graduates were doing	Percentage
Working full time in the UK	55.2%
Working part time in the UK	11.9%
Working overseas	1.8%
Working and studying	5.4%
Further study	16.1%
Unemployed and due to start work	5.1%
Other	4.5%

Source: HECSU: What do graduates do? 2017/18.[3]

A wider choice of roles

Depending on which study you read, between 50% and 70% of graduates end up in careers not directly related to their degrees. For example, a graduate in electrical and electronic (E&E) engineering could consider any of the following roles (and thousands more), although many of these roles will require further qualifications:

❝ Depending on which study you read, between 50% and 70% of graduates end up in careers not directly related to their careers. ❞

Careers in a complex world

Some career choices with an electrical/electronic engineering degree

Occupations directly related to an E&E degree	Occupations where the degree content would be useful	Other occupations where the skills gained would be useful
• Aerospace engineer • Broadcast engineer • Control and instrumentation engineer • Design engineer • Electrical engineer • Electronics engineer • Network engineer • Systems analyst	• Management consultant • IT consultant • Multimedia programmer • Project manager • Technical author • Technical sales engineer • Actuary • Patent attorney	• Accounting technician • Forensic accountant • Chartered certified accountant • Solicitor • Maintenance engineer • Doctor • Diagnostic radiographer • Radiation protection practitioner

Source: Graduate Prospects, Engineering Degree Occupational Profile[4]

Graduate choice has expanded so massively because employers are increasingly focusing on skills and grades rather than what graduates know. For example, two key skills for accountants are numerical ability and IT proficiency and these can be learned on any number of degree programmes, so entry to this occupation is incredibly diverse. Find out how to narrow down your options in Chapter 4.

How graduates are recruited

Once upon a time

For hundreds of years, graduate recruitment was based on who graduates knew and what they studied. There were so few students that recruiters tended to just reach out to HE contacts to find the best people. Students were almost universally young, white, male and drawn from the best-connected families and consequently, had no problems landing high-powered roles.

The times they are a changing

Of course, this ancient system of patronage still exists today, but a number of factors have quickly forced most employers to be more open:

- Society has increasingly demanded a more equitable approach.
- The massive growth in graduate numbers and vacancies requires more streamlined procedures.
- Students increasingly come from diverse backgrounds, making personal introductions less viable.
- Employers increasingly need to find people who can do the job, irrespective of what they've studied and who they know.

Today's focus on equality

Employers are increasingly taking care to design recruitment procedures that engender equality of opportunity, by:

(a) Drawing up clear, non-discriminatory, selection criteria for each new vacancy.
(b) Inviting candidates to prove their worth against these requirements through some sort of open application process.
(c) Choosing applicants who best match their stated needs.

This new approach gives every applicant a fair go, whatever their background, gender, race, age … etc.

The key selection criteria (your skills, commitment and knowledge)

The criteria that recruiters use to assess candidates (formally known as the 'selection criteria') tend to be connected to candidates' skills, commitment and knowledge, i.e. whether you can do the job, want to do it and know what's involved. These are the ingredients for success in any venture in life, as shown below in the triangle of success. You can find out how to promote yourself to employers in Chapter 13.

The triangle of success

Skills **Commitment**

Knowledge

The recruitment process

In the old days, graduates just sent their CVs to a few firms and crossed their fingers. This is still often the case for less professional roles and vacancies promoted by recruitment agencies but, nowadays, larger organisations often have mammoth application procedures which include the following steps:

1 Written/numerical reasoning tests and aptitude tests.
2 Application forms where you are expected to outline your skills, commitment and knowledge.
3 A first interview (often by telephone or Skype).
4 Assessment Centre exercises such as group tasks and presentations.
5 A second interview.

It's up to you to look into the usual procedures in your chosen field and prepare accordingly. Make sure you understand the ins and outs of each firm's recruitment process before starting each application.

When are people taken on?

Graduates are recruited year-round but there will be peaks and troughs in every sector, so research your chosen field as soon as possible. Most small and medium-sized businesses (SMEs) take on fresh talent as and when it is required throughout the year but many of the larger employers recruit between October and February for positions commencing the following summer, so start looking for these at the beginning of your final year. Of course, you may also be able to secure your graduate job much earlier than this if you have been working at a firm for a while or have impressed on a previous internship.

Graduates are still usually classed as 'new graduates' for two or three years after they have left university, but, make sure you can impress employers with what you've done during this time.

New graduate paths

Career journeys have also become far more flexible over recent years. Whereas there used to be one well-trodden route into each role, nowadays there are usually numerous paths to suit people from diverse backgrounds and/or situations. For example, until very recently, there was only one realistic way for graduates to get into teaching, namely a full-time Post Graduate Certificate in Education (PGCE), run by several universities. Now, you can still undertake this qualification in numerous institutions across the country but you can also:

- Undertake the PGCE course at a challenging school (School Direct).
- Train whilst teaching in a group of schools (School Centred Initial Teacher Training).
- Qualify as part of Teach First's Leadership Development Programme (see www.teachfirst.org.uk).
- Take an accelerated course (see www.getintoteaching.education.gov.uk).
- Study part-time (see www.getintoteaching.education.gov.uk).
- Find work as an unqualified teacher, perhaps at a private school or in a subject which is difficult to fill, and take the assessment-only route (see www.getintoteaching.education.gov.uk).
- Qualify overseas in certain countries and transfer your eligibility (quite a radical step!).

Unfortunately, many students and graduates never look into all their options and, consequently, never uncover all their possible options. Make sure this isn't you!

Longer graduate paths

Taking personal control

In the past, graduates tended to go straight into roles directly related to their studies and spent their whole careers at only one or two firms. This is no longer the case, as a greater spotlight is now placed on your skills (not just what you know), so you have to:

1 Choose an occupation to follow.
2 Plan your route.
3 Identify some first steps.
4 Research the skills you will need.
5 Develop those skills.
6 Promote those skills in targeted applications along with your commitment and knowledge.

You can find out more about planning your next steps in Part III.

The rise of internships

The major recruiters have traditionally hired a limited number of student interns for ten weeks or so, during their summer vacation, just before they headed back to university for their final year of study. While these original programmes still exist, you can also sign up for any number of other, less structured, programmes lasting anything from days to years. This expansion has occurred because:

- All work experience is increasingly being relabelled as 'internships'.
- Internships allow recruiters to appraise skills in real work situations, over extended periods of time.
- Skilled students and graduates are aplenty.
- Interns are cheap (and often free).

Therefore, internships are an increasingly important part of the skills mix for students, to the extent that many of the larger recruiters now recruit many, if not all, of their new graduate employees from their existing pool of interns! You can find out more about work experience and internships in Chapter 9.

Where graduates work

Which sector?

Graduates work in every sector but the proportion in each obviously changes each year according to demand and a host of other factors. The 2013 and 2017 destinations according to HECSU[5] are shown overleaf for comparison:

Type of work for those in employment 2013 and 2017

Sector	Proportion of graduates in 2013	Proportion of graduates in 2017
Arts, design and media professionals	5.8%	6.5%
Business, HR and finance professionals	9.1%	10.8%
Education professionals	6.3%	5.8%
Engineering and building professionals	4.5%	4.5%
Health professionals	14.3%	18.2%
Information technology professionals	4%	4.6%
Legal, social and welfare professionals	4.9%	5.1%
Managers	4.1%	3.9%
Marketing, PR and sales professionals	7.2%	7.7%
Science professionals	1.1%	1.1%
Other professionals, associate professionals/ technicians	4.9%	5.7%
Childcare, health and education occupations	5.7%	4.3%
Clerical, secretarial and numerical clerks	8.1%	5.6%
Retail, catering, waiting and bar staff	13%	10.4%

Source: Reproduced from What do graduates do? 2018/19 with permission from Prospects.

According to High Fliers,[6] the largest areas in the growth of graduate vacancies from 2007 to 2017, in the UK, were in the public sector (up 145%), IT and telecommunications (up 106%), retail (up 77%), consulting (up 39%) and accounting and professional services (up 9%). The biggest fallers were the media (down 53%), oil and energy (down 51%), investment banking (down 33%), law (down 23%) and the Armed Forces (down 23%).

These overall figures provide a useful, broad outline of future options and trends but, in order to gain a more in-depth understanding, you need to delve deeper into the specific roles. Resources are provided to help you research your options in Chapter 4.

Which employers?

The larger graduate recruiters feature heavily on campus but they only employ about 17,500 graduates per year (a tiny proportion of the total). The vast majority of graduates either find work in organisations with fewer than 250 employees (SMEs) or, increasingly, set up their own businesses (see Part VI).

Which region?

Students and graduates find work in every city and region across the country. Most of these roles will be in smaller or medium-sized businesses, either in 'graduate'/'professional' roles or otherwise. The regional breakdown for vacancies at the larger employers is outlined in the table here (compiled by the Institute of Student Employers).[7]

Regional breakdown of vacancies in 2017

Region	Percentage of vacancies
London	39%
South East	9%
West Midlands	8%
Rest of the World	7%
North West	6%
Yorkshire and Humberside	6%
South West	6%
Scotland	5%
East Midlands	5%
East of England	2%
North East	2%
Midlle East and Asia	1%
Europe	1%
Northern Ireland	1%
Wales	1%

Source: This data is reproduced with the permission of the Institute of Student Employers (ISE) from the organisation's Recruitment Survey 2018. Further information about the ISE is available at https://ise.org.uk/.

This table shows that major recruiters advertise vacancies all across the UK but there are massive regional variations in the actual number of jobs on offer. For example, there are very few jobs in some areas such as the North-East, Wales and Northern Ireland, and more in London than the rest of the country put together! Therefore, graduates clearly have to be flexible to chase vacancies, at least at the start of their careers. However, the picture is not so dire outside London and the South East as this table seems to imply, for two reasons:

(a) There is a much lower density of graduates outside the capital, so there is also less competition.
(b) The majority of graduates work for SMEs, which are more evenly spread across the country.

What you'll be paid

Having invested so much time and money in your degree, it's quite understandable that your future salary is uppermost on your mind. The media publish several statistics on earnings for new graduates: for example, as we head into the third decade of the new millennium, High Fliers quote an average figure in the early £30,000s. However, these raw numbers can be misleading for four reasons:

1   They tend to be weighted in favour of the salaries paid by larger recruiters (which are usually at the top end).
2   They don't tend to include the non-existing salaries of those graduates who are not working.
3   A mean measurement has limited value in a situation where salaries vary so wildly around the norm. For example, the most common starting salary for new workers could well be minimum wage! (Although this usually rises significantly over the following years.)
4   Wages clearly vary between industries and regions.

Are degrees still worth it?

This is another burning question. With the high levels of debt that modern degrees entail, you're bound to ask yourself whether it's all worth it. The answer is not so simple. On purely financial terms, degrees are still beneficial as graduates earn roughly £10,000 more per year (on average) than those with A Levels or equivalent.[8] Having said this, degrees are, of course, not just about the money. They also give you a wonderful opportunity to find out more about your favourite subject, broaden your experience, build lifelong friendships and have a lot of fun.

Future challenges and opportunities

The world is changing at a furious pace, especially in the area of employment and recruitment, for example:

● Jobs are becoming less secure.
● Wages for low-skilled (entry level) jobs have remained stunted over an unprecedented period.
● Internships tend to provide very low wages (or none at all) and are often based in the most expensive area of the country (London and the South East).
● Employers are providing fewer guaranteed hours (and zero-hours contracts) but you still have to clock on at the drop of a hat.
● An increasing number of people are technically classed as working for themselves within the 'gig' economy, but many of them are just working for unscrupulous employers who have abdicated their responsibilities to deliver decent pay and conditions.

You can mitigate these uncertainties through creativity, resourcefulness and resilience. For example, why not set up your own business? Get two jobs and volunteer in the evenings? Pursue new opportunities whilst you're still in your current job? Use your internships to network with all and sundry? Find ways to make yourself invaluable? See more about adjusting your career plans in Chapter 2.

Furthermore, artificial intelligence and robotics are quickly affecting, and even eradicating, a large proportion of current roles. The media often link these developments to mass unemployment, but this is near-sighted as previous industrial revolutions have created at least as many jobs as they have forestalled. However, there is bound to be some pain as the market adjusts. You can prepare for this shift by:

- Assessing how technology is going to impact the careers you're considering, and planning accordingly.
- Constantly developing your skills and knowledge for the upcoming requirements in your chosen industry.
- Focusing on roles where your uniquely human skills will be in demand, such as creativity, social intelligence and manipulation.
- Looking for niches to work in partnership with technology, not against it, as these will be more 'future safe'. For example, if you want to be a Careers Counsellor, you could seek out roles where you don't just provide information and advice, because a machine will probably be far more efficient in these areas; look for positions that lean on your natural human skills such as listening empathically to clients and providing targeted guidance.
- Take advantage of your position as a current student/new graduate: you're probably more in tune with modern technology so technical adjustments won't be so difficult to master. Also, you may be able to adapt your study to the new paradigm so you can plan your career, from the very start, with these changes in mind.

Useful resources

Websites

www.highfliers.co.uk – See the latest graduate market report
https://careersblog.warwick.ac.uk – See 'Graduate recruitment trends'
www.smallbusiness.co.uk – See 'Graduate recruitment trends'
www.ise.org.uk – See the graduate recruitment news
www.hesa.ac.uk
www.hecsu.ac.uk
www.universities.ac.uk

On Twitter

#graduaterecruitment
@GuardianCareers
@Recruitment
@theHRDIRECTOR

CHAPTER 2
Career planning

> ❝ There is a tide in the affairs of men which, taken at the flood, leads on to fortune. ❞
> *William Shakespeare*

What is career planning?

Career planning is about taking control of your professional journey. Therefore, it's not just about finding a job but, also, deeper issues such as what you want to do in life, what you can do and what's available. These issues can be difficult to unravel so you can quickly end up going around in circles, for example:

- How can you choose a role if you don't know what you're good at?
- How can you know what you're good at if you have no experience?
- How can you get experience if you don't have experience?

However, be reassured, this vicious circle is simple to solve by breaking it up into small manageable chunks and structuring your approach accordingly. This chapter explores various career-related theories and models in order to help you take control.

Managing any complex project

Start taking control of your next steps by reflecting on any experience you already have of managing complex projects. For example, in order to complete an essay or dissertation on a course, you will have, either consciously or subconsciously, broken down the tasks, given yourself a timetable for completion and regularly reflected on your progress.

A million things to consider

Do I have to do what mum says?
How do I target my applications?
What would I be good at?
How do I get my foot in the door?
How do I choose what to do?
How can I get experience?
What can I do with my degree?
Where are the jobs?
What would I enjoy doing?

Traditional career perspectives

A number of career theories and models have been developed over the last century to help students and graduates manage their transition into the world of work. These are a useful starting point when it comes to designing your own personal plan.

Matching theories

These frameworks link people to particular roles according to their qualities (traits) and patterns of thinking, feeling and behaving (factors). One of the most commonly used classification systems is the Holland Occupational Themes theory of occupational choice (J. Holland),[1] which links people to certain roles according to whether they are realistic (doers), investigative (thinkers), artistic (creators), social (helpers), enterprising (persuaders) or conventional (organisers). These theories have less traction now than in the latter half of the twentieth century because the job market has become so much more diverse and flexible, but they can still be effectively included in every career plan. You can view a range of jobs linked to each of Holland's traits and factors in Chapter 5 and undertake various matching exercises.

Developmental theories

Shortly after the Second World War, much of the research into career planning and development focused on the process of personal development. Donald Super[2] demonstrated that people gradually develop their vocational maturity in five clear stages as follows:

1   Growth (from birth to 14 years of age): When we become increasingly conscious of who we are and what's involved in the world of work.
2   Exploration (from 15 to 24): When we try out new experiences at school/ university/work and during our hobbies.
3   Establishment (from 25 to 44): The point when we perfect our skills and establish ourselves in our roles.
4   Maintenance (from 45 to 64): When we focus on promotion and moving up in our field.
5   Decline (65 years of age and over): As we reduce output and prepare for retirement.

As with matching perspectives, these theories are currently becoming less influential, primarily because graduates now expect to move between a number of roles as they progress through their careers. However, the process of matching still features heavily throughout this guide because growth and exploration will always be core elements of your employability and search for a potentially fulfilling role.

All change

Modern career structures have largely outgrown these traditional theories because they are now much more fluid. For example, today's graduates rarely stay in the same roles or sectors throughout their whole careers. In fact, you will typically move forwards, backwards and sideways any number of times into new jobs, positions and industries.

Therefore, new theories have been developed which focus less on planning and more on dealing with change. Three exciting new perspectives are outlined below.

Modern careers

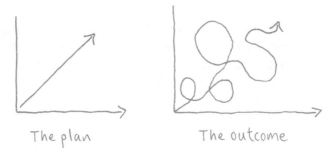

The plan   The outcome

Modern career viewpoints

Planned happenstance

John Krumboltz's recent Theory of Planned Happenstance[3] relates particularly well to the modern job market and the needs of contemporary students and graduates. It focuses on putting yourself in beneficial situations and taking full advantage, stressing the need for curiosity, persistence, flexibility, self-reflection, openness to feedback, networking and a positive attitude.

Narratives

Narrative theories (Savickas)[4] stress the links between people's careers and their personal/social relationships. Therefore, they stress the advantages of taking a step back and interpreting your life through your own experiences and the stories of others, believing this will give you the necessary perspective to trace a logical and fulfilling path.

Chaos[5]

This enlightened approach (Pryor and Bright, 2011)[6] links career planning to the scientific theories of the same name that show how real-world outcomes, in areas such as the weather, are determined by the constant flux of an infinitesimal

> **❝** This theory moves away from predicting and controlling your destiny but deals with equipping yourself for unpredictable chaos. **❞**

array of tiny variables, thus making them extremely difficult to predict in the short-run and almost impossible over the longer-term. Therefore, this theory moves away from predicting and controlling your destiny but deals with equipping yourself for unpredictable change. This involves building your resilience and flexibility, getting busy so you can see what's going on in the world, networking, becoming accustomed to change, thriving in unfamiliar surroundings and reflecting on past experiences so you're ready to take advantage of whatever comes along.

The DOTS careers framework

This model, first established by Bill Law and A. G. Watts[7] at the latter end of the last century, is an outstanding representation of the lifelong career planning process because it provides a clear overview of the internal processes involved. The model starts by assembling the full range of issues involved into four distinct headings, as outlined below.

Decision-making

Choosing suitable career options and navigating an appropriate route.

Opportunity awareness

Appreciating your full range of job options and the possible stepping stones to your destination.

Transition learning

Understanding the job market, finding jobs and making successful applications.

Self-awareness

Familiarity with personal skills, abilities and motivations.

Having collated career issues in this way, the model then expertly depicts how they interact, as shown in the diagram below.

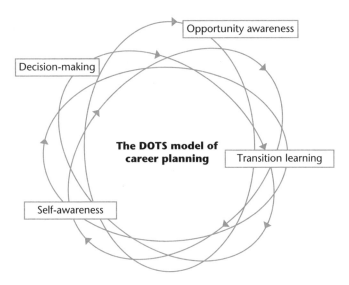

Having collated career issues in this way, the model then expertly depicts how they interact, as shown in the diagram below.

Opportunity awareness

Decision-making

The DOTS model of career planning

Transition learning

Self-awareness

As you can see from the diagram above, the DOTS model describes career planning as a constant lifelong process of 'sensing, shifting and focusing on' each of the four elements of personal growth. The four individual strands of development are interwoven in the diagram to demonstrate that this is not a straightforward cycle where you sequentially make decisions, learn about your opportunities, transit into a new position and then learn more about yourself, but a dynamic, ongoing process of constantly and simultaneously addressing and readdressing each of these four core elements that drive the career journey.

Careers in a complex world

The Careers Express Model

Sometimes, it can be too daunting to contemplate your whole career in one go. In fact, it's also probably impossible, because there are just too many variables! Therefore, the Careers Express Model (Rook) focuses solely on choosing a role and getting your foot in the door. It represents the steps as stations on a train line. Station one is the starting point where you have no idea as to what to do, and Careers Central, at the other end, is where you have successfully found your first professional role and are looking to advance. You may want to start from the beginning or anywhere down the line, depending on how much career planning you've already undertaken.

Station 1 – The starting point

At this point, get ready by making sure you have an open mind, a positive mind-set, time, energy and access to support (you may want to see a Careers Adviser).

Station 2 – Assess yourself

Identify what you personally want from a job and what you can offer. You can find out how to do this in Chapter 3.

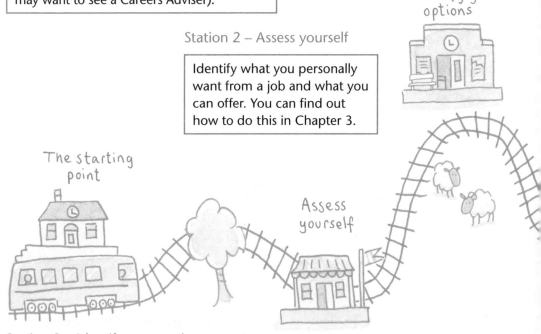

Identify your options

The starting point

Assess yourself

Station 3 – Identify your options

Now you have an idea about what you want from a job, research a wide range of occupations that look interesting. At this stage, there's no need to explore roles in detail or search for vacancies, just list your possible choices and stop there. Be ambitious – these should be the life-fulfilling roles you hope to achieve one day, not what you want to do next year. This is covered in Chapter 4.

Station 5 – Plan your route

Work out the specific steps you need to take to enter your chosen role. These could involve a vast array of activities including volunteering, internships and further qualifications. Don't just automatically choose the most obvious path; identify a route that best suites your unique personal situation and establish small, manageable steps. For example, an internship may be your fourth move, not the first, after networking, a part-time casual role and volunteering. These steps are addressed in Chapters 9–11.

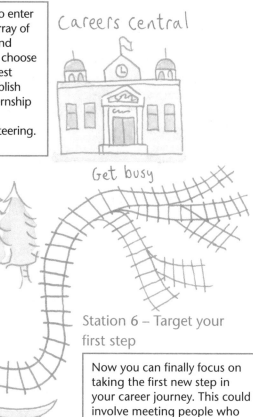

Station 6 – Target your first step

Now you can finally focus on taking the first new step in your career journey. This could involve meeting people who can help (networking), looking for a volunteer role, taking a postgraduate course, applying for an internship or, if you're ready, going for a graduate level role. See Part IV.

Station 4 – Narrow down one or two fulfilling roles/sectors

Systematically match your list of potential roles (as identified at Station 2) to your skills, interests and motivations (from Station 3) in order to narrow down one or two exciting roles/sectors. Don't panic about tying yourself down as there will be ample opportunities to change your mind later on. You can find out how to do this in Chapter 5.

Careers Central – Get your foot in the door

Once you've got your foot in the door, you're at Careers Central, and can go anywhere you want. You can carry on to your original destination or take a completely fresh track to somewhere new. The world is your oyster, as your skills will be transferable into a wide range of roles.

What theories and models tell us

The various theories and models point to the following career planning guidelines:

- **Structure your journey:** Adopt a systematic approach.
- **Break up the process:** Subdivide your plans into bite-sized chunks that are manageable and realistic.
- **Arrange your tasks in order:** Work out a logical order to tackle each bite-sized task.
- **Focus on your employability:** Systematically link each step of your journey to your skills, commitment and knowledge.
- **Create a plan B:** Consider what you could do at each stage if your original plan doesn't work. For example, if you decide to undertake a Masters but are too late to apply, maybe you could find some work experience, try a different course or study part-time?
- **Set a timetable:** Work out a realistic time frame for each step and try to stick to it – don't rush!
- **Work hard:** Leave your house and tackle each step in order – focusing solely on each specific issue at hand, before moving on.
- **Take advantage of the unexpected:** Keep your eyes open for new opportunities/paths.
- **Show resilience:** There is increasing evidence that career success is closely related to 'stickability', so stay strong when things get tough (they usually do!), work hard, find support, and look for creative solutions.
- **Keep an eye on your destination:** Regularly remind yourself about where you're headed and don't get bogged down half way.
- **Continually reassess your journey:** Set and reset your goals depending on how your journey is going.

The theory that drives this book

The advice and guidance in this guide are drawn from each and all of these theories and models listed above and others, but the structure generally follows the Careers Express Model because most students and recent graduates are primarily concerned with their first steps into the world of work. Therefore, the next chapters focus on finding your niche and planning your route.

ⓘ Useful resources

Websites

www.targetjobs.co.uk – See 'Careers Advice'

www.kent.ac.uk/careers – See 'Career Planning'

www.careers.govt.nz – See 'Career theories and models'

www.exeter.ac.uk – See 'The career development cycle'

On Twitter

#careerplanning

#careercoach

#career

#careerchat

On YouTube

'How to set your career goals' – Project Management Videos

'Donald Trump's Advice on Choosing a Career' – bluveeta

'Chaos theory explained' – Jim Bright

'How to make a career choice' – jobs.ac.uk

PART II
FINDING YOUR NICHE

This section helps you recognise what you have to offer, identify some interesting career options and link the two together to find a potentially fulfilling and successful path.

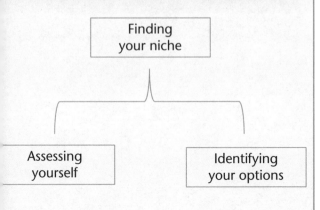

Finding your niche

Assessing yourself

Identifying your options

CHAPTER 3
Assessing your skills, interests and motivations

" Never look back unless you
are planning to go that way. "
Henry David Thoreau

Your skills, interests and motivations

The first step to finding a truly fulfilling career is to create a snapshot of your current skills, interests and motivations, i.e. what you're good at, enjoy, and want from life. These characteristics may be difficult to nail down, especially when you're just starting out, but read through the following pages to develop the best 'self-portrait' you can achieve. Start now by completing the quick two-minute test below to see how good you are already at self-reflection and consider the following advice.

Two-minute test: Your skills, interests and motivations

Quickly list two of your skills, interests and motivations (i.e. two things you're good at, enjoy and want from life). Try to avoid jargon such as 'leadership', 'organisation' … etc. (for example, instead of using the word 'communication', you could write down 'listening' or 'sharing ideas').

An example for each heading is provided to help you get going.

Skills (what you're good at)	Interests (what you enjoy doing on a daily basis)	Motivations (what you want from life)
Listening	Working with others	A profession
●	●	●
●	●	●

Reflecting on your answers: Which headings did you find the hardest to complete? How can you make sure you focus on this area when you choose a role to pursue?

Identifying your skills

Sit back and reflect

You're bound to be better at some jobs than others (you won't be much of a ballerina if you have one bad knee and two left feet!), so what are your key skills? Identify your top ten skills in the table below. As before, use simple phrases like 'work well with people' instead of jargon like 'teamwork'.

Some strategies

- Reflect on your recent achievements and identify why you were successful.
- Ask your friends, family and employers what skills you have.
- Assess your skills using online tools such as www. mindtools.com and www.kent.ac.uk/careers.
- Look at the job descriptions in some random job adverts and identify the skills you possess.
- Look at the list of skills required by employers in Part III and identify your strengths.
- Write a fantasy personal profile listing all your good points.

Are you good at ...

Multi-tasking?
Working under pressure?
Working hard?
Helping people?
Encouraging people?
Fitting in?
Getting your message across?
Taking instructions?
Working independently?
Working with others?
Sharing ideas/feelings?
Managing/Motivating people?
Organising things/events?
Planning ahead?
Teaching/Training people?
Listening?
Coming up with ideas?
Solving problems?
Manipulating numbers/IT?
Analysis/Research?
Adapting to new situations?
Practical hands-on tasks?

Self-assessment: Your top skills for work

Use the cues above to identify your best skills

Your top ten skills	
●	●
●	●
●	●
●	●
●	●

Godfrey Bloom, former MEP for Yorkshire and The Humber

You must look forward to going to work. If you dread Monday mornings, you will be unhappy and fail. Keep money at the bottom of your wish list.

Identifying your interests (what you enjoy doing on a daily basis)

Sit back and reflect

Your skills are central to your choice of career but, so too are your interests because, if you like going to work, it will make the world of difference to your level of fulfilment and, therefore, success. Complete the exercise below to identify what you enjoy doing on a day-to-day basis so you can look for relevant career options.

Some strategies

- Simply look back on recent experiences and identify the things you really enjoyed, such as writing creatively or being outdoors.
- Reflect on what you don't enjoy in life to infer what you do like, e.g. if you don't enjoy being on your own, does that mean you prefer working closely with colleagues?
- Try new things and see what you enjoy.
- Ask your friends what they enjoy on a day-to-day basis at work or university and see if that also floats your boat.
- Finish the following sentence: If I had a magic wand I would …

Do you enjoy ...
A particular hobby?
Working in an office?
Working outdoors?
Working for yourself?
Working with others?
Leading people?
Helping people?
Teaching/Training/Advising people?
Organising/Motivating people?
A quiet life/Being busy?
Organising things/events?
Researching/Analysing data?
Working with numbers/IT?
Things staying the same?
Change?
Solving problems?
Being challenged?
Being creative?
Having a laugh?
Being in a professional environment?
Learning new things?
Excitement?

Self-assessment: Your top interests

What do you enjoy doing on a daily basis?

Your top ten interests	
●	●
●	●
●	●
●	●
●	●

Identifying your motivations (what you want from life)

Sit back and reflect

The final way to assess yourself in relation to career planning, and perhaps the most important, is to identify what's important to you in life. Complete the exercise below by trying to identify your top ten drivers (and be honest!).

Some strategies

- Imagine your lifestyle in twenty years (for example, think of where you live, what your house is like ... etc.). What stands out?
- Imagine you've just arrived home after work in few years' time, with a smile on your face, and ask yourself what's made you so happy?
- Imagine you're teaching a child about what's important in life – what would you say?
- Recall the things that were important to you when you were a child – are they still?
- Think of people from all walks of life you admire and ask yourself why you look up to them.
- Brainstorm all the things you want from life and highlight the most important.

Some common career motivations ...

Autonomy/power
Working for yourself
Being a leader
Working with interesting people
Staying near your family/friends
Living in another country
Job security
An impressive job status
Helping people
Following the path of my religion
Good opportunities for promotion
A profession
Opportunities for creativity
Some money
Just enough money to be comfortable
More money than I can count
Teaching/supporting people
Time off to smell the roses
Peace
Time for a family life
Life in the fast lane
High pressure/high rewards
New experiences
A good work/life balance
A cool job that people look up to
Supporting the world
Making a difference

Self-assessment: Your top ten motivations

What do you want your career to give you in life?

Your top ten motivations	
●	●
●	●
●	●
●	●
●	●

Using your new self-awareness

This enhanced self-reflection can help you in any number of ways:

- You will become accustomed to seeing careers on your terms, i.e. finding suitable roles, not just seeing what's available.
- You will be able to identify jobs that match what you have to offer (see Chapter 5).
- You will put together more genuine applications and impress in interviews.

John Southern, new graduate at a large graduate employer

At University, I didn't have a full idea of what job to go for when I graduated and I started to worry, so I visited the careers service to ask them what to do. At the time, I thought they weren't much help because they wouldn't answer any of my questions. But, when you came in and asked me the direct question 'how can they tell, they've only known you for five minutes?' I realised, it was up to me. This realisation was a bit overwhelming and I ignored making any decisions until after the exams and the summer holidays. But then, a host of employers came on campus and I noticed they all had lists of skills they were after. At first, all these lists looked the same (teamwork ...) but, after a while, I started to notice the differences and by visiting the employer events I gained a more nuanced idea as to what suited me and what didn't in relation to the skills required and every other aspect of the roles. Eventually, I signed up for some applications and noticed that the most interesting jobs also seemed to match my skills and, on reflection, I don't think this was by accident; it was why I was interested! So I applied for a few jobs, got some advice and made some improvements (my first applications were so terrible!) and got a job!

ⓘ Useful links

Websites

www.guardian.com – Search for 'How to do a self-assessment of your skills'

www.cardiff.ac.uk – Look for 'Assessing your interests, values and abilities' in the Choosing a Career section

www.open.edu/openlearn – See week 2 of the free course entitled 'Succeed in the workplace'

www.targetjobs.co.uk – See 'Fun, prospects or money: what are you looking for? How to find and do work you love' – Scott Dinsmore

On Twitter

#careerplanning

@CareerReadyUK

CHAPTER 4
Identifying your options

> **"** The very substance of the
> ambitious is merely the
> shadow of a dream.
> *William Shakespeare* **"**

The world is your oyster

Now you have a sound appreciation of your skills, interests and motivations, you're
ready to research your full range of career options.

In this respect, you're very much in luck, because today's graduates can enter an
incredible range of roles. For example, you can choose a job linked to your
studies, stay in the same area as your work experience, branch off into a sector
close to your interests or try something completely new.

This huge choice can be
daunting for some graduates but
it shouldn't be, because you
have plenty of time and there
are several tools and strategies to
make things easier to handle.
This chapter shows you how to
calmly and systematically
research your full range of
options.

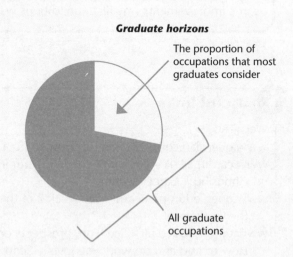

Graduate horizons

The proportion of
occupations that most
graduates consider

All graduate
occupations

Getting bogged down?

Most of us only ever consider a few of our potential career options. For example, most psychology graduates will look into psychology or counselling roles but few consider careers in media production, direct marketing or advertising. Don't let this happen to you. In order to find a truly fulfilling career, you'll almost certainly need to take the time to assess as many job options as you can and dream – what a wonderful opportunity this is!

Colonel David Thornycroft (retired)

Today's students and graduates need to have open minds about their opportunities in life and not feel confined to careers which are directly linked to what they studied at university. Employers look for more attributes than your specific academic knowledge, they are attracted to graduates because of their good all-round intelligence, the confidence to take control of events and the ability to analyse information and make logical deductions.

To test how comprehensively you've researched your career preferences so far, complete the two-minute test below and reflect on your answers.

Two-minute test

List four occupations you've considered at some time in your life (even as a child) and identify how you first discovered that they actually exist (you didn't know about them when you were born).

Four occupations you've considered	How you first discovered them
•	•
•	•
•	•
•	•

Reflecting on your answers: Most of us only discover career options in five limited ways – through our friends, family, university, TV and job pages on the Internet. If this sounds like you, read on to see how you can widen your horizons.

Daring to dream

There are several ways to prepare yourself for a successful career search, and these are outlined below. Make sure you tick each of them off before moving on.

Be open-minded

A large minority of students and graduates (perhaps even a majority) limit their own chances before they even get started, by discounting whole swathes of careers for no apparent reason. This could be because:

- They don't realise that they can pursue these roles with their particular qualifications (when they probably can).
- They already have an idea as to what they want to do (often with little research).
- They're following the most obvious path without taking the time to look for others.
- They're blindly following their peers.
- They're doing what their parents want them to do.
- They bury their heads in the sand because they're too daunted by the massive range of possibilities.
- They've plumped for any old relevant role just to stop their heads from spinning with all this choice.

If you fall into any of these categories (and we all do at some point), ask yourself what's the harm in just having a look? What great catastrophe could befall you for seeking out more options? So, find a plain piece of paper and start searching. You never know, it might be exciting to free yourself up in this way and you may even find the perfect job!

Give it time

Allow yourself as many weeks as you need to research what's out there and identify your priorities.

Find your passion

Energy and enthusiasm will carry you into a fulfilling and successful career because you'll enjoy searching and remain strong. One way of finding a truly fulfilling occupation is to:

(a) Imagine yourself, at work, thirty years from now, and ask yourself: What does 'work' look like? Where are you? Who are you with? ... etc.
(b) Identify senior roles that match these elements (these may be out of reach for now, but they'll give you something to aim for).

Raise your aspiration

Your career aspiration is your willingness to explore a full range of career options and go for challenging roles. Several factors may hold you back:

- You have little experience of professional work environments.
- You don't see yourself as 'worthy' of a dream role.
- You have few positive peers or models.
- You've been knocked back a few times and have given up trying.
- You feel that you have little chance because of discrimination.
- Your family is forcing you into a corner.

Try the following strategies to open up your perspective:

- Find voluntary roles and paid positions so you can get used to rubbing shoulders with professionals.
- Find a mentor, who's familiar with your situation, to help you search. This could be a family member, an academic, a recent graduate from your university or a member of a professional body. See if a friendly tutor or a Careers Adviser can put you in touch with someone.
- Ask a Careers Adviser for support.
- Speak to friends and peers about their plans.
- Attend employer events organised by academic departments, careers services and professional bodies.
- Pretend you're a Careers Adviser helping someone in your situation. What roles might they suggest?

See if the following exercise helps you set your sights higher.

Seeing what's out there

There is no single soothsayer who can tell you what to do in life. It's more like a treasure hunt where you pick up ideas along the way. Use each of the various strategies outlined below, to come up with two or three ideas and list them in the table provided. Don't just focus on the obvious occupations such as teaching and accountancy (although there's nothing wrong with these professions) and take your time to find truly inspiring roles, even if they're not mainstream, such as a drama therapist or park ranger. Finally, don't panic if you can't pinpoint the exact roles you may want to enter, but try to narrow down your focus to a particular industry or sector as this will really help you take control of your next steps.

Brainstorm

Just find a quiet place, sit down and see what comes to mind.

Self-assessment: Do you aspire to greatness?

Follow the arrows below to find some great career options.

A flow chart of your dreams

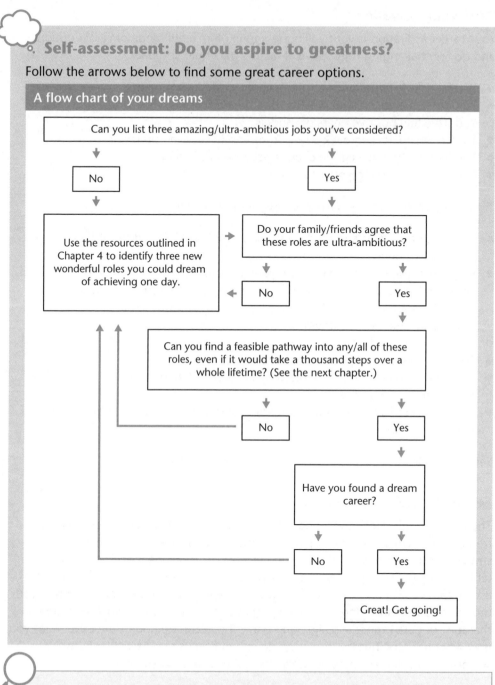

Can you list three amazing/ultra-ambitious jobs you've considered?

No

Yes

Use the resources outlined in Chapter 4 to identify three new wonderful roles you could dream of achieving one day.

Do your family/friends agree that these roles are ultra-ambitious?

No

Yes

Can you find a feasible pathway into any/all of these roles, even if it would take a thousand steps over a whole lifetime? (See the next chapter.)

No

Yes

Have you found a dream career?

No

Yes

Great! Get going!

Reflecting on your answers: If you found this exercise fun and identified numerous exciting occupations, then you're probably already a dreamer extraordinaire – so, keep it up! If you struggled, or didn't really give it a go, then you need to pinch yourself and try again. You owe it to yourself to dream.

Use your social networks

Ask friends about the careers they've always found attractive and what they suggest for you. Also, look at hashtags such as #techjobs, #jobsinoxford (if you live in Oxford!) and #guardianjobs.

Find your careers service

Pop into your university's careers service and ask for help/attend events/meet professionals in the field.

Take a look around

Keep your eyes open for new ideas. You could also get involved in new activities or just watch TV or YouTube and see what jobs come to mind, e.g. camera operators, actors, chefs, nurses and police inspectors.

See what jobs you like

Look at the vacancies on offer at temp. agencies, online job boards and graduate career websites to find any attractive roles. Links to these can be found in the chapters on job hunting.

Look up some graduate career websites

Look for interesting occupations on sites such as www.prospects.ac.uk and www.targetjobs.co.uk. Prospects also has a very useful section in its 'Job Profiles' where you can view 'Alternative careers'.

Use online diagnostic tools

Identify suitable occupations using online tools such as the 'Skills Health Check' at www.nationalcareersservice.direct.gov.uk and 'What job would suit me' at www.prospects.ac.uk. But a word of caution – make sure you take your time! Students and graduates are often quite disappointed by the feedback from these programs because they tend to include numerous suggestions that are seemingly bizarre. However, don't let this get you down. These programs can only provide a broad-brush perspective, but they do usually identify a few interesting ideas that really stand out, and you only need one! (For now.)

Identify degree relevant roles

Your careers service can tell you what individual graduates in each degree discipline have done six months after graduation. These are called 'Graduate Destinations'. Ask for information on the exact roles and companies your peers went into.

Look at some postgraduate futures

Research postgrad courses and see what interesting careers they can herald.

Finding your niche

'When I grow up …'

Try to remember all your career aspirations, even when you were a child, and identify some similar roles that look interesting. For example, if you once dreamed of being a footballer, you could consider becoming a sports coach, reporter or psychologist (or a footballer!).

Let the Internet search for you

See what comes up when you Google terms such as 'alternative careers' or 'exciting jobs'.

Identify jobs linked to your interests

Think of opportunities linked to what you do in your spare time. For example, if you enjoy listening to friends' problems, why not consider counselling or social work?

Self-assessment: Identifying possible career options

Use the strategies above to come up with a wide variety of exciting occupations.

Twenty possible careers	
1	11
2	12
3	13
4	14
5	15
6	16
7	17
8	18
9	19
10	20

Reflecting on your answers: The fundamental question here is, have you taken your time? Make sure you have access to a number of resources – there'll be something brilliant out there for you, but you have to look!

Personality types

You can also identify potentially fulfilling careers by assessing what sort of person you are and considering relevant roles. Various strategies have been developed to help you do this.

RIASEC Roles

As mentioned in Chapter 2, John Holland linked occupations to six distinct personality 'types'. These are outlined in the table below and linked to a small range of jobs. You may be able to quickly identify the type/s that apply to you by just looking at the definitions provided, but you can also research your profile further, and find additional relevant roles on the following websites:

- Career Key: www.careerkey.org – Look up 'Choose a career'/'Holland's theory of career choice'.
- Career Life Skills: www.career-lifeskills.com/pdf/jst-576530-occupations.pdf – A wide list of roles linked to each type.
- Open Source Psychometrics Project: www.openpsychometrics.org – Look down the list for the IIP RIASEC Markers questionnaire.

John Holland's Personality types	Examples of relevant roles
Realistic (doers) These are the people who put their heads down and get on with the work and, as such, they tend to have practical skills.	Carpenter, Chef, Civil Engineer, Electronic and Electrical Engineer, Early Years Teacher, Landscaper, Lifeguard, Machinist, Pilot, Radiographer, Surveyor, Tree Surgeon, Telecommunication Line Installer.
Investigative (thinkers) Investigators solve problems through their intellect and, therefore, tend to be well-versed in mathematical and scientific techniques.	Aerospace Engineer, Anthropologist, Audiologist, Book Editor, Computer Programmer, Dietician, Marine Engineer, Meteorologist, Optometrist, Prosthetic Technician, Social Researcher.
Artistic (creators) People in this cohort are original and creative, so they enjoy practical activities related to the arts.	Actor, Animator, Art Administrator, Art Director, Author, Broadcaster, Graphic Designer, Interior Designer, Journalist, Photographer, Set Designer, Technical Writer, Translator.
Social (helpers) Social people enjoy working as part of a community and nurturing others.	Careers Adviser, Counsellor, Dental Hygienist, Masseuse, Nurse, Occupational Therapist, Paramedic, Speech Pathologist, Teacher, Youth Worker.
Enterprising (persuaders) Enterprising people tend to be confident change agents suitable for roles which involve leadership, ambition and influence.	Curator, Flight Attendant, Finance Adviser, Hotel Manager, Lawyer, Office Manager, Public Relations Officer, Real Estate Agent, Retail Buyer, Retail Manager, Recruiter, Salesperson, Travel Agent.
Conventional (organisers) Individuals of this type enjoy order and systematic processes.	Accountant, Actuary, Cashier, Court Clerk, Financial Analyst, Librarian, Personal Assistant, Receptionist, Tax Technician.

Myers Briggs

One of the more reputable personality profiles is the Myers Briggs Type Indicator (MBTI®). This test was developed shortly after the Second World War in the USA by Katherine Briggs and her daughter Isabel Briggs Myers, who extrapolated Carl Jung's earlier work in the area. In essence, it allocates people to one of 16 different patterns of behaviour as follows:

1 **How people interact:** People can either be primarily 'I' for Introverted or 'E' for Extroverted, where …
   - Introverts prefer being alone; they think things through internally and tend to be private.
   - Extroverts tend to be energised by others; they think out loud and share their feelings.

2 **How people process information:** People can either be 'S' if they tend to Sense things or 'N' if they use their iNtuition, where …
   - People who sense things tend to focus on what they can actually see, hear, touch, taste and smell. They trust concrete concepts, base their opinions on established facts and prefer to use established skills so they are often described as being 'well grounded'.
   - Intuitive people tend to trust their instincts, search for new solutions, interpret facts and continually develop their skills.

3 **How people make decisions:** People can either be primarily 'T' for Thinkers or 'F' for Feelers, where …
   - Thinkers tend to be logical, objective, analytical, highly motivated and often uncaring about other people's feelings.
   - Feelers tend to make decisions according to their instincts and the feelings of others. Therefore, they enjoy pleasing people and finding compromise.

4 **How people organise their lives:** People can either be 'J' if they prefer to carefully Judge their next steps in life or 'P' if they rely on Perception, where …
   - People who use judgement strive to learn as much as they can about things before taking action. They work hard to achieve goals and enjoy the feeling of finishing projects, so they often appear to be organised.
   - Perceptive people prefer to keep their options open and therefore remain flexible about taking up new paths, learning new things and gaining new experiences.

In the following exercise, make an approximation of your particular Myers Briggs/ Jungian type based on the information provided.

You can find out more about the various personality types and lists of related occupations at:

- Keirsey: www.keirsey.com – Look up 'The four temperaments'.
- Truity: www.truity.com – View a wide range of roles in a range of sectors for each of the sixteen personality combinations.
- Career Assessment Site: careerassessmentsite.com – Click on your type to identify roles that are potentially relevant.

Two highly recommended books on this subject are: *Do What You Are* by Tieger and Barron[1] and *What's Your Type of Career?* by Donna Dunning.[2]

Self-assessment: Your personality profile

What's your personality type?

Place an 'I' in the box if you think you are more of an introvert or an 'E' if you're an extrovert.	☐
Place an 'S' in the box if you tend to use your senses to interpret things or an 'N' if you use your intuition.	☐
Place a 'T' in the box if you like to think your decisions through or an 'F' if you go with your gut instincts.	☐
Place a 'J' in the box if you focus on achieving goals or a 'P' if you prefer to keep your options open.	☐

Reflecting on your answers: Now that you have a broad idea of your personality style, look online for jobs that match by Googling 'Careers for INTJ' (or whatever you are), or look at the following links.

Useful links

Websites

www.prospects.ac.uk – See 'Job profiles' and/or 'Job sectors'

www.targetjobs.co.uk – See 'Career Sectors'

www.nationalcareersservice.direct.gov.uk – See 'Job Profiles'

www.qub.ac.uk – See '10 tips for identifying and exploring your career options '

www.sunderland.ac.uk – See 'Exploring your career options'

www.openpsychometrics.org – Look down the list for the IIP RIASEC Markers questionnaire

www.keirsey.com – Look up 'The four temperaments'

www.truity.com – View a wide range of roles in a range of sectors for each of the sixteen Myers Briggs personality combinations

www.careerkey.org

www.personalitypage.com

CHAPTER 5
Choosing a role

66 Choose a job you love, and you will never have to work a day in your life.

Confucius 99

Finding the perfect fit

Now you've identified some of your key skills, interests and motivations and created a shortlist of interesting occupations (see the previous two chapters), you can link the two together to come up with some potentially fulfilling careers, as shown in the Venn diagram below.

Matching yourself to potential careers

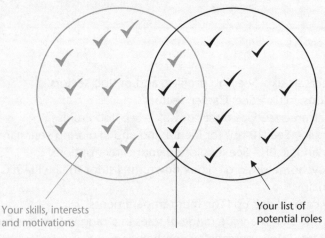

Your skills, interests and motivations

Your list of potential roles

Potentially fulfilling careers

This chapter demonstrates how you can narrow things down using several different strategies, depending on your personal decision-making style. Remember – don't be too scared to choose. You're not committing yourself for life so you can change your mind at any point, and most people do! It just helps to start your journey with a destination in mind.

Steve Rook, author of this guide

As a Careers Adviser, I have assisted people with thousands and thousands of CVs, applications, cover letters and interviews, but relatively few people have sought my help with their career choice. Therefore, it's great fun when they come along on a boring Wednesday afternoon and say something like "Hi, can you help me choose a career?" So, reach out to your Careers Service (they often have arrangements to see graduates as well as students) and ask for help – they'll be happy to see you. But hurry, once my millions of readers have read this passage, there'll be no appointments left!

I think most people avoid asking for help with their career choice for one or all of the following reasons:

- They're embarrassed.
- They don't want to show their vulnerability.
- They've placed this decision in the 'too hard to solve box'.
- They think Careers Services are just there to help with specific queries from people who know where they're going (they're not!).
- They're just too busy.
- They know what they want to do already.

Which camp do you fall in? Any of the above, or something completely different? Either way, arrange an appointment with your university's Careers Service and go for a chat. You'll find out that advisers can help you in any number of ways: they can suggest options with your degree; point towards useful resources; chat about what you enjoy/what options you've considered; provide some perspective; and, most importantly, just listen. They will not judge!

When I see people in this situation, I usually engage in activities such as those laid out in this chapter, but not necessarily with the aim of running through them to completion. I usually find that just engaging in any sort of practical process enables clients to talk freely about their personal situations and this, in turn, greatly helps them take control. Often, one of my counselling type questions immediately sets off a lightbulb in people's heads and they're off and running with ideas before we've even sat down. Of course, you can also ask these questions of yourself, things like: Why do I think career planning is so daunting? When did it became scary? Have I always found it overwhelming? What job would be perfect for me? What makes me happy? If I had a magic wand what would I choose? This last question is always very powerful because I've met so many people over the years who have subconsciously discounted their dream roles because they seem so impossible to achieve; but someone's undertaking them, so why shouldn't it be you?

A matching exercise

In the table below, you can systematically link your skills, interests and motivations to your most attractive occupations; try to find roles that score highly across the board or your results will be unbalanced. For example, you may have all the interests and motivations to be a professional footballer, but none of the skills! Thoroughly research the roles first to clarify your understanding of what they involve.

Self-assessment: Your favourite occupations

- Enter your top ten skills, interests and motivations from Chapter 3.
- Enter five interesting occupations from Chapter 4.
- Score each role from 1 to 10 on how they match each of your attributes (1 being the lowest possible score; 10 being the highest).
- Add up the totals to see which roles most closely match your skills, interests and motivations.

Five exciting careers you've discovered:	Role 1 _____	Role 2 _____	Role 3 _____	Role 4 _____	Role 5 _____
	Score 1–10	Score 1–10	Score 1–10	Score 1–10	Score 1–10
The skills you identified in Chapter 3					

Five exciting careers you've discovered:	Role 1 ____	Role 2 ____	Role 3 ____	Role 4 ____	Role 5 ____
	Score 1–10	Score 1–10	Score 1–10	Score 1–10	Score 1–10
The interests you identified in Chapter 3					
The motivations you identified in Chapter 3					
TOTAL SCORE					

Reflecting on your answers: If you've found some roles that score highly, well done! Now you can look further into the role/s that came out on top in your survey.

Making good decisions

In order to choose an appropriate path in life, it can really help to identify:

- How you usually make decisions
- How you can use this style effectively in this context.

Seven common decision-making styles are outlined below along with guidance on how you can effectively use each in your career search. See which style/s best matches your particular approach and consider how to maximise your strategy in the exercise that follows.

Decision-making styles	How they work	How you can use this style effectively to choose a career path
Intuitive	Intuitive decision makers choose options that 'feel right' at a particular moment. People with this decision-making style often have a good emotional attachment to the career they go for but may choose an occupation without looking at their full range of options or making sure that the role they've chosen fits their unique skills, interests and motivations.	Make sure you fully undertake your research into all your options and take your time. You should also find some relevant work experience before following your gut instincts.
Systematic	People with this decision-making style carefully weigh up all their options and make well thought out decisions but often take no account of how they actually feel about the jobs they're considering.	Continue to carefully research your options but get away from the websites for a while and talk to people who work in the roles you are considering; find some relevant work experience and carefully assess whether you actually enjoy doing the job.
Hesitant/ Paralytic	Career planning can be too scary for many students so they bury their heads in the sand, and hope that the whole thing goes away.	Carefully plan each of the steps you're going to take to choose a career and give yourself strict deadlines. It may also help to seek assistance from a friend or a Careers Adviser to keep you motivated. Once you start taking positive steps, you may well feel much more energised and in control.

Decision-making styles	How they work	How you can use this style effectively to choose a career path
Impulsive/ Spontaneous	People with this decision-making style often leap before they look. They find out about an interesting career one day and apply for a job the next.	Congratulate yourself for being so proactive but try to find some time to assess what you actually want to do in the long-term. You could mentally picture yourself where you want to be in twenty or thirty years and carefully research your next move by talking to people in your chosen role or seeing a Careers Adviser.
Fatalistic	The motto for fatalistic people is 'what will be, will be'. Graduates with this decision-making style often just fall into a career (or don't!) without any significant research. For example, they may just get a job after university and stick with it, or blindly pursue a role linked to what they've studied. These people often get itchy feet a few years after graduation because they haven't found fulfilment.	Find any source of income and security then take as much time as you need to dream about what you actually want from life.
Compliant/ Dependent	Some people avoid decisions like the plague and let other people take control. They may choose a certain role just to please their parents or friends and will, therefore, often make others happy but not themselves.	If you're focusing on a particular career just because someone else wants you to follow that path, try to take a step back and make sure that the role really suits you before applying. No one wants you to be miserable (hopefully)!

Now it's your turn – assess your personal approach in the following exercise.

Self-assessment: Making the most of your decision-making style

In the table below, identify:

1 Your own decision-making style (it may be one of the headings shown above, or a combination of two or three of the entries or something completely different).
2 How you can use this style effectively to choose a career path.

Your personal decision-making style (give it a name)	How it works	How you can use this style effectively to choose a career path

Reflecting on your answers: If you're happy with this approach, think of some way of making sure you stick to it – you could glue this exercise over your bed, tell your boyfriend to keep you on track, or write it down and ask your grandad to post it to you every month.

Looking more deeply

You could read every book ever written on particular careers but still have no real idea as to what they're really about on a daily basis. Therefore, once you've come up with one or two possible occupations, get out there and do what you can to confirm your decision. For example, you could find some experience in the field, volunteer, speak to people who carry out that role, and chat to people on your social networks. Of course, this experience will also help you get your foot in the door! Don't be put off if you can only find menial tasks – everyone has to start somewhere!

The Rt. Honourable Ann Widdecombe

Remember, the whole of your life is before you. What you do now does not have to be what you are doing in ten years' time. I began in industry, moved to university administration, ended up in parliament and have now been on stage at the Royal Opera House!

If you're still not sure

Don't panic if you're still confused. This is quite understandable because there are just so many options. There are a number of things you can do to break the impasse, such as:

- Get away from things for a while and refresh your perspective, e.g., travel, play football, volunteer in any area you'll enjoy.
- Take a break and return to the issues when you're refreshed.
- Aim for any role that meets a fair number of your skills, interests and motivations, but keep your options open. After all, the modern graduate recruitment market is so flexible you can refocus at any stage.
- Just jump in and try anything but keep your eyes open for interesting new directions.
- Become a 'slasher', i.e. a portfolio careerist holding down a range of roles – e.g., a journalist/web editor/PR consultant. Many slashers combine paid employment with volunteering opportunities and even set up one or two businesses. This career route is exciting because you can try little bits of what you enjoy.
- Study for an interesting night-course in an area you find interesting, or even a Masters/PhD.

Elizabeth Hunt, BSc (Hons) Chiropractic

For as long as I can remember I had always wanted to be a dentist. I liked the idea of having the option to work for myself and work in the medical profession without having to work shifts. Also, dentists always seemed to drive nice cars and this was very appealing to me as a teenager.

I was always a hard-working student, not a natural academic, but I managed to maintain good grades throughout my school years, finally achieving As and Bs in my GCSEs.

I had done my research and knew that to study dentistry at university, I would need three A levels, two of which had to be science subjects, and I would need to achieve at least two As and a B. With that in mind I chose to study biology, chemistry and modern history at Greenhead College, Huddersfield.

Throughout my time at Greenhead College I continued to work hard, but found it increasingly difficult to achieve the As and Bs I was used to gaining. I was finding that A levels were much tougher than I had anticipated and by the end of the first year it was quite evident I was not going to attain the grades I needed to study dentistry.

I was thrown into a state of panic! I had never considered doing anything else and I was supposed to apply for universities in a few months. I filled out questionnaires which were supposed to identify what type of career I was suited to, spoke to my careers adviser and spent hours researching different career pathways on the Internet. I was so preoccupied with finding myself an alternative profession that I found my grades were slipping further.

I thought I had looked into every possible career that was remotely involved in the health care profession until my dad suggested chiropractic and/or osteopathy. My initial response was 'What's that?' However, once I had looked into it further and visited several chiropractors and osteopaths, I decided it was something I could see myself doing and applied.

I did a further year at Greenhead College to improve my results, pick up a few AS levels and give myself a bit of time to confirm that I was making the right decision.

After that year I have never looked back. I started my chiropractic training in 2002, having the time of my life at university. In 2006 I graduated with an upper second-class qualification in chiropractic and got a job straight after university in my home town. I now have my own practice with an associate chiropractor and three reception staff working for me. I love my job and now, when I look back, I cannot imagine why I wanted to be a dentist. Why would I want to look in people's mouths all day?

Louis Theroux, Broadcaster

If you're not sure what you want to do with your life, just jump in and see what happens. Sometimes doing the wrong thing can help you figure out what the right thing is.

Ann Berry, Careers Adviser/Postgraduate course leader/Interim business coordinator/Event florist/Celebrant Registrar (to name but a few of my jobs)

A portfolio careerist means never getting bored doing the same old 9–5 routine, never having to think that you will have to endure yet another day in the same office chair shuffling the same office papers! It is an option for the adventurous, the enterprising and the slightly mad. The thrill of not knowing where your next project might come from or what your next task might be or even whether there will be a next task is often exciting and even more often scary. You have to balance your books, worry about cash flow, network like crazy, put yourself forward, take risks and go with the flow. It beats the full-time routine any day for me.

ℹ️ Useful links

Websites

www.prospects.ac.uk – See 'Job profiles' and/or 'What job would suit me'
www.nationalcareersservice.direct.gov.uk – See 'Skills health check'
www.thebalancecareers.com – See 'How to make a career choice when you are undecided'
www.reed.co.uk/career-advice/how-to-choose-a-career

On YouTube
'How to make a decision' – The School of Life

PART III

UPPING YOUR GAME

Now you have a role in mind, it's time to make sure you impress employers. This involves assessing your strengths and weaknesses and planning the next steps so you can improve what you have to offer.

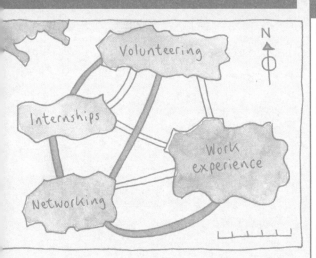

CHAPTER 6

Boosting your employability

Putting yourself in the best position to succeed

What is employability?

The term 'employability' is a recent introduction to the English dictionary and it can therefore still mean different things to different people:

- Educators tend to focus on the key transferable skills required by employers.
- Careers Advisers often include other aspects of human development such as personal attributes and the ability to take control.
- Administrators and politicians often see it as a simple statistical metric to indicate graduate outcomes.

In this book, the term is used to represent the key attributes you need to find a job and move your career forward. These are, primarily, your skills, commitment and knowledge, although they also include factors such as experience, qualifications, timing and luck, as outlined in the triangle of success below (as developed from the diagram shown in Chapter 1).

This chapter explores what's important in each of these areas and helps you improve what you have to offer. Part V, later in the book, shows you how to prove these attributes to employers.

The triangle of success

Experience and qualifications

Experience and qualifications

Skills

Commitment

Knowledge

Experience and qualifications

Luck and timing

Improving your skills

1. Identify the skills you'll need

The skills required by employers fall into two main categories as follows.

Universal transferable skills: These are the 'soft' abilities that are generally required by most employers in all sectors, a selection of those most in demand is shown below:

Transferable skills in widespread demand	
● Teamwork	● Planning
● Verbal communication	● Organisation
● Analysing	● Numeracy
● Decision-making	● Negotiating and persuading
● Written communication	● Leadership

Role specific skills: The unique set of requirements for each specific sector, role and vacancy comprising:

- The unique set of transferable skills stipulated by each employer. These could include some of the abilities listed in the table above, but also, far more wide-ranging abilities such as languages, administration and perseverance. It's up to you to figure out what they are.
- The narrow technical/task related skills that are directly linked to what you'll be doing. For example, if you want to be a seamstress, you'll need to know how to sew! These skills are often overlooked in career guides because there's no way of covering all the requirements of each individual job in just one article or book, but they are just as important!

A table has been provided on the companion website www.macmillanihe.com/rook-gcg-2e listing the key skills required in each sector. You can also use the following resources to delve deeper into the individual roles:

- Graduate career websites such as www.prospects.ac.uk, www.targetjobs.co.uk and www.nationalcareersservice.direct.gov.uk.
- The job specs in typical vacancies.
- Your contacts.
- Professionals in the field (you can probably meet them at events on campus).
- Careers Advisers.

Peter Hass, professional legal role

I finally went into law after trying any number of other careers in my twenties. Funnily enough, when I graduated I did consider this career but didn't think I was up for it and, at the time, I probably wasn't. But, it's not turned out as difficult as I thought it would be!

Last summer, I happened to be working with a few lawyers in a really boring role in a PR agency and chatted to them about the role and they encouraged me to apply. They said I shouldn't think so negatively about all the roles I had performed over the years but tease out the skills I had gained and present them confidently to employers. It seemed my professional attitude and seeming confidence would carry the day.

Therefore, I would suggest to anyone considering a career to find experience and get used to working in any position from Monday to Friday, week in/week out and pretty soon they'll realise what they have to offer.

Use the research tools outlined above, and any other resources you have to hand, to identify the specific skills you'll need in your chosen sector and role. You can do this in the exercise below. Try to find a full range of skills including wider transferable skills, the transferable skills targeted in your chosen area and the technical requirements.

Self-assessment: What skills will you need?

Identify eight specific skills required in a specific role in your chosen sector (don't worry if you're still not sure what to go into, just pick a role that looks interesting).

1		5	
2		6	
3		7	
4		8	

Reflecting on your answers: Now you've identified the skills you need, you can figure out your strengths and weaknesses and move forward.

Jenny Hasseter, Legal Trainee

During my time at university I started working for a local law firm in the general office after my dad got me a job there because his friend works there as a solicitor. I just did general filing over summer and answered the phones; that sort of thing. Frankly, I found it quite boring really and was looking forward to the new term so I could leave. However, during my leaving drinks party the partner in charge of training contracts asked me to consider their firm if I went into law. Well, we kept in touch and, when the time came, I duly applied and was given a contract and taken on part-time while I undertook my further qualifications.

At first the work was still quite boring as it involved checking paperwork and running straightforward conveyancing issues but I wanted more. So, the first lesson/skill I learned was the need to put myself forward for more interesting tasks. I did this by researching other responsibilities to the point where I was confident that I could do them. I also made sure I excelled in everything I was asked to do, went the extra mile with tasks, got to know the junior solicitors better and stayed late at work (this is common in law). In this way, more interesting work finally came my way.

I also picked up on the need to organise my work schedule every single day so I stayed ahead and improved my English which I did by just looking up websites on grammar (this was boring but it has really helped).

2. Assess your strengths

Presumably, you've chosen a particular employment sector and/or role because you have many of the skills required but, of course, there will be gaps. In the following exercise, list two skills required in your chosen field and, for each, outline your strengths and some areas for improvement. Some of the key transferable skills are expanded on the next page, if you need some help, but don't forget the extra skills you'll need that are not shown here.

Self-assessment: Assessing your strengths

1 List two skills you'll require in your chosen sector/role.
2 For each skill, outline one or two of your strengths and some areas you can improve.

Problem-solving is provided as an example.

The skills required in your chosen role	Your strengths	Some areas you can improve
Example skill: Problem-solving	● Clearly unravelling the key issues ● Researching a range of solutions	● Getting help from others ● Confidence in my conclusions
●	●	●
	●	●
●	●	●
	●	●

Reflecting on your answers: Reflecting on your skills in this way is an important skill in itself because a career is for life and this ability will help you prepare for any future challenge.

Upping your game

Some components of the key transferable skills	
The skill	**Some elements of what's involved**
Verbal communication	● Accurately hearing what people are saying. ● Clarifying and summarising what people are conveying. ● Not interrupting. ● Telephone skills (preparing what you want to say in advance and keeping business calls to the point). ● Speaking to an audience (e.g. thinking up interesting ways to put your message across, using audio-visual aids effectively, building rapport). ● Making effective use of body language, dress, conduct, speech.
Teamwork	● Contributing. ● Taking a share of responsibilities in a group. ● Being assertive, rather than passive or aggressive. ● Accepting and learning from constructive criticism and giving positive feedback.
Analysing Investigating Decision-making	● Clarifying problems before choosing what to do. ● Collecting, collating, classifying and summarising data to help you proceed. ● Condensing information/producing summary notes. ● Appropriately synthesising and applying information.
Written communication	● Preparing what you are going to say. ● Gathering, analysing and arranging data in a logical sequence. ● Developing your argument. ● Adopting your delivery for different media and audiences.
Planning and organisation	● Managing your time effectively. ● Prioritising tasks effectively. ● Setting objectives which are achievable and measurable. ● Identifying the steps needed to achieve goals.
Numeracy	● Calculating percentages. ● Multiplying and dividing accurately. ● Interpreting graphs and tables. ● Managing a limited budget.
Negotiating and persuading	● Developing a line of reasoned argument. ● Understanding the needs of your interlocutors. ● Using tact and diplomacy. ● Making concessions to reach agreement.
Leadership	● Setting objectives. ● Organising and motivating others. ● Taking initiative. ● Accepting responsibility for mistakes/incorrect decisions. ● Preparedness to adapt goals in the light of changing situations.

3. Improve what you have to offer

Now you know where you can make improvements, you can systematically up your game. Unsurprisingly, the best place to develop your skills is in a job, because this type of experience will be highly regarded by employers, but you can also enhance your offering in almost every other walk of life, such as during your networking sessions, studies, hobbies, volunteering, internships ... etc.

If you're just starting out, don't worry. You can just look out for any experience at all where you can enhance your skills and then gradually work your way up into internships and graduate roles that are more closely related to your chosen role. For example, if you want to work in event management, you could join the events committee in a club in your Student Union, work your way up to managing that committee, volunteer with a local charity, then apply for an internship. Who knows, you may well be offered a job on the way! However, be careful, you won't automatically develop your skills just by undertaking new activities. You also need to regularly reflect on how you're improving and constantly push yourself to new heights.

Developing your commitment

What commitment is

The second key recruitment criterion for employers is your commitment – this is your attitude, drive and application. Employers test your strengths in this area by gauging your true motivations such as:

- Why you want to enter their particular sector and role.
- What experience you've undertaken to find out more.
- How your studies and experience have confirmed your decision.

Faking your answers to these fundamental questions in your applications and interviews is much more difficult than it sounds, because real passion stands out, and also, what's the point? If you're not genuinely excited by a role, why go for it?

Enhancing your offering

Eight strategies for developing your career commitment are outlined below. These flow directly from your preparedness to aspire to a truly fulfilling role, and your passion, as outlined in Chapter 4.

1 **Believe in yourself (self-efficacy):** Self-efficacy is confidence in your own ability to improve your future. It is a crucial element of your career because, if you believe you'll succeed at something, then you probably will. Low self-efficacy can be caused by a number of factors, such as a lack of confidence, having a bad run of things, shyness, a lack of experience, unfamiliarity with professional environments, and moving to a new culture. You can improve your self-efficacy in your career by visualising positive outcomes; starting out with

small, achievable steps; surrounding yourself with people who succeed; and finding someone you trust to act as your coach.

2 **Stay healthy in mind and body:** It's quite easy to let yourself get run down at uni, especially if you're not looking after yourself. If you're struggling, find a safe place to rest your head, eat properly, avoid drugs and alcohol and seek counselling (available on most campuses at no extra charge).

3 **Develop your thought processes:** This involves two crucial stages, as outlined below.

   (a) **Metacognition:** This is your awareness of how you react to challenges and opportunities. For example, do you plan things carefully, or just jump in and see how they go? Think about how you tend to respond to new issues in life.

   (b) **Developing a constructive mind-set:** Once you've reflected on your unique thought processes, you can eradicate any negative processes and develop more effective ways of thinking that will help you enhance your career (and every other aspect of your life). One great way to find positivity is to consciously adjust your thought processes in insignificant areas of your life until they become second nature. For example, if you're generally apprehensive about change, you could train yourself to respond positively to friends' suggestions when you're out and about (they won't know what's hit them) until, one day, you'll start reacting this way when you face new challenges at work.

4 **Focus:** Now you're ready to dream, it's time to target the exact position you're seeking. Don't panic If you're still not sure where you're heading; just try to narrow things down as far as possible, e.g., the sector and the type of employer. This will allow you to find relevant experience and effective networks, so your applications stand out.

5 **Get busy:** Nothing demonstrates your commitment more than hard work so don't just sit at home waiting for the perfect opportunity to come and knock on your door; jump in and get involved with any vaguely relevant opportunity. For example, you could learn a useful technical skill at night-school, forge new contacts in a part-time job or drive a taxi in the evenings so you can volunteer during the day. If you make yourself busy, any number of opportunities will come your way. For example, if you take a job in a supermarket, one of your new colleagues may be happy to put you in touch with his sister who happens to work in the exact area you want to pursue. This is actually how most people find their careers! (Not necessarily in a supermarket.)

6 **Persevere/Show your resilience:** Perseverance is about maintaining your focus until you reach your destination, and not giving up when the going gets tough. This is such a crucial aspect of your commitment because the best career opportunities often go to those who've knocked on

the most doors. Learn that failure is not your enemy, but a crucial element of success. In Michael Jordan's words (the great basketball player): "I've missed more than nine thousand shots in my career. I've lost almost three hundred games. Twenty-six times, I've been trusted to take the game winning shot and missed. I've failed over and over again in my life. And that is why I succeed."[1] Therefore, if plan A doesn't work, adjust your plans and move on.

7 **Assess your progress and adapt:** If you've tried, tried and tried again but still haven't found career success, you don't necessarily have to give up and start again. Success may be very close with just minor adjustments to your strategy. Therefore, it pays to regularly assess how your journey is going and tweak things as necessary. For example, maybe you just need to approach more suitable organisations, improve your applications or get a bit more experience. You can reflect on your progress by keeping a firm eye on your destination, ticking off your achievements, being honest with yourself about why you're getting stuck and formally recording your successes and failures so as to identify a pattern.

8 **And finally ... take your chances:** Opportunities can be dressed up in any number of guises, such as a volunteering opportunity advertised in the small print of a crunched-up newspaper, a chance meeting with your friend's mum who happens to know a key local employer, or a strange job offer from a contact on Instagram. Therefore, it's up to you to keep your eyes open and creatively look for opportunities, then take them!

Expanding your knowledge

The third key ingredient of your all-round employability is an in-depth understanding of your role and how it fits in with the wider context; this can be subdivided into the following headings.

Your subject understanding

This involves any information, theories, principles and research that are relevant to your role. For example, if you want to be a maths teacher, you'll need to know the curriculum, how it's taught and the principles of good classroom management. At least, try to grasp the relevant jargon, initialisms and acronyms, which can often mark you as an insider: for example, sales jobs may involve terms such as B2B, CRM, lead qualifications and warm calling.

Your role in context

This involves a whole range of understandings including an appreciation of what's going on in the world, the culture of the society and industry where you'll be working and your commercial awareness, including:

- An appreciation of the current political affairs in the country/area.
- Popular culture such as football, TV, film ...
- How your role fits into the wider structure of an organisation and the market in which it sits.

Other key factors

Experience and qualifications

As shown in the diagram on page 57, these attributes are also crucial to success but only indirectly through the skills, commitment and knowledge you've gained. Therefore, if employers actually stipulate experience and/or qualifications on their personal specifications (as many do), outline what you've done, as requested, but also make sure you link these achievements to the skills, commitment and knowledge required. You can see how to do this in the chapters on applications.

Personal traits

Employers often use any number of other personal criteria when they choose candidates, whether or not they are fair. Examples include your looks, gender, sex, sexual preference, race and age. It's up to you to identify what each recruiter is after and act accordingly. If you're concerned about the approach being taken, speak to a Careers Adviser or someone at your Student Union to figure out how to proceed.

Timing and luck

Of course, as the triangle of success also shows, timing and luck have a big influence on career success, as in most areas of life. However, you shouldn't just sit back and hope you're lucky; you need to go out of your way to be seen and heard and create your own good fortune.

The USEM Model of Employability

Various frameworks have been designed to demonstrate how you need to combine the various aspects of employability to achieve a fulfilling and successful career. The USEM model[2] links these elements into an intuitive and practical matrix, as shown below. Take some time to make sense of the various connections, for example:

- The key inputs of employability are understanding, skilful practices, efficacy beliefs and metacognition.
- Your efficacy beliefs directly affect your skills and understanding, and metacognition.
- Metacognition, skills and understanding are all mutually dependent.

The USEM Model of Employability

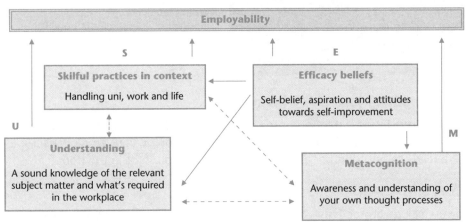

Adapted from: *Learning, Curriculum & Employability in Higher Education*, Peter Knight and Mantz Yorke, © 2003 and Routledge, reproduced by permission of Taylor & Francis Books UK.

You can find out more about linking your key employabilty attributes into a plan of action in the next chapter (Chapter 7).

ℹ️ Useful links

Websites
www.skillsyouneed.com – See 'Seven ways to improve your employability'
www.careers.ox.ac.uk – See 'Boosting your employability'
www.success.com – See '5 ways to become the person you aspire to be'

On YouTube
'How to Make a Decision' – The School of Life
'Find your dream job without ever looking at your resume' – Laura Berman/ Fortgang
'3 tips to boost your confidence' – TED-Ed
'Don't Be Afraid to Fail Big, To Dream Big' – Denzel Washington/Goalcast

CHAPTER 7
Moving forward

> " The journey of a thousand miles begins with just one step.
> *Lao Tzu* "

Your personal journey planner

Now you have found a role/sector to enter, assessed the skills, commitment and knowledge required and considered how you can improve your employability, you're ready to put together a plan of action to get your foot in the door.

What's involved

You can include any activity you want into your plan – it's your plan! But be clear about how each step is going to carry you forwards in terms of your employabilty. Some common steps are:

- Networking
- Further study
- Work experience and internships
- Further study
- Taking time out

Plus, incorporate any additional activities that meet your personal needs and interests such as hobbies, starting your own business, trying a different range of roles for a while, focusing on your family, or just asking your friends for advice. It's up to you – just take control and plan your specific steps forward.

Start from where you are now

Before making plans, make sure you have a sound appreciation of what you currently offer employers in terms of your employabity and experience. This will allow you to identify new development opportrnities at a relevant level. For example, if you're just starting out and have a very thin CV, don't just apply to a hundred blue-chip internships; start with something that's easier to achieve like volunteering or joining a local club. Alternatively, if you've already gathered extensive experience, don't just keep looking for similar roles – take a step up!

Big feet, small steps

Make sure your plan is postive and ambitious and also that each of your individual goals is manifestly achievable, keeping in mind that you shouldn't feel limited by time or circumstance and can take as many steps as you want. For example, if you want to be a personal assistant to a movie star, you may consider the following route:

- Volunteer at a charity.
- Develop your organisational and communication skills.
- Network with people from arts-based charities.
- Find an administrative role in a charity that works closely with the media.
- Move up into a PA role for a senior member of staff.
- Liaise with your media clients.
- Become a PA for one of your clients.
- Liaise with people in the film industry.
- Become a PA for a film industry executive.
- Liaise with big-time movie actors.
- Become a PA for a star.

Many students and fresh graduates get this the wrong way round; setting unambitious targets and giant, vague strategies that are doomed to fail. For example, they may settle with any admin job at all in the film idustry and establish two or three loosely defined steps to get there, such as:

- Undertaking a Masters in film production (this may help them find admin roles, but how?).
- Finding a management job in a film studio (without any management experience?).
- Living it up! (Maybe not.)

Upping your game

Now it's your turn

In the table overleaf, specify the role you want to enter (be as specific as possible) and list six steps you could take to get there. Also, enter a realistic date by which you hope to meet your target, you can then refer back to this plan as you progress over the coming months and years. Make sure you're ambitious but practical. You can use the example plans below to help you join the dots.

Some example career plans

Sam Davey – Getting into Hotel Management in the USA

1 See what the hospitality sector is like
2 Go to employer events to find out more
3 Decide whether I want to undertake that role
4 Go on a gap year in Australia and look for experience that might help me get my foot in the door
5 Come back and get some more targeted experience
6 Find an internship
7 Undertake a relevant Masters
8 Find a UK Management Traineeship
9 Become a hotel manager for an international chain
10 Get transferred to the USA

Susan Bell – Becoming a partner in a marketing firm

1 Assess my relevant skills, interests and motivations
2 See what marketing roles are suitable
3 Figure out how to specialise
4 Get my uncle Jordan to give me some experience in that role
5 Look for a relevant Masters overseas
6 Apply for an internship at a firm in London
7 Secure a graduate role
8 Move to my uncle's firm
9 Become a manager
10 Become a partner

Self-assessment: Your own personal career strategy

Plan your personal route into your career (incorporate extra steps if need be):

Your manageable steps	Completion date
Step 1:	
Step 2:	
Step 3:	
Step 4:	
Step 5:	
Step 6:	
Your destination	

Reflecting on your answers: Ask a Careers Adviser if this plan seems realistic and amend it accordingly.

Plan B

Plan A rarely works out in real life and your destination and journey may well turn out to be very different from your original plans. This can either be because you change your mind when something better comes along, or your strategies don't work. However, this isn't necessarily a problem, you just need to be resilient and creative and find new ways to move forward (see the chaos theory in Chapter 2). Therefore, many students and fresh graduates find it handy to come up with a plan B, plan C … etc. before they even get going, just in case their first approach doesn't work out.

In the following exercise, identfify a step on your career plan above that may be difficult to achieve, and draw up an alternative strategy from there on in. This may be a completely fresh approach or just a short detour to get around a roadblock, so you can return to your original plan. This back-up plan will give you peace of mind if you find yourself banging your head on a brick wall (if it's actually possible to find peace of mind whilst banging your head on a brick wall!).

Self-assessment: Career strategy: Take 2

1 Pick a step from your original career plan that you think may be tricky to achieve.
2 Design a new strategy to get to your destination from there on in.

Take as many or as few steps as you want.

The step you think will be tricky:	
Your plan B	**Completion date**
Your first alternative step:	
Your steps from there	**Completion date**
Step 2:	
Step 3:	
Step 4:	
Step 5:	
Your destination	

Reflecting on your answers: Be careful that by exploring a plan B, you don't give up too easily on plan A, but be reassured that there are almost always alternative routes to your destination. You just need patience, creativity and a positive mind-set and, if possible, don't panic!

Useful links

Websites

www.mindtools.com – See the various project management tools
www.jobs.ac.uk – See the 5-minute career action plan
www.massey.ac.nz – See 'Developing employability skills: An action plan for students'

PART IV

MAKING IT HAPPEN

Now that you have a grounding in modern graduate employment and recruitment, you can move ahead and develop the building blocks of your career. Depending on where you are in the career planning process these could involve any or all of the chapters shown alongside.

GOLDEN OPPORTUNITY

How to prepare for the job hunt

Carl Gilleard, Former Chief Executive of the Institute of Student Employers (ISE)

Beginning to hunt for jobs can be daunting for young people: many may be uncertain about what their ideal job looks like and unaware of the possibilities open to them, whilst others will have a more specific idea, but be concerned about how competitive their chosen field is.

However, those who use their time at university wisely will have ample opportunities to think through their goals, and build up an impressive portfolio of relevant experience. Students develop their employability skills all the time whilst taking part in extra-curricular activities, whether through team sports, taking a leadership role within a university society, or showing their creativity by writing for a student paper – they just need to present these skills in a clear and meaningful way to boost their CVs.

Work experience is an excellent way to prepare for job hunting. Taking on a casual job during university holiday, or volunteering for charity during a gap year, helps to demonstrate drive and awareness of working environments. The more experience students gain, the better placed they will be to make decisions about which roles are likely to suit them.

When choosing what jobs to go for, students and graduates should focus on selecting the right roles and putting in high quality applications, rather than spending time filling out multiple cut-and-paste applications for roles that don't suit them. Finally, it's important to have long- as well as short-term career goals and value your first job as an important step on the career ladder.

CHAPTER 8

Managing your networks and social media

" Skill is fine, and genius is splendid,
but the right contacts are more
valuable than either.
Sir Arthur Conan Doyle *"*

The times they are a changing

It's always been important to know the right people, especially when it comes to finding work. Therefore, well-connected students and graduates have always had the edge.

However, if your mum isn't the head of Google and your dad's not David Beckham, there is still hope. Society has diversified over recent years to allow greater interaction between different groups of people and the Internet has heralded a host of effective new channels. Therefore, there is now unprecedented scope to meet the people who can make a difference in your life; you just need to reach out and get in touch.

" You just need to reach out and get in touch. *"*

What are networks?

The *Oxford Concise Dictionary* defines networks as 'groups of people who exchange contacts and experience for professional or social purposes'. The word comes from the arrangement of horizontal and vertical lines on a fishing net and, therefore, implies that we are all connected through an ever-widening, latticework of links.

Why networks are important

Employers are investing heavily in their networks in order to effectively advertise vacancies, keep in touch with applicants and find effective staff. They're actively beefing up their online channels and finding new ways to meet students and graduates in person as well as online. This is because they realise the benefits of finding the very best applicants in a competitive market. This, in turn, enables students and graduates from every section of society (i.e. you!) to raise their profiles and get noticed. The collective value of your networks and the benefits they deliver is called your social capital.

David Griffiths, Graduate, AlphaSights

We are always actively on the look-out for people who can talk openly and honestly about working with us, as well as confidence and enthusiasm. It's absolutely crucial that we find graduates with whom we can build positive personal and professional relationships and who fit in with our teams.

Finding the courage

It can be really hard getting out there and proactively engaging with people with the sole purpose of enhancing your career because it can be scary to make contact, embarrassing to be so mercenary and often challenging to admit that you're aiming for an ambitious future (at least to yourself).

If this sounds like you, there's some bad news and some good news. The bad news is that employment is almost always, at its heart, a social endeavour and therefore relationships will always be key, so you have to find a way. The good news is, networking need not be an ego driven, forceful endeavour, so you can design your own tailored strategy. For example, if you enjoy mixing with colleagues at work but don't socialise much, look around your workplace and chat to some interesting people or, if you mainly mix with members of your own family, find ways to meet up with cousins and aunts who may be able to help.

If, for any reason, you feel like you have an inbuilt disadvantage when it comes to mixing with employers, you should ask for help from people who understand your particular situation. For example, if you're from a family with few professional contacts or you're older/from an under-represented gender or ethnic background and face prejudice, you could seek assistance from:

- People in your family.
- Your university careers service (which may be able to put you in touch with a mentor).

- Specific student societies (such as The Jewish Society).
- Local or national mentoring groups for people from your community, such as the Aspire Foundation for women at www.aspirewomen.co.uk.

Who you should know

Your personal and online networks should include your friends and family, lecturers, careers advisers, professionals, recruiters, representatives of professional organisations (such as The Chartered Institute of Marketing) and other students and graduates. You should also join up with people who share your unique character, situation and aspirations. For example:

- If a relative works in the field you want to enter then you should definitely get in touch with her friends and colleagues.
- If you want to work overseas you should reach out to people from interesting businesses and expat communities in the region.

How your contacts can help

There are several ways your contacts can help you develop your career, limited only by your own creativity and imagination. For example, they could:

- Tell you what their careers are really like.
- Tell you what skills you'll need to succeed.
- Show you how to get your foot in the door.
- Give you experience.
- Give you a job.

Of course, only some of the people you contact will be willing and able to help but, if you make enough contacts, then sooner or later, you'll get a break. Bear in mind, even if a thousand people say no to your requests for help, you only need one to say yes, so the odds are always in your favour!

What you can do for them

Effective networking is not just about getting in touch with people and asking for help, it usually comes down to a simple process of 'you scratch my back and I'll scratch yours'. Therefore, you'll get much more help from your contacts if you give them an incentive. For example, you could volunteer to help them out in some way, answer any questions they pose on social media and/or put them in touch with potential customers.

Your personal interactions

Why they're important

Nowadays, when most students and graduates think of networking, they immediately turn to platforms such as Twitter, LinkedIn and Facebook. However, you shouldn't underestimate the value of traditional methods of getting in touch, such as phone calls, letters and, of course, personal interactions.

Making it happen

What you can do

There are several ways you can expand your real-world network, as outlined below.

- Keep in touch with the people you already know.
- Get out there and make new acquaintances.
- Figure out ways of brushing shoulders with useful new contacts (for example, you could join local clubs, go to employer events, volunteer in professional settings or sign up to relevant professional organisations).
- Get your existing contacts to introduce you to people on their networks; for example, ask a friend to put you in touch with his boss and/or visit your next-door neighbour when his dad is visiting (if he's in a field you want to enter).

Be the best you can be

Before reaching out to employers, take some time to enhance your image. You don't have to abandon your character altogether; you just need to interact positively and present your best features. Above all, you should be well-spoken, attentive, friendly, professional, polite and well-presented.

Your social networks

Why social networks are important

Social media have quickly become absolutely crucial weapons in your networking arsenal as almost all employers now use them to promote their opportunities and identify talent. For example, Jobvite recently found that 93% of recruiters take candidates' social profiles into account in their hiring decisions and 55% of employers have changed their decisions based on what they've found.

Developing your online brand

Use a professional and consistent image: Upload the same picture of yourself onto each of your platforms so people get used to seeing you around. Avoid any shade or glare and sunglasses, and many experts suggest you squint your eyes slightly to achieve a more professional look. You can assess the effectiveness of your images at www.photofeeler.com.

Some example key words
Media analyst
IT project manager
London
Diploma in Social Work
DipSW
PwC
Accounting technician
BSc Chemistry
Teamwork

Keep the same name and username: Use your real name on all your profiles because this looks professional, you'll be easily found and names are used to rank profiles on search engines. Also, try to find a consistent short, memorable and descriptive username which represents what you have to offer (professionally). You can check whether names are universally available at www.knowem.com.

Managing your networks and social media

Get your profile noticed: Use any written sections to sell yourself, especially your bio/headline/summary. These constitute your 'elevator' pitch to recruiters so it's crucial you use keywords that will be picked up. One good way to find good keywords in your sector is to look through relevant job adverts. Focus on words and phrases for the following:

- Your name and job title.
- Previous job titles.
- Your target employer and previous employers.
- Your location/target location.
- Your qualifications and skills.
- Industry jargon.

Try to come up with some possible keywords for your social profiles in the exercise below.

Self-assessment: Social media keywords

List ten possible keywords for your social network profiles that will be noticed by recruiters.

Ten effective keywords for your social profiles
1
2
3
4
5
6
7
8
9
10

Reflecting on your answers: Assess your answers by Googling various combinations of the words you've identified and seeing how many job adverts you unearth.

Fully complete your profile: Be thorough, don't just fill out the main sections on each of your profiles. Additional media elements such as pictures, videos and presentations will also boost your image (as long as they're on message and support your brand).

Making it happen

Review your existing content: Make sure your online presence is clean and decent. Obviously, delete any pictures that don't put you in a positive light, and any swear words, but also remove any rants and articles/posts that are contentious and/or offensive.

Customise your background: On some channel profiles, such as Twitter and YouTube, you can upload customised backgrounds. This allows you to portray your brand even more effectively. For example, if you're an engineer, you could upload a scene where you're working on a particularly impressive project. Also, you could design a picture with extra icons and links to your other networks.

Control your settings and permissions: You have to take an active decision over who'll be able to see your information and interactions. Obviously, the wider you distribute your messages, the more effectively you can network, but keep yourself safe. To give your channels any hope of success you should release your bio, summary and profile picture.

You can find out more about networking on social media at 'Tweet your way to a job: Using social media to develop your career' at www.theguardian.com, and 'Digital networking' at www.brad.ac.uk.

Facebook/Instagram/Pinterest ...

The true 'friendship-based' social networks can be especially helpful at the start of your career journey because you can get yourself noticed and keep abreast of all sorts of opportunities and events. Even though these platforms tend to be informal, you should still make sure you're perceived in a positive light because potential employers will almost certainly look you up. So, if you're tagged in a thousand semi-clad pictures, chugging vodka, your chances may be few! Four ways to keep your brand positive and clean are as follows:

- Use a professional looking email address.
- Set appropriate privacy settings and regularly review your comments and images.
- Post regularly, presenting yourself as an outgoing, friendly person with varied interests and appropriate values.
- Post about topics related to your chosen career and report back from career relevant events and activities.

You can interact with your contacts to:

- Research employer expectations.
- Demonstrate examples of your work (such as your designs, artwork or jewellery).
- Widen your circle of friends to the sectors you want to enter and initiate professional relationships.
- Get involved in activities such as employer events on campus and volunteering opportunities.

- Communicate to find opportunities.
- Chat to professionals on an informal basis.

It's relatively straightforward to make new contacts on these platforms. You can start by just interacting with the people you already know and joining up with anyone else whose comments and contributions you enjoy. You can also look at friends' connections and see if they want to join up with you. Plus, join any groups linked to your school, university, interests and career ideas. Try this in the exercise below.

Self-assessment: Finding effective Facebook friends (or contacts on any other informal social network)

1   Google your favourite interests and industries to identify four dream Facebook contacts.
2   Figure out how you might be able to get in touch with each of them, e.g. through particular groups, or other possible contacts who are well connected (take your time to find specific links).

Who you'd love to contact	How you could possibly get in touch.

Reflecting on your answers: So, what's stopping you? Get in touch!

Twitter

Twitter has also quickly become one of the best tools for students and graduates at every stage in their career journeys whether they're just starting out or looking for blue-ribbon internships. This is because it's a great tool to research occupations and find a job. Twitter's success is down to its democratic, non-hierarchical structure and the strict limit on the length of messages (280 characters). This gives you quick and easy access to people and organisations in any area of industry and recruitment, including:

- Professionals.
- Professional organisations.
- Recruiters.

- Students and graduates.
- Trainees.
- Careers Advisers.

Making it happen

The jargon on Twitter can take a bit of time getting used to – but don't let this put you off. Some of the key terms are outlined in the table below.

A glossary of Twitter terms	
Tweet	These are your messages – you're allowed up to 280 characters of text plus photos, videos and links.
Username/Twitter handle	What you call yourself – it's always preceded by the @ symbol, e.g. @stevenrook.
Hashtag (#)	Words or amalgamations of words which are preceded by a '#' symbol such as '#jobs' and '#CareerPlanning'. Hashtags are very useful because they generate a theme of tweets which you can augment and search through (via the search tool) to research issues and promote yourself where you'll be seen. Anyone can allocate hashtags, including you!
Followers	The people and organisations who've subscribed to other users' accounts so they can see their tweets. Any registered user can normally 'follow' any other (unless you've been blocked). Just click the 'Follow' button next to a user's name or on their profile page.
RT (Retweet)	These are tweets you forward to your followers. There are various ways to retweet where you can either just forward the message or add your own comments. The retweet button has two circling arrows and looks like a recycling symbol.
DM (Direct Messages)	Private messages between users or groups.
Favoriting	Indicating you like tweets. This lets the users who've shared them know you've approved, and stores them together so you can access them at any time.

A fuller appendix of terms and guidelines can be found at www.twitter.com.

Twitter gives you two names, which appear next to all your tweets. Your account name can be fifty characters long and doesn't have to be unique so you can just choose your real name, even if it's very common, e.g. 'John Smith' or 'Joe Soap'. Usernames, on the other hand, can only be fifteen characters long, have to be unique and are preceded by an '@'. So, again, you can simply choose your name, e.g. '@jsmith' or '@JoeSoap' but, if your name is already taken (as these examples probably are), you could amend it to promote something like your blog, a society you belong to or your business; for example, you could call yourself 'Joeysoap' or '@TaxAccountant'.

You have just 160 characters in your bio to introduce yourself and outline what you have to offer/the job you're seeking, so think carefully about how you can use keywords to attract your target audience (i.e. recruiters). You may want to include the following:

- Your university (especially if it's well regarded in your subject or the career you want to enter).
- Who you work for and what you do.
- Any awards you've gained.
- Your relevant interests.
- A link to your LinkedIn page, or your website, so people can find out more.

Once you've signed up, follow relevant recruiters and gradually get involved in their discussions. You can then expand your network by seeing who your immediate contacts are following and retweeting. Research some useful Twitter links for your chosen industry in the exercise below. Look up 'Twitter' on www.ed.ac.uk, if you want to find out more.

Self-assessment: Interesting Twitter usernames and hashtags

In the table below, research your target career and identify:

(a) Four interesting Twitter users (individuals and/or organisations) who publish useful tweets and retweets.
(b) Four useful hashtags.

Users with interesting Twitter threads	Useful hashtags
@_____	#_____
@_____	#_____
@_____	#_____
@_____	#_____

Reflecting on your answers: Ask yourself how these links can help you develop your networking and jobsearch strategy (be specific).

LinkedIn

Why it's so useful

LinkedIn is used by almost all of the UK's big firms to find talent (and most of the small ones too!). Therefore, it's also a valuable tool for students and graduates to network, research occupations, industries and career paths and find a job. Your LinkedIn page is also a brilliant place to outline everything you have to offer, in detail, and can therefore be used as your virtual CV, especially if you use it as your 'landing page', i.e. you link to it from all your other social networking sites.

Filling in your profile

LinkedIn profiles tend to be more substantial than most other platforms. Here are some tactics to make yours stand out:

- Sell yourself by saturating every section with appropriate keywords.
- Create an 'All-star' profile, as indicated by a circle at the top right-hand corner of your page, by thoroughly filling in every section. This is important because, when employers search for talent with certain keywords such as 'London', 'accountant' 'and 'intern', they'll get thousands of hits but the 'All-star' profiles will be on page one – and who looks past that?
- Focus on your skills, experiences and achievements that are relevant to the career you want to follow.
- Create an attractive headline (this is the short section just under your name, where you can attract employers' attention) and make it clear you're looking for a job! (unless you don't want your current employer to know). For example, you could write something like: 'Student at Warwick University | Digital marketing specialist | Seeks internship | Experience of social media, PPC, SEO, video, content, PR and advertising.'
- Provide a targeted summary. LinkedIn advises you to: 'Describe what motivates you, what you're skilled at, and what's next.' This is your opportunity to outline your accomplishments, strengths, ambitions and interests and tie them to the work you're seeking. Also, upload images, video or other multimedia elements to add a bit of colour.
- Secure some recommendations from employers, academics and influential contacts.
- List up to twenty skills that are relevant to your industry so people can endorse you as these can dictate the types of vacancies that turn up in your jobs folder.
- Contact people using your own personalised text (i.e., avoid the platform's default messages) and tailor what you write to the situation and your existing relationship. For example, if you've just met someone at the rugby club, you could write: 'Hi Brian. I really enjoyed meeting you and Florence after the match on Saturday – it would be great if we could link up on LinkedIn.'

To find out more about networking on LinkedIn see 'Using LinkedIn' on www.ed. ac.uk and 'The 31 best LinkedIn profile tips for job seekers' on www.themuse.com.

Selina Begum, UK Head of Resourcing, Springer Nature

Social media platforms such as Twitter, YouTube and LinkedIn are a great way for you to find out what it's really like to work for a company! Companies use social media tools to convey their employer brand and they upload some great content such as employee video interviews and 'Day in the Life' blogs, so my tip would be to follow their channels to get a real insight into who they are and their values. Social media is a great alternative to the traditional job boards for HR Professionals like myself to attract talented candidates who are engaged with our brand and upon interview will show real interest in joining us as they have been keeping up to date with our latest content. A lot of companies use LinkedIn to advertise their vacancies and to headhunt candidates, therefore my advice would be to get ahead and create your LinkedIn profile. Think of LinkedIn as your personal advert, and use it to describe your professional self to the world. LinkedIn works like a search engine, so use the platform wisely and choose the right descriptive words so you can be found by the right people. Include your achievements too: they will really help you stand out against other candidates. Lastly, check your spelling and grammar, as how you present yourself is an indication to the reader of how you may perform in the role.

Blogging

Blogs are personal online platforms where you can stand out from the crowd by developing a unique online presence and post about anything you want. They can be an especially powerful tool if you write well and market your other channels. However, you should only commit to a blog if you have the time to engage with it properly and maintain a consistently impressive product. Some possible areas to focus on are:

- Your area of interest (e.g. your love of animals if you want to be a vet).
- Your creative output (if you're an artist).
- Your situation (e.g. life as a Vietnamese student in London).
- Your experience journey (e.g. what jobs you're doing, who you're meeting …).

You can set up blogs on www.blogger.com and www.wordpress.com and find in-depth advice on www.writersdigest.com.

Making it happen

A joined-up networking strategy

So, you have numerous opportunities to create powerful networks in both your real-life interactions and your social networks but, you need to integrate your approach and develop a unified strategy. The

> **You need to integrate your approach and develop a unified strategy**

best way to do this is to settle on a universal 'brand', place a detailed profile on one of your social platforms (usually LinkedIn or your own website), then slowly and systematically build up mutually beneficial relationships before finally asking for help. Don't just jump in and ask everyone for a job! An example strategy is outlined below.

1. Get ready

- Decide how you want to be perceived by employers (your brand) and dress/conduct yourself accordingly.
- List all the people you know who may be able to help you in your career and make sure your relationships are on a sound footing.
- Establish yourself on Twitter, Facebook, LinkedIn and any other interesting platforms in line with how you want to be perceived, and get used to interacting.
- Manage your online presence through a program that links all your social networks together, e.g. www.hootsuite.com.
- Chat to your contacts (in real life and online) about career related issues.
- Ask your friends, family, peers and existing contacts to put you in touch with useful contacts either in real life or on your online networks.

2. Get set

Once you feel comfortable chatting about careers and managing your brand, both online and in real life, it's time to interact and raise your profile. For example, you could:

- Link your career-hunt to your wider experiences so it's connected to everything you do: for example, if you're in a band and you want to work in business, chat to promoters, DJs and event managers – they're bound to know someone who can help.
- Look for any opportunities (either in real life or online) to expand your network. For example, if you want to be a journalist, collect blogs and join in with every possible journalism related hashtag.
- Join professional organisations and Internet groups connected to the career you want to enter, such as those on LinkedIn (see www.linkedin.com/directory/groups).
- Find groups connected to your own particular needs. For example, if you identify yourself as being female and want to be an engineer, you could join The Women's Engineering Society.

- Join university student societies that have links with employers, such as your student law society.
- Meet people through your interests. For example, if you're into wine, you could join some local wine-tasting groups and chat to wonderful contacts over a subtle Sancerre.
- Get used to meeting your online contacts and vice-versa.
- Get involved with any career-related activities at your university such as careers fairs, employer workshops and talks.
- Raise your profile and build deeper relationships by publishing career relevant information, joining key conversations and providing positive feedback to contacts' posts, tweets and messages.
- Help people out; for example you could drive your cousin to the airport, help employers at university events and join in with any of their interactive online initiatives.

3. Go!

Once you've built strong relationships and a good reputation, you can leverage your way into work. Again, it's best to try this one step at a time as suggested below.

Ask for a chat: Ask contacts if they can spare five minutes to talk about their career, or if they can put you in touch with someone who can. Don't tell them you're looking for a job because this will probably scare them away, just say you're trying to find out more about a particular role. This is quite a simple request to grant and people will usually agree because they'll be flattered.

Don't just always rely on your immediate contacts talking to people on your behalf, you may have much more success by getting people's details and taking the initiative to contact them yourself (but still ask the person who recommends you get in touch with them to let them know you'll be calling and that you're a good egg). Although, you could consider conducting these meetings online or on the phone, it's usually far more beneficial to meet in person. For example, if your friend's father is a barrister and you want to go into law, send his dad an email to ask if you can visit him in Chambers for a five-minute chat, and ask your friend to back you up.

One way to maximise your chances of success is to give your new contact various times when you could meet (but don't be too demanding). For example, you could say, 'I'm in London next week and can see you on Tuesday at 9.00 a.m.,

Wednesday at 2.00 p.m. or Thursday at 3.00 p.m. – which time works best for you?' This is an old salesman's technique to make your contacts think they don't have a choice.

During your meetings with your contacts, you could ask questions such as what their jobs are like, what skills you'll need, how they got their careers started and how they recommend you get started. This last question can be very effective because they'll probably suggest employment experience, which you can then, immediately, request (and how can they say no?). Whether or not an interaction leads to bigger and brighter things, ask everyone you meet to give you details of further contacts who might be able to help.

Shadow: Once you've met and impressed your contacts you could ask to shadow them for a day or two at work. This just involves hanging around to see what their job is really like. While you're at their workplace, be prompt, dress appropriately and demonstrate good manners with everyone you meet. Make sure you ask intelligent questions, help out where you can and show that you have a brain. Try to identify any specific tasks where you could lend a hand such as mundane jobs no one else wants to do or something related to your skills/degree. Then, you'll be in a great position to make your next move.

Volunteer: Now you've formally met your contacts and seen what their businesses involve, offer to support them on a voluntary basis, especially if you've identified a specific project where you can make a difference. While you're there, you can then continue to impress and build rapport so that, one day, they'll see you so often they'll offer you a pay cheque.

Steve Rook, author of this guide

I decided to become a university Careers Adviser whilst running my own graduate recruitment agency in Perth, Western Australia. During this period, I regularly liaised with all sorts of university personnel and thought the careers advisory role was fantastic. Therefore, I decided to join their ranks. However, instead of just immediately applying for jobs, I decided to plan and execute a strategy to get my foot in the door. My journey involved the following steps:

1   Building stronger relationships with the Careers Advisers I had met.
2   Shadowing the Careers Advisers while they counselled students.
3   Volunteering to help.
4   Getting advisers to be my referees.
5   Applying for a part-time position in the UK (where there were far more jobs). I chose Southampton because it's expensive and out of the way so I didn't think many people would apply.
6   I got the job.
7   I gained a full-time job up north.

This journey demonstrates my newfound wisdom at this stage in my life to take control of my next steps in life – not just look for interesting jobs and apply at random.

Move into employment experience/a graduate job: Of course, once you've got your foot in the door of an organisation, you can continue to impress and establish yourself as a valued member of the team so that, when a vacancy arises, you will be in the right place at the right time and be offered the post. This process is far more common than you might imagine and explains why over 50 per cent of jobs in the UK are never advertised.

Other approaches: Now you've engendered a good reputation, you can also request assistance in any number of additional ways – for example, you could ask contacts to:

● Help with applications.
● Recommend you to their contacts.
● Give you a job.
● Find you a position further afield.
● Pass around a speculative application (see Part V).
● Provide references in your job applications.

In the exercise below, think of three existing contacts with whom you have a good relationship and consider how you could ask them for help (e.g. you could ask for a chat; ask them to put you in touch with someone; let you shadow, or volunteer; give you a job).

Self-assessment: Your networking strategy

1 List three good contacts.
2 Think of the help you could elicit from each (where they're likely to say yes).

Who	What help you'll ask for
1	
2	
3	

Reflecting on your answers: Are your strategies realistic/too optimistic/not optimistic enough? Once you're ready, don't hesitate to contact the first person on your list.

Once you're in a job

Just as your career doesn't end in your first job, neither does networking. In fact, work is probably the best place to network as you have access to an unprecedented range of useful contacts including colleagues, competitors, allied professionals, clients and customers. So, don't just rest on your laurels when you get your first pay cheque, step up your networking efforts from day one and see where they take you!

Jonathan May, Student

When I started university I felt so awkward talking to people. I come from a little village and I've known most people there my whole life. So, meeting employers and business people was quite daunting. I didn't know what to say, what to wear or how to act so I just avoided any interactions. However, once I met a few friendly employers on my course and at work, I started to feel more comfortable and started to chat to professional people whenever I got the chance. Now, I don't feel so uncomfortable in my suit and can chat more naturally so looking for a job isn't nearly so stressful.

And finally …

Of course, every conversation you have won't lead to a graduate job, and more often than not you won't even get past stage two, but every contact you make could be the one that makes things happen. For example: over time, your lecturer may have lost all his useful contacts in industry, but his wife might be able to help, your vet's brother may be happy to talk about nursing or your uncle's accountant may be happy to have a chat. You won't know until you ask people if they can help, or if they know someone else who can.

What to do now

Take a selfie and ask yourself what you represent. Then, think what you want to change to present your best self to employers (which is both fun and professional), then get out there and start making friends. You can find out more about social networking in *Social Media for Your Student and Graduate Job Search* (Kelly, 2016).[1]

ℹ️ Useful links

Websites

www.targetjobs.co.uk – See Networking tips for graduate job hunters

www.grb.uk.com – See 'Networking to find graduate jobs'

www.theguardian.com – See 'Our experts said: How to network your way into a graduate job'

www.enterprisealive.co.uk – See 'A beginner's guide to networking' (advice on meeting employers at careers fairs)

www.themuse.com – See '10 Ways to use social media for your career – not just for killing time'

www.topresume.com – '7 Tips on How to Use Twitter effectively for your career'

www.jobs.ac.uk – In the Careers Advice tab, search for 'How to Use LinkedIn to Full Advantage'

On YouTube

'Networking: tips from a graduate recruiter' – University of Nottingham

'The introvert's guide to networking' – Charisma on command

'How to hack networking' – David Burkus

'How to use your social media to get a Job!' – How to Adult

Experience and internships

Contents

So much choice

You need experience but don't panic if you don't have much to put on your CV, at this stage, because you can undertake any number of activities and work your way up the ladder. As you follow this path, you will gradually nail down your career decisions, develop a stronger self-esteem, focus your career search, build your networks and impress employers. A wide range of experience opportunities is outlined over the following pages; see what sparks your interest and list it here:

☁ Self-assessment: What experience are you after?

List a range of specific activities you could undertake.

-
-
-
-

🔍 **Reflecting on your answers:** Look over your activities and see if they are realistic, varied and exciting.

> *Laura Lodwick, Operations Manager, BJSS Limited*
>
> We look for candidates who have a good academic background but we are especially attracted to those who also have a wealth of experience – people who have gone out of their way to get wider experience and some general business awareness.

> *Graduate from 'Big 4' accountancy firm*
>
> You can impress employers by demonstrating an in-depth understanding of their organisations and what they bring to the market.
>
> Due to the expansion in the Internet and the range of social media, it's very easy to learn the basics about organisations and what they offer. Therefore, today's recruiters expect you to delve a little bit deeper. You should research the organisations that interest you and reflect deeply about what you discover in order to develop your own views, judgements and ideas.
>
> Start early. In your first year, you should get some relevant experience and develop a real understanding of how businesses work. In your second year, try to get an internship. In this way, by the time you are looking for a graduate job, you will be ready to relate to interviewers and business contacts.

Activities at university

There are a number of things you can do to get experience during your studies:

- Pick activities/modules that will enhance your skills. For example, if you need to develop your team skills, you could target group-based assignments.
- Pick activities/modules that are related to your favoured career.
- Sign up for any career/entrepreneurship modules on your degree.
- See if your university runs an employability skills award, i.e. a module which links employability skills to a period of employment experience.
- Visit university/local events related to your chosen career. For example, if you want to go into marketing you could see what the local branch of the Chartered Institute of Marketing is getting up to in your area.

Making it happen

Expanding your interests

Employers are very attracted to applicants who have gone out of their way to get involved in extra-curricular activities. It's also a great way to meet new people and get the most out of your time at university (and once you've graduated). You can get involved in everything from archery to Zoroastrianism, and if a club hasn't yet been invented to suit your unique interests then why not set one up yourself? Some of the more popular activities are shown below. See what ideas come to mind and list them in the table on page 96.

Student societies

All universities run a wide range of sporting and cultural clubs that are open to all students. Look up your Student Union website to see how you can get involved.

Local groups

Look out for interesting groups in your area. For example, if you live in Huddersfield, you could get involved in the Halifax Amateur Radio Society, the Rothwell Shokotan Karate Club or the Skelmanthorpe Historical Society (or all three!).

Volunteering

Volunteers work for free but their expenses are sometimes paid. Just under twenty million people in the UK formally get involved at least once a year, so, why don't you? You could try something connected with your personal interests or a particular career. Either way, try to find opportunities that will help you enhance the specific skills you need to develop, and build contacts with people who can help. For example:

- If you want to be a graphic designer, you could help a charity out with their branding.
- If you dream of becoming a solicitor, get in touch with some legal eagles during your time at Amnesty.

Here's how you can get started:

- Just ask interesting people and organisations if you can help out.
- Ask your department if they need any support with open days, field trips ... etc.
- See if your university has a volunteering office.
- Search for 'volunteering' on your university website.
- Ask for help from your current/local HE careers service.
- Look for ideas on general student/graduate career websites such as www.prospects.ac.uk, www.thestudentroom.co.uk and www.milkround.com.
- Google 'volunteering in ... (your area)'.
- Attend volunteering events and fairs and see what's going on at your local careers service.

You can also find useful information and a wide range of opportunities via the following links.

- Volunteering Matters: www.volunteeringmatters.org.uk – A massive organisation offering opportunities in social or health care, education and youth justice.
- Do-It: www.do-it.org.uk – Search opportunities by postcode.
- Timebank: www.timebank.org.uk – Volunteering focused on youth/social issues.
- Idealist: www.idealist.org – A massive database of volunteer opportunities, jobs and internships across the globe.
- Elevation Networks: www.elevationnetworks.org – Events, mentoring, internships and volunteer opportunities for students/graduates from minority ethnic backgrounds, women, and those affected by a disability.
- *The Guardian*'s Volunteering pages: www.theguardian.com/voluntary-sector-network.
- Vinspired: www.vinspired.com – Volunteering website for 14–25-year-olds.

Susan Davies – Primary School Teacher

Unfortunately, the first time I applied for teacher training, I was knocked back. For a while I was depressed and angry but eventually I pulled myself together.

I decided to apply the following year but make sure, this time, I'd have what it took. I got in touch with various people to see what skills I would have to develop and demonstrate. This included course providers, careers advisers, head teachers and friends.

I concluded I'd have to get a much more practical understanding of teaching and consequently got a volunteer role in a school, twice a week, for a full year. I learnt so much, and, when I applied again, I passed with flying colours.

Finding paid employment

Employment experience is especially valuable because it proves to employers that you have the skills and commitment to succeed in the workplace. Students and graduates have access to a number of job opportunities. Your university probably has a 'job shop' and, as with voluntary experience, you can make speculative applications and ask for help from contacts (see Chapter 8). Other student/graduate vacancy sources are outlined below.

> 66 Employment experience is especially valuable because it proves to employers that you have the skills and commitment to succeed in the workplace. 99

Social networks

Keep on top of your social media channels as more and more student opportunities are being advertised on these platforms. Twitter is a great source of opportunities across the board – just find the relevant recruitment and industry usernames and hashtags in your chosen sector and keep your eyes open. LinkedIn also has a great database for more formal experience opportunities, internships and graduate roles at www.linkedin.com/studentjobs.

Agencies

The UK has a wealth of excellent recruitment agencies. Some national chains offer vacancies across the board. Others focus on specific regions and sectors. Find some that suit you at www.rec.uk.com. Local papers also usually list agencies in each town and your careers service will probably be happy to recommend the best local firms. Furthermore, your university may well also have a 'job shop', and finally, don't forget Jobcentre Plus at www.direct.gov.uk. Some of the larger national agencies are shown below:

- Total jobs: www.totaljobs.com – A wide variety of vacancies in all sectors.
- Office Angels: www.office-angels.com – Secretarial and office support and a gradually broadening range of opportunities.
- Michael Page: www.michaelpage.co.uk – Diverse vacancies in roles from accountancy to retail and life sciences.
- Reed: www.reed.co.uk – Another giant with a similarly wide remit and good career planning/job-hunting advice.
- Hays: www.hays.co.uk – Jobs in a massive range of sectors from casual to executive, plus good job-hunting advice.
- Jobsite: www.jobsite.co.uk.

Some agencies that focus on holiday jobs are as follows:

- Indeed: www.indeed.co.uk/Seasonal-jobs – Temporary posts in a wide range of sectors.
- E4s.co.uk: www.e4s.co.uk – Holiday jobs/long-term positions.
- Summer-jobs.co.uk: www.summer-jobs.co.uk – Activity based roles throughout the year.

Many agencies look for people with specific employment experience and competencies such as the ability to type more than fifty words per minute or mix concrete (but not usually both!). You'll probably need to develop these skills in other voluntary or paid roles before applying. Be careful when you sign up for agencies. Don't pay a registration fee, make sure the websites are regularly updated and, above all, if no work is forthcoming, move on. Finally, remember that the lowest salary you say you'll consider, will be the highest you'll ever be offered!

University careers services

Careers services tend to advertise experience opportunities formally on their websites and informally through word of mouth and their social networks.

Professional organisations

Professional organisations are a good source of industry-specific news and 'hidden' vacancies. For example, the Chartered Society for Designers at www.csd.org.uk lists agencies and vacancies and also offers a 'find a designer' service.

Individual organisations

Take some time to bookmark the websites of the specific businesses and third-sector organisations where you'd like to work, join their social networks and keep abreast of what's going on. This will not only highlight any vacancies but also help you prepare for any future employment trends.

Search engines

Why not spend half an hour a week Googling terms relevant to your chosen career such as 'jobs in catering', 'volunteer marketing positions' or 'seasonal jobs'?

General student/graduate websites

Look at the following sites for find internships, graduate training programmes and permanent graduate vacancies.

- Graduate prospects: www.prospects.ac.uk – A highly respected and comprehensive website because of its links to the Association of Graduate Careers Advisory Services.
- Milkround: www.milkround.com – A student-friendly site with focused advice and useful forums.
- TARGETjobs: www.targetjobs.co.uk – A comprehensive website with tips on applying to specific employers.
- Graduate-jobs.com: www.graduate-jobs.com – A narrower range of vacancies but with some good forums and blogs plus links to other graduate vacancy websites.
- Student job: www.studentjob.co.uk.

On the high street

Back in the day, if you wanted to find work, or any sort of voluntary experience, you needed a good pair of shoes, a bag full of CVs and a map. You'd pop into every shop, warehouse, theatre, bingo hall (ask your parents) and office with a smile on your face and ask if they're hiring. Your chances of success at each interaction were small, but the more people you saw, the luckier you got. Surprisingly, this approach still bears fruit today, especially with less formal roles, as it shows enterprise, drive and good communication. At first, it can be challenging just walking up to employers and trying your luck, but you'll soon get the hang of it.

Try to avoid nervously handing over your CV and running out with your tail between your legs. Chat to the people you see about their jobs, try to speak to the manager or someone in charge and don't forget to get some contact details before leaving, so you can follow up and say thanks.

Many local shops also still have noticeboards promoting opportunities, for example:

- Corner shops may have adverts for local jobs such as cleaning and working in retail.
- Specialist retailers, such as music shops, may be on the lookout for skilled people in their particular sector.

Newspapers and magazines

Newspapers, magazines and trade publications still carry job ads, plus they can be really useful sources of news and information about future vacancies. For example, if 'The Stage' reports that more actors may soon be needed to train doctors – you could make contact with the relevant training managers on LinkedIn or give them a call. *The Guardian*'s recruitment pages are especially useful, see www.jobs. theguardian.com.

What are internships?

Internships are short-term, structured opportunities that provide some sort of training as well as employment experience. They have traditionally been designed for students nearing the end of their degrees, but in recent times, have morphed into a range of diverse opportunities, from short-term menial tasks for little or no salary to lucrative summer-long placements. They are popular with employers, students and graduates. For employers, they are cheap labour and a great opportunity to see if people are up to the mark; for interns they are a chance to confirm a career choice, gain relevant skills, develop networks and find a potential pathway into graduate work.

> " Internships are short-term, structured employment experience opportunities that provide some sort of training as well as employment. "

Katerina Vlkova, Economics and History student

During my first year I applied for jobs everywhere for the summer holidays and got an internship at Pershing, a financial services firm. At the end of my second year, I was invited back for an internship with their parent company, the Bank of New York Mellon, and now I am hoping to work there in a customer-facing role.

My advice would be to try to get as much work experience as you can before graduating and be curious about what´s outside the top 100s. Before my first year, I had never heard about Pershing, but thanks to the first internship I am now more clear on where I would like to work and what I would like to do in the future.

What internships look like

Nowadays, internships come in all shapes and sizes and there are opportunities for almost everyone at any stage in life (see the film 'The Intern').

Traditional internships/placements

Vacation placements are the customary internship option in the UK. They are typically structured to fit into the spring, summer or winter university vacations and last from a few weeks to two or three months during the summer break at the end of students' penultimate year of study, but many are also available at other times.

Summer internships at larger employers are usually advertised from October onwards for the following year's intake. Therefore, you'll need to apply as soon as you start your penultimate year at university. Applications are often viewed on a first come, first served basis. SMEs are more likely to accept applications throughout the year.

Introductory events

A number of organisations offer short-term opportunities during the winter, spring and summer vacations that are open to first-year students who are considering certain careers. They typically last from a few days to a couple of weeks. For example, JPMorgan Chase & Co. offers a 'Spring Week' of activities to demonstrate what's involved in investment banking and risk management (look up their UK careers section at www.jpmorgan.com/country/GB/en/jpmorgan).

Study placements

An increasing number of undergraduate and postgraduate degree programmes now include academic placements in industry. On these courses, you're typically asked to complete some sort of research for the organisation or undertake a specific project linked to your study. For example:

- The BSc Computing degree at Edge Hill University offers a second-year module in employability during which you will work in industry.
- The Bank of England has a PhD internship scheme for people currently researching a PhD in fields related to monetary analysis and financial stability.

Sandwich courses (often called placements/industrial placements)

University sandwich courses offer undergraduates the chance to undertake an extended 'industrial placement' for a period of between six months and two years, usually in between their penultimate and final years of study. Some Masters courses also offer this opportunity. These extended internships confer extensive experience and the majority of interns are taken on permanently once they've graduated. During your time away from campus you are usually treated as a current student but your fees will be reduced. Funding for overseas industrial placements is currently available from Erasmus at www.erasmusprogramme.com but this may change after Brexit. Check with your department as early as possible to see if they will facilitate such opportunities.

Modern internships

Graduate internship opportunities have grown massively in the UK over the last decade or two. They comprise short-term work opportunities that vary greatly in terms of the work and training provided, and include opportunities that were once only open to current students, for example:

- Barnardo's offers a 12-week placement for students or graduates who are under 25 in various sectors of their business.
- Barclays Capital offers a variety of short-term and six-month internships at both Analyst and Associate level that are open to students and graduates.

Finding internship vacancies

You can use the following resources to find internships:

- Your academic department.
- Your university's careers service.
- Ratemyplacement: www.ratemyplacement.co.uk – An excellent site with jobs, advice and reviews on all kinds of student and graduate internships.
- Inspiring Interns: www.inspiringinterns.com – Another popular site with vacancies, advice and a CV drop box.
- InternTown: www.interntown.com – Internships across the globe including many in the UK.
- Graduate Talent Pool: https://graduatetalentpoolsearch.direct.gov.uk – The Government's own job board for graduates who want to take up internships, covering a wide range of opportunities, primarily in England.
- STEP: www.step.org.uk – A well-regarded organisation that coordinates project-based internships including short-term undergraduate work placements, sandwich placements and graduate internships.

- Your university: many universities, themselves, now also run internship programmes for students and/or graduates.

You should also ask your contacts for help and send out speculative applications. A good approach with small and medium-sized employers (SMEs) is to approach them with specific offers of help over the summer: for example, you might suggest that you could develop their website, write a marketing plan or improve their industrial processes.

Internships for specific groups

A number of organisations offer internships for particular groups, often because they are under-represented in the workforce, for example:

- City Solicitors Horizons runs a three-year training, mentoring and work-experience scheme for disadvantaged first-year students considering a career in law (see www.citysolicitorshorizons.org).
- Women Deliver offers five-month, part-time internships in various fields for women (see www.womendeliver.org).
- The Civil Service offers internships of 6–9 weeks for undergraduates and graduates from diverse backgrounds (see www.faststream.gov.uk/summer-diversity-internship-programme).
- Fidelity Worldwide Investment, at www.fidelityrecruitment.com, offers a Women's Investment Insight Week for women from any academic background (primarily first year degree students).
- The Windsor Fellowship offers a 'Leadership Programme' for second year undergraduates from minority ethnic groups (see www.windsor-fellowship.org).
- The Royal National Institute of Blind People (RNIB) Scotland offers internships to school, college and university leavers who are blind or partially sighted and live north of the border (see www.rnib.org.uk).

One way to seek out these opportunities is to Google 'Internships for X (name the group on which you would like to focus)', e.g. women, ethnic minorities or the blind. You can also ask for help from any organisations linked to the sector you want to enter.

Internships overseas

A number of organisations offer overseas internships in conjunction with other services such as training, induction, visas and accommodation. The first place to look is Erasmus+ at www.erasmusplus.org.uk, a European Commission programme which aids cross-border cooperation across the European continent and all points beyond. Through this initiative, students and recent EU graduates from partner universities (which are listed at www.erasmusprogramme.com) can work abroad for a period of from three to twelve months and receive a grant to cover expenses (of course, this programme may be affected by Brexit). In the UK, this programme is currently coordinated by the British Council (see www.britishcouncil.org). Positions are promoted on www.erasmusintern.org. The British Council also coordinates internships around the globe for a range of other organisations.

Other useful sources of posts include:

- AIESEC UK: www.aiesec.co.uk – A youth-led independent organisation providing internships in over 110 countries.
- The International Exchange of Students for Technical Experience (IESTE): www.iaeste.org – Paid international opportunities (usually over summer) for students of science, engineering and applied arts.
- International Internships: www.international-internships.com – Opportunities in Africa, Asia, Europe and both North and South America.
- Glassdoor: www.glassdoor.co.uk – A database of internships across the globe.
- Graduateland: www.graduateland.com – Internships at major employers in Europe and beyond.

Of course, you can also apply directly to organisations themselves for any opportunities but this may necessitate securing some sort of work visa (you can find out more about visas in Chapter 11). You could either apply to the UK offices of international organisations or directly to their bases in the other countries. The advantages of contacting bigger firms are that they will be comfortable with the paperwork and will have systematic recruitment processes; the key disadvantage is that they tend to also apply extremely tough criteria such as extensive experience. Small and medium-sized firms, on the other hand, may be very intrigued by your creative approach.

As with other vacancies, it can pay to look for organisations that are linked to your interests: for example, if you like horse-riding and you want to work in France, why not try the Fédération Française d'Équitation at www.ffe.com, or, if you love dogs, the Canadian Kennel Club at www.ckc.ca/en. Remember, application procedures differ in each country but you could just start out by networking with people in your chosen area and getting in touch online. Some useful local hints and links for a host of countries can also be found at www.prospects.ac.uk/working_abroad.htm.

If you're getting an internship as part of a degree programme, make sure your overseas position fits in with your university's guidelines. Remember, you'll also have to fill out a lot of forms such as the EU residence permit, and you may need to sign joint contracts between you, your employer and your university. These are required in many countries, such as France where they're called a Convention de Stage. Ask for help from your Department and your Careers Service to see where people have worked before and what paperwork may be required.

What are interns paid?

Many employers now provide a living wage but some will still expect you to work for nothing. If you're prepared to undertake an unpaid internship, there are a few things you can do to make sure it's a beneficial experience.

Before you start:

- Check out the specific internship on forums such as www.thestudentroom.com.
- Clarify exactly what you'll be doing.
- Try to negotiate payment for expenses.
- Set parameters such as how long the internship will last and the hours you'll be expected to work.
- Make sure you'll have an opportunity to develop the specific skills you require.

Once you get going:

- Maximise your learning opportunities and make good contacts.
- Talk your way into paid work.

ⓘ Useful links

Websites

www.telegraph.co.uk – See 'Getting experience without experience'
www.kent.ac.uk/careers – See 'Internships and Work Experience'
www.ed.ac.uk – Look up Look up 'Internships and work experience'
www.volunteers.manchester.ac.uk
www.prospects.ac.uk – See 'volunteering'
www.theguardian.com – See 'Why temping is tempting'/'10 things every graduate should know before they start job hunting'
www.thecompleteuniversityguide.co.uk – See 'Working part time'
www.student-jobs.co.uk
www.e4s.co.uk
www.ratemyplacement.co.uk
www.goingglobal.com
www.bath.ac.uk/careers, search for the 'Directory of Charities, Volunteering and Gap Year Opportunities'
http://uclu.org/volunteering/directory

On Twitter

@GdnVoluntary	@studentjobsUK
@joininUK	#UKjobs
#volunteer	#jobsearch
#Volunteering	#ukjobs

On LinkedIn
www.linkedin.com/studentjobs

CHAPTER 10
Further study

66 An investment in knowledge pays the best interest.
Benjamin Franklin 99

Contents

What's covered in this chapter
Will it enhance your career prospects?
Is it right for me?
Finding a course
Choosing a course
Funding
Applying
Making the most of your course

What's covered in this chapter

This chapter is designed to help you decide whether further study is right for you and plan your next steps accordingly.

Will it enhance your career prospects?

As we head into the third decade of the twenty-first century, more and more people are undertaking postgraduate study; however, further qualifications will only usually help your career if they are part of a well thought through plan and strategy. For example, a Postgraduate Certificate of Education will definitely help you get into teaching and a Masters in Risk Assessment may well help you find a relevant role in the City, but extra qualifications will not necessarily improve your chances of gaining entry into many graduate training programmes. This is simply because employers are generally more concerned with your grades, skills and employment experience than with what you know.

66 Further qualifications will only usually help your career if they are part of a well thought through plan and strategy. 99

104

> *Susan Davies, Primary School Teacher*
>
> I have studied two postgraduate courses – a Masters in Environmental Law and a Postgraduate Certificate in Education (PGCE).
>
> I enjoyed my Masters and it has recently impressed employers but, at the time, I didn't use it effectively to further my career. I imagined the qualification would help me somehow, but I put little thought into how. In retrospect, I should have networked more effectively with the leaders in the field who were teaching me, and reflected on the skills I was gaining so I could target relevant roles.
>
> I decided to become a primary school teacher after working for many years in the cash office of a music store in central London. I only got onto a PGCE course after volunteering for a year in a school during my time off from work. Now I'm a very happy and dedicated teacher.
>
> Each of these experiences has given me a very favourable impression of further study, but also an appreciation of the benefits of planning how I'm going to make the most of the experience.

Is it right for you?

Some of the more common motivations for taking up further study are outlined below along with advice on their validity vis-à-vis your career success. Once you've read through the list, try to honestly identify your personal motivations in the exercise provided, and consider how you can make sure your study enhances your career. For example, you could:

- Use your extra study time to network with professionals in the field.
- Study part-time.
- Wait for a few years so you can first get some experience.
- Find study that relates directly to a particular career (such as teacher training).
- Study online.

Studying a subject you love

This is a pure and noble reason for signing up for another period of study, and it's hard to knock. However, you should determine whether you can afford more debt and the course fits in with your career plans. You may also consider studying your chosen subject on an informal basis (at least at first) while pursuing your existing job.

Buying more time

After a lifetime in education it can be very difficult to face your next steps in life but this shouldn't hold you back because, in a year or two, it will be even more difficult to leave and you'll be in even greater debt! On the other hand, you may believe that you are now more mature and able to make the most of such a great opportunity.

Refocusing your career

One reason for taking up postgraduate study is to go into a new field. This is a risky decision, so make sure your chosen qualification will actually help and that it is accredited by the appropriate professional body. Good conversion courses are a real plus if you want to enter some professional sectors such as journalism and IT; however, relevant employment experience is often more useful, even if the role you want to enter is unconnected to your first degree.

Freshening up your qualifications

This is a common motive for graduates who have been away from university for a while and are unhappy with their lot. They often sign up for a course in the hope that a further qualification will reboot their careers and give employers a new respect for what they have to offer. If this is your plan, make sure the extra qualifications will, indeed, be useful, and dedicate yourself to readjusting to student life.

Getting a professional qualification

Many professions such as teaching and clinical psychology require further professional qualifications. If you're considering this route, make sure you're happy with your career choice before applying and consider whether it's worth confirming your decision through some relevant experience, before signing up.

Undertaking ongoing professional training

Further study can really enhance your career, especially if you agree your options with your managers. For example, you may want to develop a particular expertise or slide into a slightly different role, but make sure the career prospects in this new direction are strong and ongoing.

Making up for a disappointing first degree

Further qualifications may persuade recruiters that your previous poor grades were a glitch, but most of the larger employers won't have the flexibility to consider your personal situation and will still focus on your original degree classification. Some people even consider starting another undergraduate degree if they didn't perform well on their first course but, again, employers will still probably give more credence to your original grades. Furthermore, if you have already completed one and a half years of an undergraduate degree, you may well be liable for the full fees up front if you want to start afresh.

Becoming an academic

If you're considering staying on at university to become a lecturer or researcher, make sure you look at the pros and cons of this career route, just as you would for any other. In other words, don't just start a PhD because an academic has told you how wonderful you are and has asked for your help.

Studying overseas

There are many benefits to upping sticks and studying in another country, such as:

- Discovering another culture, lifestyle and educational system first hand.
- Developing international experience, foreign language capabilities and a global perspective so you stand out amongst your peers.
- Working in an internationally recognised faculty or institution.
- Moving lock, stock and barrel to another country (if this is your passion).
- Saving some money (overseas courses are often cheaper, as is the cost of living).

Obviously, English-speaking nations such as the USA and Australia teach in English as do many institutions across Europe and Asia.

If you're considering this route, make sure you know exactly what you're letting yourself in for and, if possible, try to speak to students and alumni from your chosen institution. Also, check that you can use the qualification back in your home country. If you're still at university, you could also consider studying in Europe as part of your undergraduate course. You can find out more on the Erasmus website, see www.britishcouncil.org/erasmus.htm.

Now you've seen the common motivations for taking up further study, identify yours in the following exercise and see how you can make the most of your studies.

Self-assessment: What's your motivation?

Identify two of your personal motivations for considering postgraduate study and consider how you can make sure your study leads to a fulfilling career.

Your top two study motivations	How you can make the most of your study
•	•
•	•

Reflecting on your answers: Having undertaken this exercise, do you feel more confident about your next steps? If not, can you figure out why? Do you need to research things more or talk to someone?

Finding a course

Postgraduate study in general

Look up the following links:

- Prospects' course directory – www.prospects.ac.uk/search_courses.htm.
- Target courses – http://targetcourses.co.uk.
- Course directories for individual institutions, which will be on their websites.
- Courses overseas: www.prospects.ac.uk/country_profiles.htm.
- Hotcourses Abroad directory of courses in the UK and overseas, including English-language courses in other countries – www.hotcoursesabroad.com/sitemap.html.

Taught courses

Taught Masters courses (MA, MSc, etc.) are the most common postgraduate study option. They generally last for one year, full-time (or two years, part-time). You can either focus on a favoured aspect of your undergraduate degree or take up a conversion course in a subject specifically related to a particular area such as magazine editing or human resources. Either way, most course providers will expect good grades in your initial degree. See the links above to find some suitable courses.

Vocational courses

You can study professional courses in everything from acting to youth work. It is also possible to train for certain roles such as medicine through accelerated postgraduate courses. However, you should keep in mind that new qualifications do not automatically get you a job!

Applications for work-related qualifications are usually made through central application bodies. Some of these are listed below but you'll also find more on the companion website.

- Teaching: UCAS at www.ucas.com/teaching-in-the-uk.
- Becoming a solicitor: www.lawcabs.ac.uk.
- Medicine/Dentistry/Social work: www.ucas.com.
- Clinical psychology: The Clearing House for Postgraduate Courses in Clinical Psychology at www.leeds.ac.uk/chpccp.
- Speech therapy: The Health and Care Professions Council at www.hpc-uk.org/apply.
- Journalism: The National Council for the Training of Journalists at www.nctj.com/accredited/course-application-forms.

Masters by Research (MRes)

These typically last for up to two years and usually combine taught courses with intensive training in research methodology. They are often taken as a precursor to a career in research. You can usually find these opportunities on individual university websites or on the FindAMasters international Masters directory: www.findamasters.com.

Doctorates (PhDs)

PhDs take three years or more to complete and are usually the first step to a career in research. They involve new research in a specific field, resulting in a thesis and oral exam (viva). You can find PhDs by discovering where your favoured research is being undertaken and approaching academics (start at your own institution). You can also look for them in the FindAPhD international directory of research programmes: www.findaphd.com.

Masters in Business Administration (MBAs)

These are one- or two-year courses primarily tailored for graduates who already have experience and want to develop careers in management. You can start looking for them at:

- Top MBA directory: www.topmba.com.
- *Financial Times* rankings: search on http://rankings.ft.com.

Short courses

Here, you can learn specific skills linked to the sector you want to enter, such as web authoring software or bookkeeping. Local councils organise a wide range of courses at different times and venues in your local area such as schools, colleges and village halls. You can usually find them on your local council's website.

Choosing a course

You can apply a number of filters to your course shortlist in order to identify the best one for you, as follows:

- Check which institutions will accept your grades.
- See which locations you prefer (or can afford).
- See which courses most closely match your academic/professional objectives (find out by reading prospectuses and contacting academics).
- Check each course's reputation within the academic community: look them up on the website of the Research Assessment Framework (RAF) (www.ref.ac.uk/2014), and ask for direction from research staff in your own department.
- Research what courses are most highly rated by employers.
- Ascertain each course's employment prospects: speak to the admissions tutors and relevant supervisors to find out where past graduates have ended up.
- If you're planning on undertaking a PhD, check out each of the departments and supervisors. For example, visit them and see how supportive they're likely to be; compare each department and supervisor's enrolments over the last five years with the number of doctorates they have awarded (to assess their success rates); see which supervisors have had supervisor training and find out how long each supervisor is prepared to spend with you.

○. **Self-assessment: Which course is for you?**

Identify three dream postgraduate courses of any kind.

Three interesting courses (including where they're based)

●

●

●

Reflecting on your answers: Are you ready to get in touch and find out more?

Funding

Postgraduate student loans

There are now loans for postgraduate students along the lines of those provided for undergraduates. These are administered by Student Finance England (or the equivalent bodies in Wales, Scotland and Northern Ireland).

> **❝** There are now loans for postgraduate students along the lines of those provided for undergraduates. **❞**

You will receive sufficient funds for the fees and a whole range of other costs. These loans are not based on your income and are paid directly to you. Of course, the bad news is that you will have to pay them back (subject to similar rules for undergraduate loans). The loan repayments are currently charged at 6% when your annual income is over a similar threshold to that of your undergraduate loans. Of course, these arrangements may well change, especially as they are a relatively new initiative, so research the current rules and provisions at www.thestudentroom.co.uk/student-finance/postgraduate and www.gov.uk/funding-for-postgraduate-study.

Institutional funding

Research Councils provide funding to university departments for a number of research and taught programmes. Institutions also offer a number of scholarships, research assistantships and teaching assistantships, where they pay your fees and provide you with a salary for undertaking specific duties. If you cannot gain access to these funds at the outset of your course, you may have a good chance of picking up some sort of salary as the years go by. Opportunities are often advertised on www.jobs.ac.uk and www.postgraduatestudentships.co.uk.

Bursaries, scholarships and grants may also be available for vocational courses such as social work, teaching and a range of health care courses. Check with the relevant professional group responsible for applications in your chosen field; some of these are shown above in the 'Vocational courses' section and on the companion website (www.macmillanihe.com/rook-gcg-2e). A number of universities themselves also offer grants to students in certain situations, such as those with no family history of Higher Education. Universities in the United States typically offer a number of grants you can access as an international student.

Start by contacting institutions themselves to see what's on offer.

Charities and trusts

A number of charitable organisations will support your study; for example, the Royal National Institute for the Blind has funds available for blind students. However, charities can usually only give you a few hundred pounds at most. You can find relevant grant providers at www.fundingeducation.co.uk and www.scholarship-search.org.uk.

Employer-funded study

Training budgets are usually quite tight nowadays, but if you can make a good argument as to why further study will improve your performance, you will probably get your employer to stump up some of the funds.

Applying

Depending on the course, you either need to apply directly to the institution or through a central admissions service (e.g. UCAS in the UK). In either case, places can fill up quickly, so you often need to apply well in advance. Therefore, clarify application procedures for your target courses at least a year before they commence. If you don't have this amount of time, you can look for late opportunities or get some experience and apply for the following year's intake.

Before putting pen to paper (or fingers to keystrokes), try to meet your future supervisor and/or the course director to discuss what's involved and ask how you can appropriately focus your application.

Your personal statement

As with your undergraduate application, you may well be asked to complete a statement to back up your application. Here, you should clearly and systematically address what's required. For example, you may be asked to outline your relevant skills and experience, why you want to take up that particular course and/or what you can offer. If no specific request is made and you are simply asked to write a personal statement, outline your skills, knowledge and commitment (why you want to study the course) and prove each through your relevant academic/professional experience. This will demonstrate to course providers that you will succeed on the course.

For example, the following personal statement is for a taught Masters course on 'Politics in the USA'.

Making it happen

Please outline your relevant skills, commitment and knowledge (500 words)

Address the specific attributes required and stick to the word limit

Thank you for discussing this stimulating course when I visited you last month. I particularly enjoyed sharing everyone's enthusiasm and genuine love for the subject. In the following paragraphs, I have systematically outlined my relevant skills, commitment and knowledge.

Introduce your statement – not yourself

My relevant skills are an ability to conduct in-depth qualitative and quantitative social science research, good written communication, teamwork, flexibility and focus. I recently demonstrated these attributes by gaining 73% in my undergraduate dissertation where I juxtaposed the hope and promise presented by President Kennedy's inauguration with the compromise that marked his tenure.

Relate each personal statement to the specific skills required in each different application

I demonstrated my research skills through my ability to explore this subject in depth. For example, I was able to draw from hard copy and online resources in both the UK and the USA and direct testimony from a number of influential US politicians and journalists such as Senator Alan Dixon and Bob Woodward.

Outline *how* you demonstrate each of the skills required and give specific examples of when you have demonstrated them (you can use bullet points, but don't overdo them)

My writing style is positive and accurate and I clearly convey complicated theories and concepts through short sentences and focused paragraphs. I have demonstrated these skills in a number of essays during my undergraduate study and as editor of my university's student newspaper. In teams, I can be relied on to listen to colleagues and encourage them to succeed: for example, when I worked closely with three colleagues in the Enterprise Society at university to win the National Student Enterprise Award. My flexibility and focus are best demonstrated by my ability to maintain high grades at university whilst balancing a range of technical jobs and outside interests such as website development and writing historical articles for several publications.

My commitment to this course is demonstrated in three key ways:

- My longstanding interest and proactive drive to study US politics during my secondary and tertiary education.
- My recent visit to the department where I discussed the programme with Professor Tim Loghley and Doctor Franks.
- My clarity over the specific modules I will choose, i.e. Nationalism, The Senate and The Recent Presidents.

Show that you have researched the course

Having studied US politics during my A levels, degree and in my spare time, my relevant knowledge is extensive. For example, I understand the federal political system, the checks and balances on

Use a simple structure including a straightforward introduction, paragraphs for each of your attributes and a summary

the power of the President, and the drivers of parties and factions such as the Democrats, the Tea Party and the Grand Old Party.

In summary, I have the research and communication skills to succeed on this course as well as a burning ambition and the appropriate knowledge. I look forward to hearing from you soon. Please feel free to contact me by phone or email if you have any questions.

Research proposals

Providers of Masters by research and PhD programmes tend to require a formal proposal. This is a document (usually a form of about ten pages) in which you outline information such as:

- The aims of your project.
- A literature review.
- Your objectives.
- Your proposed methodologies.
- References.
- A timetable.
- Some sort of personal appraisal of your skills.
- A reflection on any ethical issues that may be raised.

You should be able to find the appropriate form on university/department websites. These proposals help supervisors assess several issues, such as:

- Whether your project is germane to their personal (and departmental) research interests.
- Your appreciation of the issues involved.
- Your academic skills.

Try to avoid just sending your proposal to the university on spec. You should contact the department before putting pen to paper, find out who will be supervising you and get in touch. If you speak to your future supervisor beforehand, they will give you advice on what they want to see and you will get a chance to see if you will get on.

Making the most of your course

Making plans

Whether or not your career is your primary motivation for taking up further study, you should plan for the day you leave from the day you sign up (as it will come soon enough) then, set incremental goals so you can gradually ensure you achieve your aims. For example, if you're studying to be a teacher then, at the start of the course, quickly ascertain where you want to work, the skills you will need to demonstrate, when you should apply for your first post, how to put together effective applications and with whom you need to network. This will mean that when you leave, you'll be ready.

You should also start planning as soon as possible because important dates often occur early on in your study. For example, if you sign up for a Masters and you then want to apply for a graduate training programme, you'll need to apply as soon as you start!

Networking

One of the hidden benefits of further study is the opportunity to make valuable contacts who will be at least as useful in your career as what you've learned, especially if you want to go into academia or a related industry. Make sure you take advantage of this chance to network, whether it's for career reasons or just to chat to people you admire. You can do this by:

- Asking for their help in your research.
- Asking your tutors to introduce you to interesting contacts.
- Getting involved in the wider activities of your department.
- Getting involved in the wider research community allied to your subject.
- Meeting employers who visit your department and university.

Useful links

Websites
https://help.open.ac.uk/further-study
www.kent.ac.uk/ces – See 'Further study'
www.prospects.ac.uk/postgraduate-study
www.findamasters.com
www.findaphd.com
www.nationalcareersservice.direct.gov.uk – Search for 'Course directory'
   (short courses in any number of subjects around the country)

CHAPTER 11
Taking time out

Contents

Finding perspective

Time out can be another useful stepping stone on your way into a career because it can help you see all your options and find perspective (at what can be such a confusing juncture in your life). This chapter shows you how to make the most of your time away from your usual life and outlines a range of possible activities.

Making the most of the experience

A good rule of thumb is to:

- Clarify why you want to get away.
- Plan accordingly.
- Keep track of how things are going.
- Stay on the lookout for new opportunities.
- Make sure you return home at the right time to kick-start your career. For example, if you want to apply for a graduate training programme on your return, or take up further study, you probably need to be in the country from October onwards.

Various motives are discussed in the table below along with advice on how you can make the most of the experience; see which ones relate to you.

Your reasons for taking time out	How you can make the most of the experience
You just need to rest and have some fun!	What a pure and noble motive – and you deserve it! If this sounds like you, don't just pick the first idea that comes along, ask yourself what you'd really love to do and look for appropriate opportunities, even if it's just sitting on a beach for two months!
	Furthermore, during your actual break, take stock of what you enjoy, as this may also help you plan your next moves when you finally return. For example, you could find out you love hospitality, hate working indoors, or prefer working alone. In this way, your time out will help you appreciate more about what makes you tick, so appropriate careers will start to organically appear.
You want to get away from things so you can identify some career ideas	While you're away, keep your eyes open and chat to people about their future plans. They may have some incisive observations (especially if you're sharing a cask of wine in front of a campfire).
You've planned your next steps in life but want a break	In this situation, the first thing to do is to make sure you get back in time to set yourself up properly for your next step. However, you could also find ways to develop the skills and contacts you'll need upon your return. See the quote below from Jenny Archielle.
You want to get some useful experience	Figure out the sort of experience you want and look for relevant opportunities. You don't need to restrict your search to organised gap year opportunities; for example, you could contact people yourself before leaving. See the quote below from Grace Lander. When you promote your experience to employers, make sure you stress your initiative as this will help you stand out.
You can't find any decent work and are sick of doing nothing	If you're in a rut, then it can be a great idea to completely change your lifestyle, for a period, so you can view your problems from a new angle and find solutions. However, make sure you maintain this new-found energy when you return to your previous life (if you return) and don't just fall back into the same old ways.

Jenny Archielle, Graduate working in retail

Working in retail is fulfilling but full-on. Once you start you are on a treadmill to greater things but there's no chance to get off, so enjoy yourself and travel before you start so you can focus on your job when you eventually get going.

Grace Lander, Recent graduate (1st class)

As part of my degree in Wildlife Conservation with Zoo Biology I was given the opportunity to spend a year in industry. I decided to pursue a perfect placement somewhere interesting. I chose three months in Key West, Florida, and six months in Anchorage, Alaska (USA). By finding something for myself, I could really tailor what I got up to. In both Key West and Alaska, I lived onsite at an animal rehabilitation centre, which was a lot of responsibility!

The best part of tailoring something for yourself is choosing what you want to do and how you want to do it. Just make sure you agree terms with your employer in writing so you get as much out of your trip as possible. Due to USA visa requirements I couldn't be paid for my work, so saving up enough to fund the internships was a challenge. The upside is that when you offer yourself up to work for free, people really appreciate the work you're doing and it looks great on your CV.

The most valuable experience I gained was the time spent learning veterinary procedures and techniques with the team in Alaska. Getting that sort of experience, even as a volunteer in the UK, is next to impossible. It was a fantastic opportunity to get really involved helping with surgical procedures and after-care. Public educational presentations in Alaska gave me the opportunity to work with live eagles, owls and other birds. While the public speaking practice was great, I was also trained in bird handling, a unique skill on my CV! Liaising with the public in both locations and educating large groups about wildlife and nature has given me the confidence to apply for jobs in wildlife education, a passion which was seeded during my placement.

Where to go and what to do

You can go nowhere, anywhere or everywhere. Some backpackers visit a specific region whilst others get a round-the-world ticket and head off in search of adventure. The choice is yours. Some common destinations are France, Italy, Asia, Australia, the USA and Canada. You can also undertake any activity (if you can find the money). For example, you could learn French in New Caledonia, help children in Bogotá or teach English in Laos. What would you love to do?

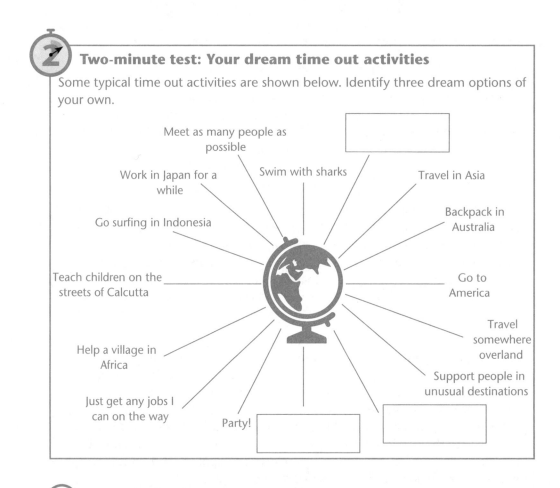

Two-minute test: Your dream time out activities

Some typical time out activities are shown below. Identify three dream options of your own.

Meet as many people as possible

Work in Japan for a while

Swim with sharks

Travel in Asia

Go surfing in Indonesia

Backpack in Australia

Teach children on the streets of Calcutta

Go to America

Travel somewhere overland

Help a village in Africa

Support people in unusual destinations

Just get any jobs I can on the way

Party!

Reflecting on your answers: Are you really dreaming big? If not, read on to expand your horizons.

Finding opportunities

The first thing to decide is whether you want to use some sort of agency or find your own opportunities – or try a little bit of both. There are pros and cons to each approach, as outlined below.

Third-party agencies

There are several private, government and public agencies that will help you get involved in time out activities. These agencies will deliver peace of mind and sort out all the paperwork, but they could also stifle your own creativity and sense of adventure! Some of the more popular agencies, that focus on different activities, are listed over the following pages. Before making contact, you should make sure organisations are reputable by:

- Seeing how long they've been in business.
- Checking that their online presence is up to date and professional.
- Making sure they have an actual residential address.
- Googling their name and the word 'complaints'.
- Checking them out at your careers service.

Creating your own openings

If you don't want to find an option through a third-party agency, there's usually nothing stopping you from sorting things out yourself. You could try anything from roles linked to your current experience, the career you're chasing, or try a mini-adventure such as photographing butterflies in Orkney, office-work in Gibraltar, bookkeeping in Tanzania or fishing in Sri Lanka. Of course, you'll have to sort out all the logistics yourself, including travel, accommodation and visas (if required).

There are several ways you can identify possible activities, such as:

- Sit back and dream.
- Copy the projects currently being offered by the various gap year companies.
- Think of accessible roles that will help you develop the career skills you want to develop.
- See what other people are doing on the various traveller websites and social networking groups.
- Identify roles linked to humanitarian/environmental issues that are close to your heart.
- Identify the needs in the countries you want to visit.
- See what opportunities are available in your chosen region.

Once you have some individual volunteering ideas, you need to tee them up. You can either contact people and organisations before leaving or see what turns up on the road. The advantages of organising things before you go are that you can unearth specific opportunities and create a more secure itinerary. Contact people through email or the appropriate social media, tell them a bit about yourself and ask if you can come and help out. Businesses, charities and individuals are often very impressed by such an enterprising approach and will respond positively.

If you decide to look for opportunities as you travel, you'll derive the benefits of spontaneity and seeing what you're in for before making any commitments. You can also ask around and find something that's been highly recommended. However, the activities may well be less structured or less directly related to what you really want to do.

Options at home

Getting more experience

Find out about voluntary and paid experiences, in the UK, in Chapter 9.

Developing your hobbies

If you have an all-consuming interest or hobby, this is your chance to take it further and, who knows, this may even lead to a really fulfilling career or business idea. For example, you could learn French by working in a café in the French Riviera, develop your Taekwondo skills at an internationally acclaimed school, or learn to fly a plane. Any one of these activities could lead to thousands of fulfilling roles.

Looking after relatives

Having relied on support from your family and friends to get through your degree, you may want to give something back. For example, you could look after your sister's infants while she looks for work, or care for your ailing grandfather. Carers can get an allowance from the government for their effort and this could be your chance to cement your family's future. Find out more at https://carers.org.

Going down the pub

It's quite natural to let your hair down once you've finally graduated but be careful that your time out isn't just an excuse to totally 'Turn on, tune in, drop out.'[1]

Have a pint or two, or an appletini, but then slowly turn your thoughts back to what's next.

Options abroad

Some of the more common activities and destinations are outlined below.

Teaching English

English is easily the world's dominant second language. Therefore, you could use your familiarity with your mother tongue to find some interesting positions. If you're looking for casual work or voluntary opportunities, you can just approach overseas English language schools before you travel or once you've landed, but you will have much more chance of success if you take a formal TEFL qualification (teaching

English as a foreign language) and sign a contract (for a year or two) before leaving.

TEFL qualifications come in all shapes and sizes, but most schools around the world will expect you to have a postgraduate certificate incorporating 120 hours of study and practice. Many British TEFL students take the Certificate of English Language Teaching to Adults (CELTA) awarded by Cambridge ESOL (see www.cambridgeesol.org) or the Certificate in Teaching English to Speakers of Other Languages (Cert. TESOL) awarded by Trinity College, London (see www.trinitycollege.co.uk). These qualifications can be studied online or at numerous venues throughout the country and overseas.

Common teaching destinations include China, Japan, South Korea, Brazil and numerous countries in Europe. The following websites will give you a good idea of what you're in for:

- Cactus TEFL: www.cactustefl.com – Everything from information and advice to jobs and a useful blog.
- Esl Base Teach English: www.eslbase.com – Good all-round guide with a useful glossary of terms.
- University of Kent Careers and Employability Service: www.kent.ac.uk/careers/tefl.htm – Extensive list of useful resources.
- Japan Exchange & Teaching Programme: www.jet-uk.org – Long-term teaching positions in Japan.

Steve Rook, author of this guide

While backpacking in northern Thailand many years ago I bumped into some volunteer workers in a hostel. They were performing a number of supporting tasks in a refugee centre on the Thai–Myanmar border. I asked if I could come along and help. They agreed and I spent the next two months teaching English to enthusiastic children. It was a wonderful experience and later gave me the motivation to become a primary school teacher.

I'm so glad I got involved, not least because the experience eventually gave me an idea of what to do in life!

Making it happen

Volunteering

There are millions of charities across the globe. You just need to find one that matches your interests and offer your services. You can either do this in advance or turn up unannounced. One simple way to find opportunities is just to Google what you want to do and where – for example, a simple search for 'Kolkata charities' comes up with 196 results, including the following …

- Mother Teresa of Calcutta Center: www.motherteresa.org.
- Calcutta Rescue: www.calcuttarescue.org.
- Calcutta Children Charity: www.calcuttachildren.org.

Here are some other useful links …

- Charity Choice: www.charitychoice.co.uk – Database of UK charities in different sectors.
- Wikipedia: www.wikipedia.org – Search for 'worldwide list of charities'.
- Erasmus Plus: www.erasmusplus.org.uk.
- UNICEF: www.unicef.org.uk.
- Volunteer South America: www.volunteersouthamerica.net.
- The International Citizens Service: www.volunteerics.org.
- Voluntary Services Overseas: www.vsointernational.org.
- The European Voluntary Service: www.europa.eu/youth.
- EU Aid volunteers: www.ec.europa.eu.

Au pair work/Nannying

This is where you look after children and/or adults, either in the UK or overseas, and get paid for the privilege. Being an au pair is generally a domestic, household role with, perhaps, some language tuition thrown in, whilst nannies are typically more professional child-minders who often have good references and relevant qualifications, such as a level three diploma in home-based childcare. Find work by contacting agencies that have vacancies where you want to work. The website for the Association of Nanny Agencies provides advice on training and finding work at www.anauk.org. These are a few of the agencies in the UK and the USA:

- Gap 360: www.gap360.com/work-au-pair-america.
- Royal Nannies: www.royalnannies.co.uk.
- Nanny Job: www.nannyjob.co.uk.
- Au Pair in America: www.aupairinamerica.com.
- America's Nannies: www.americasnannies.com.

Gap year projects

This is where you get involved in some sort of exotic placement in a far-flung corner of the world, usually to help the environment or disadvantaged people or animals. For example, you could find yourself looking after kangaroos in Australia (where else?), building schools in Africa or supporting medical professionals in Japan.

If you book these activities through any of the thousands of 'gap year providers' (as most people do) you will pay a pretty penny but find some amazing projects. However, as with all business transactions, it's up to you to make sure everything's above board. For example, you should check out whether the projects you're considering will actually help the local groups they propose to serve (many don't) or indeed whether they will deliver the experiences you're expecting. Some popular organisations are listed below ...

- Raleigh International: www.raleighinternational.org.
- Year Out Group: www.yearoutgroup.org.
- Personal Overseas Development: www.podvolunteer.org.
- The Gapyear Company: www.gapyear.com.
- Real Gap Experience: www.realgap.co.uk.
- Action Aid: www.actionaid.org.uk/adventures.
- Coral Cay Conservation – Reef and tropical forest conservation: www.coralcay.org.

Government/Quasi-Government initiatives

If you're not attracted to working for a private sector organisation but still want the benefits of a tailored voluntary programme, there are also various governmental alternatives. These activities are usually more extensive but involve less active adventure. Some ideas are listed below.

- The International Citizens Service – 'A UK government-funded development programme that brings together 18 to 25-year-olds from all backgrounds to fight poverty in overseas and UK communities.' See www.volunteerics.org.
- Voluntary Services Overseas – Unique roles in developing countries linked to your specific qualifications and experience. See www.vso.org.uk.
- The European Voluntary Service – Projects in The EU and beyond for 18–30-year-olds. These are unpaid but expenses are covered. See www.europa. eu/youth.
- EU Aid volunteers – Online support and active roles for humanitarian organisations around the world. See www.ec.europa.eu.
- British Council European Voluntary Service – Opportunities for 17–30-year-olds, of varying length around the globe with expenses and a monthly allowance. See www.britishcouncil.org.

Working at theme parks/resorts

Theme parks and resorts rely on students and new graduates to keep the doors open. There are usually numerous roles open to hardworking individuals, ranging from cleaning chalets and washing dishes to entertaining clients and running activities for children. Typical jobs can be found by contacting resorts directly or through a number of websites, such as 'Resort Work' at www. resortwork.co.uk.

Helping out at events

Major music, sporting and cultural events regularly occur across the globe and many of them rely on temporary and volunteer workers. This is a great chance to take part in a vibrant activity closely linked to your personal interests, and meet lots of like-minded people. Sporting events include the Summer and Winter Olympics and the Football and Rugby World Cups. Music events include the Roskilde Festival in Denmark and the Big Day Out in Australia. You can find opportunities by looking through the event websites well in advance. Some useful sites listing European festivals and events are also shown below.

- E Festivals: www.efestivals.co.uk/info/working.shtml.
- The Guardian's event jobs page: Search on https://jobs.theguardian.com.
- BugBog: www.bugbog.com/festivals/european_festivals.html.

Summer camps

This is where you look after children or disabled people who are on holiday, especially in the USA. This work involves a range of roles from cleaning and cooking to teaching, counselling and running activities. In return, you are typically given accommodation and a small wage. The following organisations offer a number of programmes around the globe.

- BUNAC: www.bunac.org.
- CCUSA: www.ccusa.com.
- Camp America: www.campamerica.co.uk.
- Lourdes volunteers: www.lourdesvolunteers.org.

Anything and everything

A large number of backpackers just get any work they can to pay their rent. For example, a quick survey of gap year travellers in a Sydney hostel, reveals that the following roles were being undertaken ...

● Bicycle courier	● Telesales
● Waitress	● Driver
● Bar tender	● Mechanic
● Bouncer	● Marketing assistant
● Office temp	● Accountant
● Lifeguard	● Teacher
● Shop assistant	

Where to stay

- If you're going on an organised trip either in the UK or overseas, rudimentary accommodation will probably already be organised. Otherwise, you'll probably have to stay in a rented flat, backpacker's hostel, hotel or tent.
- Hostels are a great place to stay and meet people, but you'll probably have to share a dormitory with three or four other people who snore and have a strange fascination for plastic bags at three o'clock in the morning! Some hostels are party central, others are filled with workers who want to get to bed early, and official Youth Hostels are often quiet and clean, so choose your accommodation carefully.

Visas

If you travel abroad on some sort of organised placement (whether paid or unpaid), your host will probably arrange any visas you may need. However, if you choose to travel independently, this will be down to you. For now, UK citizens can freely work in any European Economic Area country (but this may change after Brexit). This comprises:

Austria	Greece	Malta
Belgium	Holland	Norway
Bulgaria	Hungary	Poland
Cyprus	Iceland	Portugal
Czech Republic	Ireland	Romania
Denmark	Italy	Slovakia
Estonia	Latvia	Slovenia
Finland	Liechtenstein	Spain
France	Lithuania	Sweden
Germany	Luxembourg	

However, there will still be plenty of paperwork! For example, if you stay anywhere in Europe for more than three months, you'll need to apply for an EU resident permit from the relevant authority. This usually involves submitting a whole tranche of documents to the local authorities.

Outside the EU, every country has its own rules and procedures. Some don't allow visitors of any kind but others have limited work agreements and a few have no rules at all! So, it's down to you to research what's allowed and make appropriate provisions. This process can take many months, so start early! Some good places to start your research are www.gov.uk and the Working Abroad section on www.prospects.ac.uk. Country-specific information can also be found on the relevant government/state department websites or by Googling 'working/living in xxxxx'. You may also want to visit a reputable visa service such as Trailfinders at www.trailfinders.co.uk/visas.

Making it happen

Some popular visas for young students and graduates include:

- Australian working holiday visas for young people (18–30) from a range of countries (including the UK and Ireland) to work and travel for a year or two. However, work must not be the main purpose for the visit (note this when you fill out the application!). See www.immi.gov.au.
- New Zealand working holiday visas: A similar scheme to Australia's with a fixed limit of one year and a possible allowance for people up to thirty-five years of age. See www.immigration.govt.nz.
- Canada: The International Experience Canada programme allows UK citizens to work and travel for up to two years. See www.cic.gc.ca.
- The USA: You're allowed to work under a range of visas including the J1 (Exchange) visa programme, which allows you to take up temporary work when you've just finished your degree, in roles such as any casual work, camp counselling or internships. However, you must sign up for the visa through a recognised sponsor such as BUNAC, CCUSA or CIEE. A list of sponsors can be found at http://j1visa.state.gov/participants/how-to-apply/sponsor-search.

Note: the visas listed above often have a quota for each year's intake that tends to fill up quickly, so check them out well in advance!

Linking the experience to your personal development

When you've finished with your time out activity and you're ready to advance in your career (if you can pull yourself away), you'll have to demonstrate the skills, commitment and knowledge you've gained to your future employers and/or course providers. For example, you may have developed teamwork skills during a school building project or administration skills in an office job.

In other words, you can't just expect people to infer what you've learned, you need to prove it! You can find out how to do this in Part V.

> ### ⓘ Useful links
>
> Websites
> https://help.open.ac.uk/further-study
> www.telegraph.co.uk – See 'Gap Year 100 company directory'
> www.prospects.ac.uk – See 'Gap year'
>
> On Facebook
> Sign up for the group: 'Backpacking'
> @gapyeardotcom
> @gapyear365
> @backpackertravel
>
> On Instagram
> #backpacking
> #backpackers
> @backpackermag

PART V

FINDING A JOB

Now you've chosen a career and planned your journey it's time to look for a job. Graduate vacancies come in all shapes and sizes, and this section shows you how to find them and effectively promote yourself as the right person.

CHAPTER 12
Searching for graduate jobs

" You become a champion by fighting one more round. When things are tough, you fight one more round.
James J. Corbett **"**

Contents

What are graduate jobs?
Where you'll find vacancies
If at first you don't succeed

What are graduate jobs?

In the 'good old days', graduates tended to immediately enter a narrow band of clearly defined, skilled roles in areas such as medicine, banking and law. Nowadays, graduates can no longer just expect to fall into fulfilling graduate jobs as soon as they leave university and often have to embark on far more meandering journeys. The good news is that degree holders still tend to earn far more than non-graduates over their lifetimes, whatever career route they follow.

" Nowadays, graduates can no longer just expect to fall into fulfilling graduate jobs as soon as they leave university and often have to embark on far more meandering journeys. **"**

Consequently, a 'graduate job' can now mean almost anything, from a highly prized position to any job at all that may lead to better things. This chapter outlines the full range of employment options for graduates in the modern recruitment market.

Graduate training programmes

Graduate Recruiters, Slaughter and May

The qualities we look for in our trainees include common sense, a sharp intellect, independent thought, judgement and a good sense of humour. To thrive here, you will also need enthusiasm, commitment, a willingness to accept responsibility and the ability to get on well with others. Our work is intellectually demanding so the minimum standard we look for in our applicants is three very strong A-levels (or equivalent) and either a good 2.1 or a 1st in your first degree. The international nature of our practice means that our trainees have the opportunity to work abroad and although proficiency in a foreign language is a bonus, it is not a requirement.

Our trainees come from a range of universities: it is the quality of the candidate, not your university, which is important to us. A law degree is not essential – approximately half of our trainees have not studied law at university.

All future trainees must study the LPC at BPP Law School in Holborn, London. Those who have not studied law will also be required to study the Graduate Diploma in Law at BPP.

Many of the larger graduate employers recruit graduates into organised training programmes. These schemes are very popular because they provide a secure route into work, good prospects and a relatively high salary. They are offered in a range of sectors but are especially prevalent in traditional professions and finance/business-related roles such as accountancy, law, banking, investment banking and management consultancy.

Graduate training programmes are widely advertised and typically offered to candidates with excellent potential, as demonstrated by good grades, relevant skills and a burning commitment to succeed. They are available throughout the year and positions tend to start the following summer once students have graduated. However, you'll find that vacancies usually peak over the winter months from September to February. Therefore, if you're still studying, you need to be ready to apply as soon you start your final year. If you left university in the last two or three years then you are also usually still welcome to apply, especially if you have made the most of your time since graduating.

Application procedures for these positions are understandably long and convoluted and only the most appropriate candidates are hired. New recruits are trained in every aspect of the business for a year or two and then given specialist management/technical roles.

You should note that, even though these graduate training programmes are widely presented on campus and beyond, they only constitute a small proportion of today's total graduate opportunities, this is because:

- Many sectors, such as publishing and community work, do not generally favour this method of selection.
- Small and medium-sized firms (that employ the vast majority of graduates) tend to recruit candidates with particular skills, directly into specific roles.

Two current examples of graduate training programmes are as follows:

- EY: www.ukcareers.ey.com/graduates/our-programmes/graduate-programmes – Roles in actuarial, assurance, consulting, law, tax, technology and transactions opportunities.
- Unilever: www.unilever.co.uk/careers/graduates – Become a 'future leader' in marketing, customer management, human resources, supply chain management, financial management, research and development and technology management.

Other graduate jobs

Mark Hanrahan, Business Development Director, Nomenca Limited

We are not a massive organisation and most people have never heard of us, but we hire graduates every year into a range of exciting roles. Therefore, we get less applications and recruitment is carried out on a more personal basis whereby we look for proactive people who have gone out of their way to find a fulfilling role.

The number one recommendation I would make for graduate job hunters would be to take a step back and look for opportunities across the industry where you want to work, including SMEs, not just the obvious companies who have recognisable brands.

Many larger employers and the majority of small and medium-sized firms do not run graduate training programmes, but instead recruit people with specific skills as and when they're required. Also, many blue-chip companies now prefer to recruit new talent from their pool of interns. Vacancies outside the formal training contract programmes appear in every conceivable area of the economy but two common areas are sales and junior skilled positions.

Sales/Support roles

These positions tend to have a high turnover and the work is usually based on commission: i.e. you get paid according to how much you sell. Sales can be a cut-throat business, but if you have the gift of the gab it might be for you. If you choose this path, make sure you nail the employer down about how much you'll be paid before you start. You should also check out the firm on forums such as those provided at www.thestudentroom.co.uk. Two recent examples of sales positions that have called for graduates are shown below:

- Trainee/Graduate Recruitment Consultant. Salary: £24,000–£26,000 per annum + bonus and benefits. After following the training programme and on achieving specific targets, you will be promoted to the position of Recruitment Consultant.
- Graduate Sales Executive. Competitive salary structure and commission plan. We are looking for individuals of a graduate calibre with the right attitude, drive and determination to succeed in a demanding sales role.

Junior-level positions

Entry-level graduate roles are very attractive because they will probably give you the chance to develop your skills and experience in a supportive professional environment. Therefore, vacancies of this type can be very competitive and are ironically usually secured by the most experienced applicants. Consequently, so-called 'entry-level' positions are often actually the second or third step in a graduate's career journey.

Two examples are shown below:

- Trainee Graduate Process Engineer. Salary unspecified. As a Graduate Process Engineer you will be required to implement several projects and manage/ supervise contractors.
- Graduate PPC Marketing Analyst. Salary – up to £19,000 per annum. This is an exciting role for a graduate with excellent analytical skills and an interest in search marketing.

Non-graduate jobs

Of course, numerous jobs are also offered every year that don't require a university degree at all. These jobs are often unskilled, and you may wonder why you should even consider them when you've earned a degree. However, you shouldn't turn up your nose as they're a great opportunity to:

- Pay your bills and take the pressure off your career search.
- Get used to the work environment (and getting up in the morning).

- Network with key contacts (especially if you can find work in the sector you want to enter).
- Talk your way into a more substantial role.
- Gain the skills and experience you need.
- Enhance your CV and job applications (especially if you highlight the more professional and relevant tasks you undertake, rather than those you may perform most of the time).
- Keep your family happy.

Two recent examples of non-graduate vacancies that may turn out to be the first step towards a fulfilling career are shown below:

- Health Care Assistant required for a Domiciliary Care Department. Successful applicants will have a minimum of six months' experience as a Health Care Assistant. £8–£10 per hour.
- Support Services Adviser. Due to continued growth, the Support Services Advisers will assist the existing Support Services Team in taking incoming calls to the help desk. Salary: £8 per hour.

The scenic route

As outlined throughout this guide, you shouldn't panic if you can't find a fulfilling permanent job straight after university because there is still another well-trodden career path. This winding journey involves gradually enhancing the skills and experience you gained at university through activities such as networking, volunteering, training, temporary employment and internships.

Many graduates who follow this path find themselves in rewarding careers almost by accident, whilst others develop their skills and confidence to such an extent that they are then ready to apply for graduate training contracts or other graduate vacancies.

You just have to be ambitious, patient, dogged and focused.

Where you'll find vacancies

Graduate vacancies in the UK are advertised on a massive patchwork of websites, social networks, directories, agencies and at campus events. Major employers tend to annually advertise their posts on numerous high-profile platforms but small and medium-sized firms usually recruit graduates as and when they are required through limited channels such as job agencies and their personal networks.

Many of the more common sources of graduate jobs are outlined below. Use them to list your favourite sources of vacancies and some interesting vacancies in the following exercise.

Self-assessment: Your favourite graduate career websites

Identify your favourite two graduate career websites and list a current vacancy on each that looks interesting.

Your favourite graduate career websites	Some attractive vacancies currently on offer
●	●
●	●

Reflecting on your answers: Well done if you looked widely but, if you just picked the first jobs you saw that relate to your degree/experience, you owe it to yourself to undertake a deeper search so you can find some new, exciting ideas!

Graduate career websites

These sites provide general careers advice and advertise graduate vacancies at major recruiters in both the public and private sectors. The databases are usually set up so you can look for jobs in specific industries and/or regions and sign up for regular job updates. These popular websites, and the recruiters they promote, maintain a lively presence on campus and produce shiny brochures and posters because they have plenty of money. However, you should always remember that they tend to only focus on the needs of larger recruiters in a narrow range of sectors. Some of the more popular sites are shown below:

- Graduate Prospects: www.prospects.ac.uk – A highly respected and comprehensive website with professionally written advice.
- Milkround: www.milkround.com – A student-friendly site with focused advice and useful forums.
- TARGETjobs: www.targetjobs.co.uk – A comprehensive website with tips on applying to specific employers.
- Graduate-jobs.com: www.graduate-jobs.com – A narrower range of jobs but some good forums and blogs and links to graduate vacancy websites.
- Inside careers: www.insidecareers.co.uk – Great advice and a wide range of roles.

Focused websites

A number of websites focus on a particular aspect of the graduate job market such as the more popular graduate employers (see www.top100graduateemployers.com) or LGTB+ inclusive employers (see www.proudemployers.org.uk).

You can find others by Googling appropriate terms and/or asking at your careers service. However, take some time to look through websites to make sure they're up to date and well-resourced (and don't ever hand over any money!).

University careers centres

Careers services advertise local and national graduate vacancies. Many of them automatically link you to the vacancies advertised on the Prospects website but they also tend to promote specific vacancies for their students and graduates that are not generally released. They may also be able to point you towards vacancies they've heard about through the grapevine.

Most careers centres will see their own graduates and you may also be able to get help from the careers centres at other universities, although some institutions may charge you for this service. You can find contact details for all the nation's centres on the AGCAS website at www.agcas.org.uk.

Visit your local careers centre and see how they can help you in your job search, plus enter some interesting vacancies they are currently advertising.

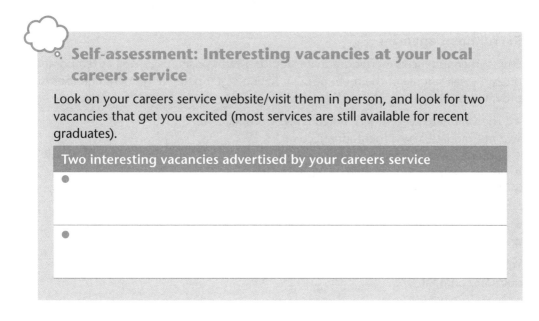

Self-assessment: Interesting vacancies at your local careers service

Look on your careers service website/visit them in person, and look for two vacancies that get you excited (most services are still available for recent graduates).

Two interesting vacancies advertised by your careers service
●
●

Professional organisations

Professional organisations are another good source of industry-specific information and vacancies plus they can also provide excellent networking opportunities. For example, the Royal Society of Chemistry at www.rsc.org offers a dedicated careers advisory service, links to several jobsites and opportunities to rub shoulders with professionals in the field. You can find a full list of the professional organisations in each sector on www.prospects.ac.uk.

Self-assessment: Useful professional organisations

Identify the two most useful professional organisations in your chosen sector and list two specific ways they can help you find a job.

Two useful professional organisations in your chosen sector	How they can help you find a job
●	●
●	●

Reflecting on your answers: Now you've got used to looking around for interesting vacancies, find some way to keep up to date, e.g. you could sign up for their vacancy alerts for regular updates.

Recruitment agencies

Employment agencies recruit graduates for long-term positions as well as temporary ones. A small sample of the more popular national graduate recruitment agencies is provided below:

● The Graduate Recruitment Bureau: www.grb.uk.com.
● TheGraduate: www.thegraduate.co.uk.
● Gradplus: www.gradplus.com.
● Reed Graduates: www.reed.co.uk/graduate.
● Total Jobs: www.totaljobs.com/graduate – Jobs in all business areas, particularly finance, IT, sales and administration.
● Meta-Morphose: www.meta-morphose.co.uk – Business to business positions.
● Matchtech: www.matchtech.com – Technical roles.

You can search for agencies in your area/chosen sector on www.rec.uk.com. Find out more on page 97.

Individual organisations

Many organisations don't advertise their vacancies but rely on people to contact them directly. You can find relevant organisations through professional organisations in the appropriate sector, by looking up directories such as www.yell.com or by Googling terms such as 'publishers in London' or 'UK banks'. You can then target the specific organisations by:

● Contacting individual employees and asking for help (see Chapter 8).
● Asking your existing contacts to put you in touch.

- Attending events where you might be able to rub shoulders with key staff.
- Joining relevant groups on social networks.
- Sending speculative applications.
- Securing casual roles at the organisations and gradually moving up the career ladder.
- Camping out on their doorstep and asking for a chance (but don't get arrested!).

Working overseas

Thousands of graduates find work outside their home countries as soon as they leave university. They either find positions on the general recruitment hubs of larger companies or apply directly to SMEs where they're based. Other graduates work in their home countries for a few years before seeking internal work transfers to their region of choice. Either way, if you want to head overseas, put together a list of organisations in your chosen sector that operate where you want to work, and research what they have to offer/the best way in. The following links may also be useful:

- Prospects Working Abroad: www.prospects.ac.uk/working_abroad.htm.
- Going Global: www.goinglobal.com – International graduate advice and jobs.
- Graduate Jobs in Europe: www.graduatejobsineurope.com – Excellent information and advice for graduates seeking work.

If you're arranging work off your own back, consider the following:

- Are you allowed to work in that country? (If you're British you can currently work anywhere in the European Economic Area – see Chapters 9 and 11.)
- What are the administrative procedures you have to go through to work in your chosen country?
- Do you need to speak the language? And can you?
- How do recruitment procedures differ (such as CV expectations)?

If at first you don't succeed

If you find yourself unemployed and lost when you finish your student days, make sure you take care of yourself. The last thing you should do is give up and sit at home watching day time television. Getting into your career is about reflection, hard work and perseverance, so you need to continually refocus your approach and improve your applications until you get to your destination. Consider the following strategies.

- Reassess what you have to offer and identify possible new roles or paths.
- Get used to taking control in other areas of your life so it becomes second nature.
- Get busy with any activities at all so you can develop your skills, get ideas and stay positive.

- Ask for help from everyone you can think of, such as Careers Advisers, your mum and dad, your brother and your friends.
- Consider going back to university or night school for a further course.
- Have a break and recharge your batteries.
- Set up your own business (see Part VI of this guide).

You may also want to refer back to the advice and guidance in Part III.

ⓘ Useful links

Websites

www.prospects.ac.uk – See 'How to find a job'

www.careers.manchester.ac.uk/findjobs/graduatejobs

www.grb.uk.com – See 'How to find a graduate job'

www.savethegraduate.org – See '7 places to find graduate schemes'

On LinkedIn

www.linkedin.com/jobs/graduate-scheme-jobs

https://uk.linkedin.com/jobs/graduate-job

CHAPTER 13
Promoting yourself effectively

❝ All the world's a stage.
William Shakespeare **❞**

Putting your best foot forward

Job applications shouldn't be long, boring autobiographies of everything you've ever done in your life. They should be effective marketing tools that clearly show you're right for the job. This chapter gives you the essential tools to promote yourself to employers at every stage in the application process. The following chapters show you how to apply this understanding to specific application tools such as CVs, applications and interviews. You can explore how to develop your key employability attributes in Chapter 6.

❝ Job applications shouldn't be long, boring autobiographies of everything you've ever done in your life. **❞**

❝ Send out a few excellently targeted applications rather than hundreds of duds! **❞**

139

Quality not quantity

Many graduates complain that they have to send off countless applications so don't have the time to spend hours on each one, but they're missing the point! You only need one job (usually) and you should be getting interviews with at least one in three applications. If this is not happening, stop and re-appraise your approach. Are you going for jobs outside your reach or are you sending out weak applications? (or both?). As a guide, you should spend at least twenty hours on each vacancy (for graduate level jobs). This is because, you need to:

- Carefully identify what employers are after (the skills, commitment and knowledge).
- Prove you have what's required.
- Engage the reader.
- Spell everything correctly and use appropriate grammar.

Graduates often baulk at this commitment to each application, especially if employers could then discard them after 20 seconds, but what's the point of applying if you don't seriously want to give it your best? Anyway, when you focus in this way on only the most exciting vacancies, you will send far fewer applications, so this approach does not take any more time after all, i.e.:

3 x 20-hour applications = 20 x 3-hour applications

SAME TIME – MORE SUCCESS!

Giving employers what they want

Blair England, Graduate Marketing Officer, KPMG

Here at KPMG in addition to your academic qualifications we look at nine key Behavioural Capabilities. These are the skills and behaviours which you will need to demonstrate to be successful at KPMG. These are the same capabilities that all KPMG employees need to demonstrate across the globe. This includes assessing whether a candidate is enthusiastic about a career at KPMG, whether the person builds relationships internally and externally and works collaboratively to achieve success. KPMG is a high performing culture and we are looking for candidates who show self-awareness, are forward thinking, curious and creative. A positive approach to self-development and awareness of the external marketplace are also extremely important. KPMG staff are continually growing and developing and our future depends on nurturing great individual talent and providing an environment where people can flourish personally and professionally.

For employers, the modern recruitment process is quite straightforward; they simply want to find the best people for the job based on its unique requirements. Therefore, they systematically identify candidates by assessing everyone against clear and objective selection criteria. Selection criteria are usually based on the three elements of success in any field: your skills, commitment and knowledge.

Proving your skills

Employers seek a wide range of skills including:

- Advanced transferable skills, such as teamwork and commercial awareness.
- Technical competencies relevant to the specific job, such as the ability to cook if you want to be a chef.

You can find more information on transferable and technical skills in Chapter 6.

It's harder to prove your skills than it sounds, but it gets easier with practice. This is because it's not sufficient to just list various examples of where and when you have demonstrated them, you also need to outline your specific strengths, i.e.:

- HOW you perform the skill to a high level.
- WHEN AND WHERE you have performed the skill well (provide a specific example).

For example, you could describe your teamwork and Photoshop skills as follows:

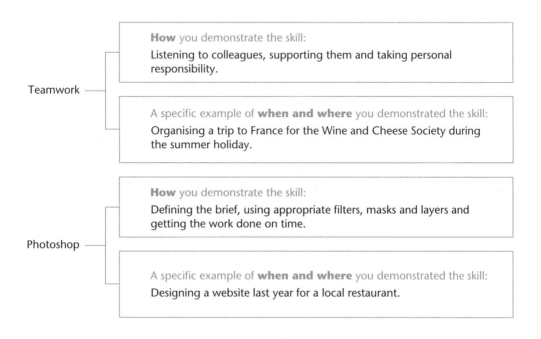

Teamwork

How you demonstrate the skill:
Listening to colleagues, supporting them and taking personal responsibility.

A specific example of **when and where** you demonstrated the skill:
Organising a trip to France for the Wine and Cheese Society during the summer holiday.

Photoshop

How you demonstrate the skill:
Defining the brief, using appropriate filters, masks and layers and getting the work done on time.

A specific example of **when and where** you demonstrated the skill:
Designing a website last year for a local restaurant.

Now you've seen how it's done, try it for yourself. In the exercise below, describe how and when you have performed two of the skills required in your chosen career.

Self-assessment: Demonstrating your skills

Prove you have a technical and a transferable skill required in your chosen career.

Technical skill required:

How you demonstrate the skill (list three ways):
1
2
3

A specific example of **where and when** you've demonstrated the skill:

Transferable skill required:

How you demonstrate the skill (list three ways):
1
2
3

A specific example of **where and when** you've demonstrated the skill:

Reflecting on your answers: If you're still finding this tricky, look back at Chapter 6 and persevere – it's a valuable skill and easy, once you know how. You're also welcome to contact the author for advice at steventhomasrook@ yahoo.co.uk.

Proving your commitment

Commitment is about your genuine interest in the specific career, organisation and vacancy. This is absolutely vital to employers because they are always on the lookout for passionate candidates who are able to proactively take control of their own careers and make a difference. You can usually prove your commitment by demonstrating that you know what the job entails and have a genuine passion, you can prepare as follows:

1 **Research the job:** Look into the role, sector and specific vacancy using the following sources …
   - Graduate career websites such as www.targetjobs.co.uk.
   - The websites of professional organisations (see the companion website at www.macmillanihe.com/rook-gcg-2e).
   - Organisations' individual websites.
   - Contacts at the organisations themselves, such as the recruitment manager.
   - Contacts who know about the sector you want to enter.
   - Forums on websites such as www.thestudentroom.co.uk.
   - Social networking sites and groups.
   - Employers at careers events.

2 **Demonstrate why you want the job:** Clearly outline what attracts you to the particular industry, organisation and role. This demonstrates that you've done your research and reflected on why you are suitable.

3 **Show how you've targeted that specific role:** Demonstrate how you have actively gone about preparing yourself for this career path and reflect on how your experience, so far, has confirmed your decision. For example, you should be able to clearly relate your degree and your previous employment experience to the role.

4 **Plan for the next five years (if you get the job):** Here, you can impress employers by demonstrating that you're looking for more than a job, i.e. you're interested in forming a mutually beneficial long-term partnership.

Proving your knowledge

Knowledge is clearly related to your potential success in the recruitment process, but, it's not usually as important as your skills and commitment. This is because, if you have the ability to do a job and want to do it, then you'll soon learn what's required. Nonetheless, many employers still call for relevant degrees and/or technical knowledge, especially in highly complex roles. You can prove your knowledge by:

- Learning the key concepts, methods and data.
- Outlining exactly where you picked up the necessary knowledge (e.g. during a particular module at university or as part of your role at work).
- Describing what you know and how it relates to each specific vacancy. For example, if you need to know which inorganic compounds are produced when decomposing tissue oxidises, you could state that you studied this process in detail during your biochemistry final-year module, and outline your specific understanding in relation to the role (this is one area where the author of this guide definitely cannot help!).

Selling your experience

Some employers focus heavily on your experience and don't necessarily mention your other key attributes. This could be for several reasons including the following:

- They assume that, if you've done the job before, then you'll probably be able to do it again.
- They just want to limit the number of applications they receive!

If employers focus on your experience, it's up to you to outline what you've done and relate it to the requisite skills, commitment and knowledge. For example:

- If an advert simply states that an organisation needs a barman with six months' experience, list your relevant positions and relate them to the qualities you will need in that specific organisation, such as ability to pull a pint or make cocktails.
- If a manufacturing firm says they need people with two years' sales experience, cobble together all your roles that feasibly fit (and a few more), and outline how they have given you the ability to engage clients, build rapport and sell (i.e. your skills).

Targeting specific jobs

You can use a wide range of resources to research what's required in specific roles. Some of these are listed below.

Job adverts

Adverts generally include the key attributes required in a vacancy. Selection criteria are usually clearly stated but some may be hidden. You need to get used to teasing out the exact requirements. For example, the following attributes are required in the advert below:

- Skills: An outgoing personality, the ability to pick things up quickly and competence with C# or VB.net, SQL Server or Oracle and web technologies.
- Commitment: A passion for IT, a strong desire to learn new technologies and a commitment to developing your skills and career.
- Knowledge: C#SQL.Net, Oracle knowledge and an IT degree.

Trainee Software Developers

Big-Box software developers are looking for recent graduates with IT-related degrees coupled with C#SQL.Net knowledge. You will have a real passion for IT and a strong desire to learn new technologies. You will have an outgoing personality and an ability to pick things up quickly. This is a great opportunity for a graduate to secure a position with a company that is committed to developing your skills and your career. Skills required: C# or VB.net, SQL Server or Oracle knowledge and web technologies.

Job specifications and personal criteria

Most graduate employers provide formal personal specifications. These include job descriptions that outline the specific tasks involved and selection criteria, which are the formal benchmarks they will use to assess applicants. Examples of these are provided in the following activity. See if you can identify all the skills, commitment and knowledge required (the answers are provided at the end of the exercise).

☁ Self-assessment: Untangling personal specifications

Identify the skills, commitment and knowledge required for the following teaching position.

Job description/personal spec for a maths teaching role

We can offer you:
- The opportunity to work in an outstanding school.
- Well-motivated children.
- The full support of a professional team of staff.
- The benefits of working in an innovative and forward-thinking school.
- Professional development to support you in your career.
- An attractive rural location in semi-rural Cheshire.

Are you someone who:
- Is an inspirational and passionate teacher of maths?
- Has a desire to further improve a strong faculty?
- Wants to make a real difference to the lives of young people?
- Is passionate and committed to continually improve?
- Can teach the full range of age and ability across KS3, GCSE and A level?

Answers:
- *Skills:* Outstanding teaching, being able to motivate children and support colleagues plus being an inspirational and passionate teacher with the capacity to teach the full range of ages and ability.
- *Commitment:* Being forward thinking, committed to professional development, happy to live in a rural community, a desire to improve the faculty and make a real difference to young people's lives, committed to professional development and high standards.
- *Knowledge:* Maths curriculum across KS3, GCSE and A level.

Reflecting on your answers: Get some more practice by seeing how the CVs in the next chapter target the specific attributes required.

Direct contact

Sometimes, you can find out a lot by just contacting employers and asking for an informal chat. This will give you the opportunity to ask about any aspects of the job that are not obvious in the advert or the job description, for example:

- The key skills they're seeking.
- How your experience will help you fit in.
- Where you'll be based.
- Any professional training you'll be able to undertake.

This approach will help you target your applications more effectively but also impress employers and they'll probably remember you when you make further contact. However, before you contact anyone, make sure you've done your research and know what you're talking about! You may also want to thank employers for any help they've provided when you finally get round to writing your cover letters, as this will remind them of your previous conversations (see Chapter 16).

Making the most of low grades

As more and more students gain a 2.1 or higher each year in their degrees (currently about 75%[1]), so many employers are stipulating that they will only consider this level of qualification (and high A level grades). If you don't think you will get a 2.1, talk to your tutors to see what you can do to improve. If that doesn't work, or it's too late to make a difference, seek out the larger firms that will consider lower grades and look for jobs at smaller employers as they're usually more flexible.

Dealing with prejudice

It is illegal for employers to act prejudicially against people from particular groups, such as younger people, women or people with a disability. If you suspect this is happening to you, you could apply elsewhere or speak to a Careers Adviser/your Student Union about how you can stand up for your rights.

Are you being targeted?

Employers often target students and graduates from particular universities such as the top Russell Group universities (see www.russellgroup.ac.uk) or specialist centres in your area of expertise (such as Bradford for Peace Studies or Optometry). If relevant employers aren't targeting your institution (e.g. they're not running any events on campus), then make sure you network with them yourself and try to meet them when they visit neighbouring seats of study. Also, go out of your way in your applications, to relate your course to the role.

If you have a disability

If you have a disability that hinders your capacity to complete your applications online, such as dyslexia, get some help from the relevant university service. You should also consider asking the employer to take your disability into account or to provide an alternative application procedure.

It's largely up to you whether you declare your disability at the application stage. On the whole, larger recruiters will do whatever they can to ensure you are given the same opportunity as other candidates but small and medium-sized firms may be less conscientious. Organisations that carry what's called a 'two ticks' symbol will definitely interview disabled candidates who meet the minimum qualifications for the role.

Some quick English revision

Spelling

Employers (or their computer programs) specifically look for poor spelling in applications. For your part, there's no excuse for any mistakes because you can check your work with your word processor's spell-check facility and a dictionary. However, when using a spell-check program make sure of the following:

- You don't correct the word to something completely different. For example, if you spell 'connection' incorrectly, your computer may automatically change it to 'confection'!
- The language on your computer is set to English UK not English US (you can do this in Word by clicking on Tools>Language>English UK).

Dictionaries are especially useful when you want to check which version of a word to use when two or more words sound very similar but have different meanings, depending on how they're spelt (homophones). For example: *Where/we're/were*; *its/ it's*; *there/their/they're*; *dear/deer*; and *practice/practise*. Finally, make sure you spell everyone's names correctly!

Punctuation and grammar

It should go without saying, but you need to write sentences that make sense! Advice on four common problem areas is provided below:

- **Commas:** Use when you want to list items, join two phrases together, avoid repeating words and mark off weak interruptions of sentences.
- **Capital letters:** Use in the following instances...
  - The first word of a sentence.
  - The first word of a direct quotation which is a sentence.

- The first word, and each significant word, of a title (e.g. 'Where the Wild Things Are').
- The name of a day or a month (e.g. Monday).
- The name of a language (e.g. English).
- A word expressing a connection with a place (e.g. British).
- The name of a nationality or an ethnic group (e.g. Jews).
- A proper name (e.g. Huddersfield).
- The name of a historical period (e.g. Elizabethan).
- The name of a holiday (e.g. Christmas).
- A significant religious term (e.g. Passover).
- A brand name (e.g. Macmillan).
- The pronoun 'I'.
- **Apostrophes:** Use when you want to indicate possession or combine two words (e.g. shortening do not into don't).
- **Tenses:** Use the tense appropriate to the situation and stick to it!

Style

English is a wonderfully flexible language that can be used in an infinite number of ways. For example, academics use convoluted sentences and long words whilst texters often avoid vowels, initialise much of what they write and use as few words as possible. Job applications also have their own unique style that takes a bit of getting used to. Some pointers to remember are:

- Write formally and avoid colloquial phrases.
- Avoid contractions such as 'don't' or 'can't'.
- Use short sentences and short paragraphs.
- Use simple words.
- Use positive action words such as those listed below.
- Avoid phrases like 'I think...' and 'I believe...' as they indicate doubt.

Positive action words

Positive words leave a positive impression, especially if you back up any claims. For example, consider the impression created by each of the following three statements and stick to the third style in your applications.

- I am good at communicating. (Boring!)
- I am an effective and enthusiastic communicator. (More dynamic, but shallow.)
- I demonstrate effective and enthusiastic communication skills by carefully listening to clients and diligently adjusting my message to meet their needs. (Skills are outlined in a positive, upbeat style.)

Some examples of positive adjectives and adverbs are shown below:

Ability	Create	Experienced	Keen
Accomplished	Decisive	Flexible	Knowledgeable
Actively	Dedicate	Focused	Launched
Adaptable	Demonstrate	Fresh	Leadership
Advanced	Dependable	Friendly	Logical
Ambitious	Design	Generate	Maintain
Analysed	Determined	Goals	Manage
Analytical	Develop	Guide	Mature
Approachable	Diligent	Happily	Motivated
Aptitude	Discipline	Hardworking	Negotiate
Calculate	Discover	Help	Nurture
Capacity	Dynamic	Highly	Objective
Careful	Eager	Honest	Observe
Caring	Effectively	Implemented	Open
Clearly	Efficient	Independently	Opportunity
Collegiate	Encourage	Influence	Plan
Committed	Energetic	Initiative	Praise
Composed	Enquiring	Innovative	Relentless
Comprehensive	Enterprising	Inspire	Reveal
Conduct	Enthusiastic	Interested	Sustain
Confident	Evaluate	Intuitive	Tenacious
Coordinate	Excel	Judgement	Wise

Structure and format

There are a number of things you can do to make sure your applications stand out and look attractive, as follows:

- Use a consistent style and headings.
- Make sure the key points stand out and are easily identifiable from a quick scan.
- Use good quality white paper and black ink from a good printer.
- Consider spacing your lines by at least a factor of 1.15.
- Use basic bullet points.
- Type in an easily readable 'sans serif' font such as Arial or Verdana, make sure the size of your text is easy to read and avoid italics or using bold words in the middle of sentences.

- Leave enough white space on each page so the reader isn't daunted by how much she has to read (more text isn't necessarily better). You can do this by maintaining sufficient margins.
- Perfectly align the text using the tabs (see below).

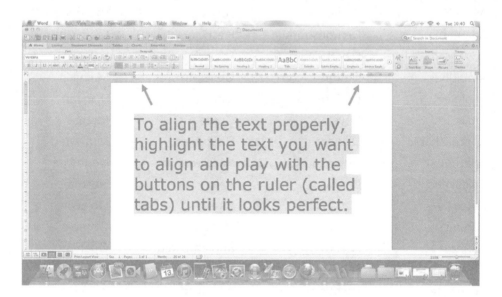

To align the text properly, highlight the text you want to align and play with the buttons on the ruler (called tabs) until it looks perfect.

Updating your work

Always make sure your applications are up to date and focused on the specific vacancy in hand. Don't just cut and paste previous applications without updating what you've written. For example, you won't get a job at Sky TV if you send them a copy of a previous BBC application where you outlined why you want to work for a public service broadcaster!

Drafting and checking

You should expect to make several drafts of your applications before sending them off, as you will probably have to refocus them several times and correct numerous mistakes. Use the following process:

> ❝ You should expect to make several drafts of your applications before sending them off. ❞

1 Allow your creativity to flourish and write your applications freely without worrying about any errors; then edit later (at least twice).
2 When you've finished, make sure you've addressed all the attributes required.
3 Once you've personally edited your applications a few times, get someone else, such as a Careers Adviser, to check them again (but stress you want them to be thorough). This is very important because you won't notice many of your own errors as you're so familiar with what you've written.

ℹ Useful links

CHAPTER 14
Targeting your CV

> *"* I have no skills at the moment but I hope to develop them at your firm.
> *Extract from a genuine CV! "*

What is a CV?

CVs are your shop-window advertising, giving you a wonderful opportunity to quickly and effectively promote what you have to offer. This chapter shows you how to construct impressive marketing documents that will help you advertise your attributes, secure interviews, and hopefully, get a job!

Five example CVs are provided later in this chapter and four more are shown on the companion website (www.macmillanihe.com/rook-gcg-2e).

What is a good CV?

Rebecca Taylor, former MEP for Yorkshire and the Humber

In both job-hunting and recruiting, I have learned the importance of tailoring each job application. When recruiting, it is immediately obvious when someone has sent a generic application, which has probably been sent to 50 other employers. This gives the impression that the job hunter wants any job rather than the role in question. This kind of application, which is very easy to do in an era of email/online applications, will rarely get you an interview, never mind a job.

In my experience as a job hunter, applying for fewer jobs, but tailoring each application to the specific role and employer in question, is a far better approach. Doing this results in a greater number of interviews than the scattergun approach of applying for anything and everything with the same CV and letter.

Another somewhat linked point is about attention to detail. Always check you are referring to the right person, job title and organisation. It may seem obvious, but as an MEP I have received job applications where the letter was addressed to another MEP from a different political group! I have also received job applications where the role referred to is incorrect, probably a result of amending another application. When I worked in a consultancy firm with a female MD, we sometimes received applications addressed to 'Mr X', indicating that the person had not bothered to visit our website, which included a message from the MD along with her name and photo. This may sound harsh, but applications with such basic errors end up in the bin.

About 80 per cent of CVs are quickly discarded within seconds, a further 10 per cent are dismissed after further consideration, and the remainder are considered for interview. This statistic can sound quite sobering but it's actually good news to anyone who is prepared to put in the work and produce high quality applications, because good CVs get results!

Poor CVs

Inadequate CVs tend to be long random lists of people's skills and experience that are unrelated to the vacancy on offer. These documents are typically discarded in a matter of seconds because recruiters can immediately see that the skills they require are not proven. Poor CVs also tend to contain numerous spelling mistakes and are poorly formatted. You can see a typical example of a poor CV later in the chapter, labelled Example CV1.

Average CVs

Average CVs at least relate the person's experience to their skills, but not the specific attributes required. They tend to outline as many skills and experiences as possible in the hope that some of them will hit the mark but, of course, most of them don't! Therefore, such catch-all CVs also tend to be quickly discarded. Example CV2, later in the chapter, is a typical average CV.

Good CVs

Good CVs (Example CVs 3, 4 and 5, plus the CVs on the companion website) are effective marketing tools that contain the following elements:

- They are tailored to the specific attributes required in each specific role.
- Previous experience and education are clearly linked to the specific skills, commitment and knowledge required.
- Only relevant skills are outlined in full (see Chapter 13).

CVs – The good, the bad and the ugly

GOOD CVs (10%)
Relate experience to the specific skills required

AVERAGE CVs (10%)
Relate experience to random skills

POOR CVs (80%)
Just list experience

When to use a CV

CVs can be used in the following circumstances:

- When you meet an employer or contact.
- When organisations ask for one.
- If organisations give you the choice to send one with your application form.
- If you're making speculative applications.

Rules and conventions

There are no rules to CVs, but there are several conventions that are very important, because employers will quickly dismiss CVs that don't follow an easily recognisable form. This has become especially important in the Internet age because recruiters are increasingly scanning text for important information rather than conscientiously reading through it from start to finish.

These are the key rules to follow:

- Use two pages unless:
  - you have been otherwise advised.
  - you are applying for academic roles, in which case you can generally use three.

- you are applying for business roles such as management consultancy, where one page will do.
- you are applying for a role overseas where other guidelines prevail (see www. prospects.ac.uk/country_profiles.htm).
- Make sure your headings are clear and well highlighted.
- Put key information at the top of each page.
- List everything in reverse-chronological order, i.e. the most recent events first.
- Use your name as the main heading and don't bother writing 'Curriculum Vitae'.
- Make sure your key attributes stand out at first glance.
- Make sure dates are easy to see and that there are no unexplained gaps.

What to include

The distinct advantage of CVs over other job applications is that you can stress your strengths and obscure your weaknesses. For example, if your A Level grades aren't up to scratch, then maybe you could just list the subjects. Also, you don't have to stick to the common headings if you can tailor yours more appropriately. For example, your education section could be headed 'Qualifications', 'Education and Qualifications', or 'Undergraduate study'/'Postgraduate study'; whichever puts you in the best light.

Usual sections

Most CVs will have the sections listed below. Look at the example CVs on the following pages and those on the companion website to see how they look in practice.

Personal details

Include your name, email address, phone numbers, how you can be contacted on social networks, and your address. If you live somewhere different in the holidays, or you're going to move when you graduate, then state clearly when you will be at each address, as in Examples CV3 and CV4. Create a professional voicemail reply message and email address incorporating your name (sexychops@hitmail.com won't really give a good first impression – hopefully!). As a rule, do not include information relating to your age, sex, nationality, marital status or health unless this information is overtly requested (and you are comfortable to comply) or it is customary to do so where the role is being advertised (see Going Global at www.goingglobal.com). You might want to put all your contact details at the top of your CV, as in many of the example CVs provided, or just put your key contact information at the top and your full address nearer the end, as in Example CV7 on the website, thus freeing up some valuable advertising space at the top of your document.

Education

In this section, you should record the names of each institution you attended since secondary school including the towns, dates, qualifications and grades (especially if they're good). If you studied overseas you should also include the name of the country and the UK grade equivalent, which you can find at www.naric.org.uk (your university's careers office should have the password).

Once you've listed the course details, briefly relate your qualifications to the attributes required in the specific vacancy. If you're going for a job that's closely related to your degree, as in Example CV3, you should relate your key modules to some of the technical skills mentioned in the job description. If the vacancy is unrelated to the job you're seeking, as in Example CV4, then you could link your studies to your relevant transferable skills. Allow more space for recent and relevant studies. For example, you could devote one line of your CV to your GCSEs, two for your A Levels and five for your degree. Most students and new graduates promote their education above their employment experience on their CVs because their degrees are their main selling point.

Employment experience

Outline the names of each organisation, where they are, when you worked there and what you did, using the same format as your education section. Remember – all experience counts whether it's paid or unpaid. Focus on your duties and responsibilities that are most relevant to the job you're seeking, even if they weren't your major tasks, as in Example CV3. Finally, relate what you've done to two or three of the specific skills required.

People use a wide range of headings in this section and often break it up into separate headings to suit their personal situation. For example, if you have a great deal of experience, but most of the more relevant roles were conducted some time ago, you could make it more noticeable by splitting your employment experience into two sections entitled 'Relevant Experience' and 'Additional Experience', as in Example CV7.

If you're struggling to come up with any experience to put in this section, you really need to get out there and get a job or some voluntary experience. In the meantime, you could list anything you've done on your degree or in your spare time that could loosely be described as work.

Interests

Relate your hobbies and pastimes to the job you're seeking and the skills required. This is usually a good section to focus on transferable skills such as communication, teamwork and organisation.

Referees

If you're still studying, or you've recently graduated, provide the contact details for a professional referee (a current or recent employer) and an academic referee (a tutor or your personal tutor). If you graduated a while ago, list two professional referees. If you have a good reason for not including the details of your referees, such as, you don't want your boss to know you're looking for another job, you can just write 'References available upon request'. Make sure you get permission from your referees before including their details on your CV and keep in touch with them about the work you're seeking. Include all contact details including phone numbers and email addresses.

Optional sections

As previously stated, you can create any sections you want in your CVs, especially if they increase your chances of finding a job. Here are some options.

Personal profile/Career objective

CVs are increasingly prefaced with a personal profile and/or career objective, usually placed just below the personal details section. Such summaries can be a good way of highlighting your abilities and experience but they are often verbose and self-indulgent. If you do decide to include a profile and/or career objective, then make it short (two or three lines) and focus on your personal qualities, experience, skills and personal strengths. Also, make specific, substantiated claims, frame it in the third person (don't refer to yourself as 'I' or 'my'), and use positive 'action' words. See Examples CV3 and CV4.

Skills

If you want to highlight your relevant skills, one option is to outline them in a specific section, following the skills-based CV format rather than the chronological/traditional style. This is a good way to bring your skills to the fore but, if you do this, you should avoid mentioning them in other areas of your document as this could create confusion. See the guide on different CV formats below.

Additional skills

This is a good section to have if you've already covered all the important skills that are required but have some extra competencies that will help you stand out, such as an ability to speak languages, or a driving licence. See Example CV6 on the website.

Achievements (also often labelled 'Awards' or 'Prizes')

This is the section for all you over-achievers who have impressive accomplishments to promote such as scholarships, professional accolades and/or business triumphs. See Example CV3.

Other popular headings

You can incorporate any headings you want, so be creative, for example you may want to include: 'Positions of responsibility', 'Personal attributes', 'Relevant qualifications', 'Relevant interests', 'X skills' (i.e. attributes targeted at a particular sector, such as 'Digital skills' or 'Coaching skills'), 'Additional skills', 'Qualifications', 'Research', 'Publications'.

The two main CV formats

Employers are accustomed to seeing two main types of CV – chronological/ traditional and skills-based. These are described below. Unfortunately, graduates often assume that chronological CVs focus on experience, whereas skills-based CVs emphasise your key attributes. This is not true. Traditional and skills-based CVs should both highlight your key experiences and prove that you have the requisite skills, commitment and knowledge; they are just structured differently.

> 66 Traditional and skills-based CVs should both highlight your key experiences and prove that you have the requisite skills. 99

Chronological/traditional CV

As shown below, in Example CV3 (and CV6 on the website), this type of CV directly links your education, work experience and interests to your relevant skills. It is a particularly effective CV format if you have a great deal of relevant work history because it highlights your experience.

The usual structure of a chronological/traditional CV:

Name

Personal details
Outline your contact details.

Education
Outline what you've studied and use your education to prove you have some of the skills required.

Employment history
List the jobs you've done and use your experience to prove you have a few more of the skills required

---

Page 1

Interests
Outline your pastimes and hobbies and, again, relate them to the requisite skills.

Referees
Provide the contact details for two referees

Page 2

158

Skills-based CV

Skills-based CVs outline your relevant education, employment experience and interests in one section and collate your skills together under an additional heading. The skills section should therefore have examples from every aspect of your life, especially your time at work. This type of CV is especially useful if you don't have much experience or it's not particularly relevant but you have all the relevant attributes. See Examples CV4 below and CV7 (on the website).

The usual structure of a skills-based CV:

Name

Personal details
Outline your contact details.

Education
Outline what you've studied.

Employment history
List the jobs you've done.

Interests
Outline your pastimes and hobbies

Page 1

Skills profile
Prove you have the 7/8 skills required in each vacancy using examples from each walk of your life.

Referees
Provide the contact details for two referees

Page 2

Name

Personal details
Contact details

Education
Your studies

Employment history
The jobs you've done

Skills
Focus on your key abilities.

Interests

Referees
Contact details for two referees

The usual structure of a one-page CV

One-page CVs

As shown alongside and in Example CV8 (on the website), one-page CVs usually resemble skills-based documents but all the information is squeezed into one side of A4. Therefore, you have to be very brief, focusing on your most relevant education, employment experience and three or four skills.

This one-page résumé, popular in North America, is quickly becoming the norm in a range of finance-related industries such as management consulting, investment banking and even corporate law. Most of these industries have application forms for students and graduates so this issue rarely arises but, if this is your area of interest, you should certainly have a one-page CV for networking purposes.

Academic CVs

CVs for academic posts (as shown below and in Example CV9 on the website) usually contain a third page. The first two sheets follow the pattern of the traditional or skills-based CV shown above and the third page is an appendix of your research/teaching achievements such as an academic abstract, publications, and conferences/courses attended.

Academics tend to prefer more formal CVs in the traditional format and you should be very careful to highlight your relevant attributes and experience. It's very important to have a good understanding of the research/teaching involved in the post before you apply.

The usual structure of an academic CV:

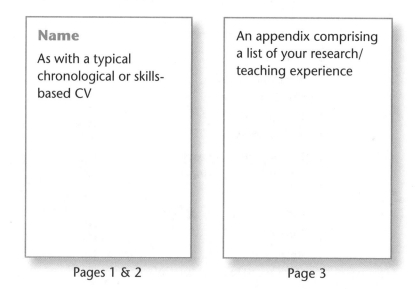

Name

As with a typical chronological or skills-based CV

An appendix comprising a list of your research/teaching experience

Pages 1 & 2   Page 3

Online CVs

Most CVs are viewed online, so why not develop a permanent and up-to-date marketing document on a landing page somewhere, and link to it throughout your online presence. Most students and graduates either place their online record on their own websites or adapt their LinkedIn profile to perform this function. This is an especially valuable tool if you're in a creative industry, such as graphic design, as you can link freely to examples of your work.

For advice on LinkedIn profiles, see Chapter 8. For web-based documents, consider the following guidelines:

- Refer to your digital CV throughout your networking activities.
- Clearly link to your portfolio of work and any online reviews/recommendations of your work.
- Tailor your style and links to the needs of the employers in your chosen sector.
- Arrange a straightforward address for your landing page.
- Keep your document simple and use a universal file format such as pdf.

You can find further guidance on promoting yourself online at:

- www.digitalmarketinginstitute.com (see 'How to write a great digital marketing CV').
- www.geekflare.com (see '16 tools to create an outstanding visual résumé').
- www.michaelpage.co.uk (see 'Six steps to writing a great digital CV').

Video CVs

These are also especially valuable in creative industries where your personality takes centre-stage, such as the media, advertising, sales and marketing. All you need is a good digital camera and an attractive, well-lit space. Follow these guidelines:

- Prepare (look for four examples of 'video CVs' on YouTube and Vimeo, then get going).
- Get used to seeing yourself on video and critiquing your performance.
- Get the lighting sorted and make sure your video looks good on different screens.
- Briefly promote what you've done by highlighting your relevant skills, commitment and knowledge (see the previous chapter).
- Learn your lines off by heart – don't read from a script!
- Make several takes until one clicks.
- Maintain a cheery, positive attitude and direct eye contact.
- Make sure every element looks ultra-professional; good enough is not good enough!
- Be yourself but make sure you clearly demonstrate your brand (see Chapter 8).

Finally, make sure your video has a simple web address and is easily accessible.

You can find further guidance on video CVs at:

- www.theguardian.com (see 'How to make a great video CV').
- www.prospects.ac.uk (see 'Create a great video CV').

Putting your CV together

Now you know what CVs are, you can quickly put one together using the five-stage process outlined below. You can use the examples CVs as templates but make sure you tailor them to your own specific needs.

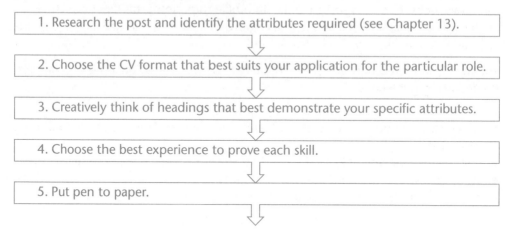

1. Research the post and identify the attributes required (see Chapter 13).

2. Choose the CV format that best suits your application for the particular role.

3. Creatively think of headings that best demonstrate your specific attributes.

4. Choose the best experience to prove each skill.

5. Put pen to paper.

Example CVs

Five example CVs are provided over the next few pages and four more are shown on the companion website www.macmillanihe.com/rook-gcg-2e, as follows:

Example CV1 – A poor CV
Example CV2 – An average chronological CV
Example CV3 – A good chronological/traditional CV
Example CV4 – A good skills-based CV
Example CV5 – A good CV from someone just
        starting out, looking for work
        experience

> On the following pages

Example CV6 – Another good chronological/
        traditional CV
Example CV7 – Another good skills-based CV
Example CV8 – A good one-page CV
Example CV9 – The format for an academic CV

> On the companion website

Brief job details and personal specifications are provided for each example so that you can see how well (or badly) they have been targeted at the particular vacancy. You should also note:

- The first seven CVs are from the same fictitious person so you can clearly see how they have been targeted and adapted to focus on different jobs.
- The first three CVs are for the same job so you can see a gradual improvement.

Example CV1 – a poor CV

The CV below is allegedly targeted at the publishing role listed alongside but, as you can see, it represents almost everything that could (and does) go wrong with modern CVs.

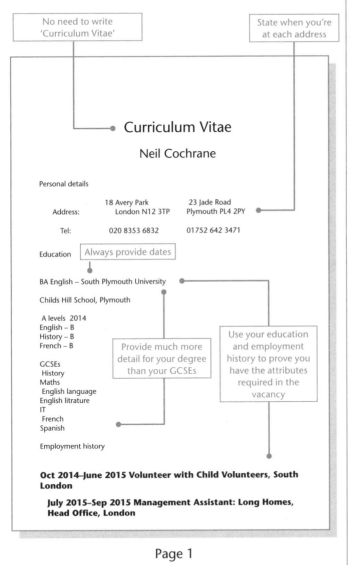

No need to write 'Curriculum Vitae'

State when you're at each address

Curriculum Vitae

Neil Cochrane

Personal details

Address:	18 Avery Park London N12 3TP	23 Jade Road Plymouth PL4 2PY
Tel:	020 8353 6832	01752 642 3471

Education   Always provide dates

BA English – South Plymouth University

Childs Hill School, Plymouth

A levels 2014
English – B
History – B
French – B

GCSEs
History
Maths
English language
English litrature
IT
French
Spanish

Provide much more detail for your degree than your GCSEs

Use your education and employment history to prove you have the attributes required in the vacancy

Employment history

Oct 2014–June 2015 Volunteer with Child Volunteers, South London

July 2015–Sep 2015 Management Assistant: Long Homes, Head Office, London

Page 1

Job description (For CVs 1–3)

Graduate Media Publishing Assistant

You will assist with all aspects of content development for books, journals and digital publications.

Key duties:

- Day-to-day development of content, including liaison with authors and editors
- Scheduling, i.e. chasing authors, editors and other contracted services
- Assisting editors in a fast-paced environment
- Supervising interns and volunteers when required

Experience/skills required:

- Experience of managing freelance editorial and production work
- A relevant degree
- An interest in media, especially films
- Quick, accurate and effective editing skills
- Excellent English skills and a second language
- Good communication skills
- An ability to build relationships with a wide range of people
- Good IT skills, including knowledge of Adobe InDesign and Photoshop

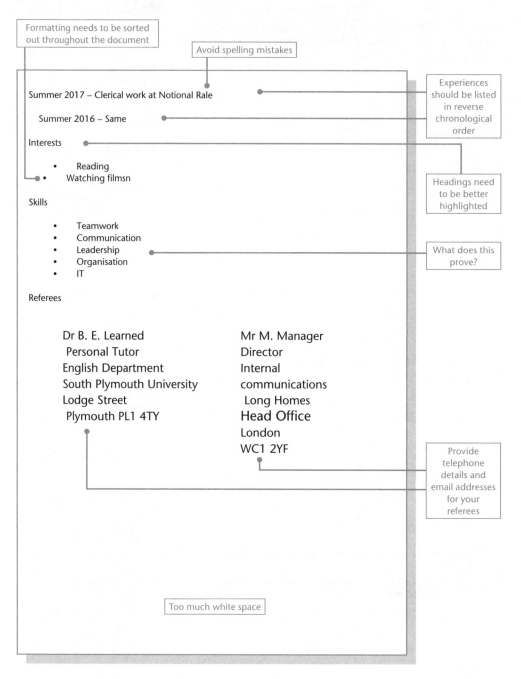

Formatting needs to be sorted out throughout the document

Avoid spelling mistakes

Summer 2017 – Clerical work at Notional Rale

Summer 2016 – Same

Interests

- Reading
- Watching filmsn

Skills

- Teamwork
- Communication
- Leadership
- Organisation
- IT

Referees

Dr B. E. Learned
Personal Tutor
English Department
South Plymouth University
Lodge Street
Plymouth PL1 4TY

Mr M. Manager
Director
Internal
communications
Long Homes
Head Office
London
WC1 2YF

Experiences should be listed in reverse chronological order

Headings need to be better highlighted

What does this prove?

Provide telephone details and email addresses for your referees

Too much white space

Page 2

164

Example CV2 – an average chronological CV

The CV below is formatted appropriately and everything is spelt correctly. It also makes a better job of outlining the person's experiences and relating them to skills required in the workplace. However, no attempt has been made to relate the person's experience to the specific attributes required.

Neil Cochrane
n.cochrae@gigig.com

Personal details

Address:	18 Avery Park Plymouth PL4 2PY (Until 18/06/12)	23 Jade Road London N12 3TP (After 18/06/12)
Tel:	01752 642 3471 07565 678 6551	020 8353 6832 07565 678 6551

Education

2015–2018   **South Plymouth University, BA English**

Relevant modules
• Creative writing   • Gender politics
• Rise of the modern novel   • Medieval romance
• Autobiography   • English poetry

Dissertation
Do good books make good films?

2009–2015   **Childs Hill School, Plymouth**

A Levels
English B, French B, History B
GCSEs
7 GCSEs including English, IT, French and Spanish

Employment history

Summer 2017   **Notional Rail, Euston, London**
Commercial intern
Training provided in all aspects of project management

Summer 2016   **Notional Rail, Euston, London**
Clerical assistant
Supporting colleagues with activities such as filing, typing and IT demonstrating an ability to work in an office and work in teams

Page 1

Job description (For CVs 1–3)

Graduate Media Publishing Assistant

You will assist with all aspects of content development for books, journals and digital publications.

Key duties:

- Day-to-day development of content, including liaison with authors and editors
- Scheduling, i.e. chasing authors, editors and other contracted services
- Assisting editors in a fast-paced environment
- Supervising interns and volunteers when required

Experience/skills required:

- Experience of managing freelance editorial and production work
- A relevant degree
- An interest in media, especially films
- Quick, accurate and effective editing skills
- Excellent English skills and a second language
- Good communication skills
- An ability to build relationships with a wide range of people
- Good IT skills, including knowledge of Adobe InDesign and Photoshop

Dates are easy to see

Consistent formatting

Summer 2015   **Long Homes, Head Office, London**
Management assistant
Promoting our website to our commercial partners

Good use of
bold text

October 2014–   **Child volunteers, South London**
June 2015   **Volunteer support worker**
Teaching and supporting underprivileged children
demonstrating good organisational skills such as an
ability to responsibly manage a wide range of
different projects

Good outline of
organisational
ability (even if it
isn't mentioned
in the job
description)

Interests

* Modern British literature and film
* Reviewing modern art

Make more of
this wonderful
experience!

Additional skills

* Teamwork – Listening to others and encouraging them to succeed
* Communication – Speaking clearly and getting my point across
* Leadership – Managing small teams
* Organisation – Successfully working in a busy environment
* IT

The skills here
are outlined in
some detail but
this section is
still ineffective
because:
* It isn't
focused on
the skills
required in
the post
* The skills are
not linked to
specific
experiences

Referees

Academic
Dr B. E. Learned
Personal Tutor
English Department
South Plymouth University
Lodge Street
Plymouth PL1 4TY
01752 645 3456
learned@splymouth.ac.uk

Professional
Mr M. Manager
Director
Internal Communications
Long Homes
Head Office
London
WC1 2YF
0207 564 6778
m.manager@longhomes.ac.uk

Full details
provided

Page 2

Example CV3 – a good chronological/ traditional CV

The CV below stands out. The formatting is uniform and clear, everything is spelt correctly and the content is unmistakably targeted at the specific attributes required in the job. The skills are also proven with reference to specific experiences.

Highlight any useful social network addresses/ personal websites/ blogs …

Key contact details clearly presented

The personal profile is written in the third person, i.e. without using the pronouns 'I' or 'me'

Neil Cochrane

07565 678 6551   n.cochrane@gigig.com
www.linkedin.com/in/neilalexandercochrane.

Personal profile
Dedicated English graduate with a strong interest in the film industry, substantial editorial and production experience, qualifications in French and Spanish and relevant IT skills.

Personal profile sums up specific skills, interest and experience relevant to the role

Personal details

Address: 18 Avery Park   23 Jade Road
            Plymouth PL4 2PY   London N12 3TP
            (Until 18/06/12)   (After 18/06/12)
Tel: 01752 642 3471   020 8353 6832

Education

2015–2018   **South Plymouth University, BA English, 2.1**
             A highly relevant degree focusing on the contemporary use of English in modern media

Degree is effectively linked to the specific role

             Relevant modules
             • Creative writing   • English poetry
             • The rise of the modern novel   • Autobiography

             Dissertation: 'Do good books make good films?' A 5000-word report linking contemporary literature to ersatz American screenplays.

             Demonstrated a clear and accessible critical style and a deep understanding of good written communication in a wide range of contexts.

2009–2015   **Childs Hill School, Plymouth**

             A Levels: English B, French B, History B
             GCSEs: 7 including English, IT, French and Spanish

Employment history

Summer 2017   **Notional Rail, Euston, London**
               Commercial editorial intern
               • Developed and edited content for the firm's annual report in a high-pressure environment.
               • Successfully liaised with a wide range of colleagues and managed freelancers by building strong relationships and keeping in touch.

Try to get your key experience on the front page

Don't let the contents of the last entry on the first page spread onto the second

Job description (For CVs 1–3)

Graduate Media Publishing Assistant

You will assist with all aspects of content development for books, journals and digital publications.

Key duties:

- Day-to-day development of content, including liaison with authors and editors
- Scheduling, i.e. chasing authors, editors and other contracted services
- Assisting editors in a fast-paced environment
- Supervising interns and volunteers when required

Experience/skills required:

- Experience of managing freelance editorial and production work
- A relevant degree
- An interest in media, especially films
- Quick, accurate and effective editing skills
- Excellent English skills and a second language
- Good communication skills
- An ability to build relationships with a wide range of people
- Good IT skills, including knowledge of Adobe InDesign and Photoshop

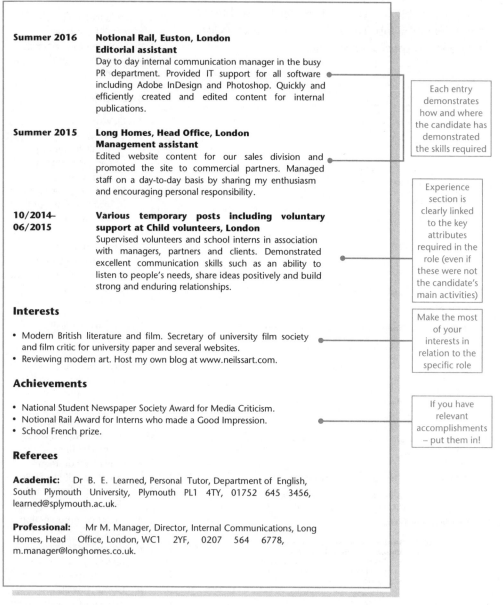

Summer 2016   **Notional Rail, Euston, London**
Editorial assistant
Day to day internal communication manager in the busy PR department. Provided IT support for all software including Adobe InDesign and Photoshop. Quickly and efficiently created and edited content for internal publications.

Summer 2015   **Long Homes, Head Office, London**
Management assistant
Edited website content for our sales division and promoted the site to commercial partners. Managed staff on a day-to-day basis by sharing my enthusiasm and encouraging personal responsibility.

10/2014–   **Various temporary posts including voluntary**
06/2015   **support at Child volunteers, London**
Supervised volunteers and school interns in association with managers, partners and clients. Demonstrated excellent communication skills such as an ability to listen to people's needs, share ideas positively and build strong and enduring relationships.

Interests

- Modern British literature and film. Secretary of university film society and film critic for university paper and several websites.
- Reviewing modern art. Host my own blog at www.neilssart.com.

Achievements

- National Student Newspaper Society Award for Media Criticism.
- Notional Rail Award for Interns who made a Good Impression.
- School French prize.

Referees

Academic: Dr B. E. Learned, Personal Tutor, Department of English, South Plymouth University, Plymouth PL1 4TY, 01752 645 3456, learned@splymouth.ac.uk.

Professional: Mr M. Manager, Director, Internal Communications, Long Homes, Head Office, London, WC1 2YF, 0207 564 6778, m.manager@longhomes.co.uk.

Each entry demonstrates how and where the candidate has demonstrated the skills required

Experience section is clearly linked to the key attributes required in the role (even if these were not the candidate's main activities)

Make the most of your interests in relation to the specific role

If you have relevant accomplishments – put them in!

Page 2

Example CV4 – a good skills-based CV

This CV separates the candidate's experience from his skills because his degree and employment are not clearly related to the vacancy. This allows the candidate to show how he has demonstrated the required skills in all aspects of his life. The other advantage of this format is that recruiters can easily check off your relevant skills.

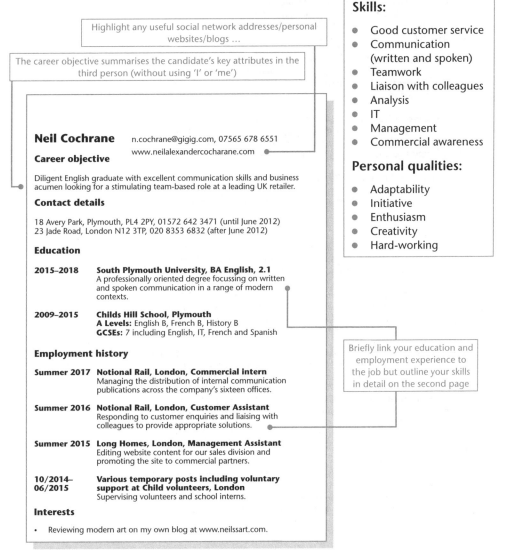

Highlight any useful social network addresses/personal websites/blogs …

The career objective summarises the candidate's key attributes in the third person (without using 'I' or 'me')

Neil Cochrane   n.cochrane@gigig.com, 07565 678 6551
www.neilalexandercocharane.com

Career objective

Diligent English graduate with excellent communication skills and business acumen looking for a stimulating team-based role at a leading UK retailer.

Contact details

18 Avery Park, Plymouth, PL4 2PY, 01572 642 3471 (until June 2012)
23 Jade Road, London N12 3TP, 020 8353 6832 (after June 2012)

Education

2015–2018   **South Plymouth University, BA English, 2.1**
A professionally oriented degree focussing on written and spoken communication in a range of modern contexts.

2009–2015   **Childs Hill School, Plymouth**
A Levels: English B, French B, History B
GCSEs: 7 including English, IT, French and Spanish

Employment history

Summer 2017   **Notional Rail, London, Commercial intern**
Managing the distribution of internal communication publications across the company's sixteen offices.

Summer 2016   **Notional Rail, London, Customer Assistant**
Responding to customer enquiries and liaising with colleagues to provide appropriate solutions.

Summer 2015   **Long Homes, London, Management Assistant**
Editing website content for our sales division and promoting the site to commercial partners.

10/2014–   **Various temporary posts including voluntary**
06/2015   **support at Child volunteers, London**
Supervising volunteers and school interns.

Interests

• Reviewing modern art on my own blog at www.neilssart.com.

Briefly link your education and employment experience to the job but outline your skills in detail on the second page

Page 1

Job description

Graduate Trainee (retail)

We are looking for graduates from any degree discipline with the following attributes:

Skills:

- Good customer service
- Communication (written and spoken)
- Teamwork
- Liaison with colleagues
- Analysis
- IT
- Management
- Commercial awareness

Personal qualities:

- Adaptability
- Initiative
- Enthusiasm
- Creativity
- Hard-working

Make sure the headings stand out

The list of skills should be copied directly from the job description, but some can be amalgamated into one heading so there are 7/8 titles in total

Specific experiences should be taken from every walk of life, but primarily from your employment experience

Skills profile

Customer service/Commercial awareness: Strong ability to increase sales by listening to customer needs and responding quickly and effectively as demonstrated by excellent feedback from customers and managers at Notional Rail and Long Homes.

Written communication: My English language degree and communication experience in a number of professional contexts have given me excellent spelling/grammar and an ability to tailor messages for different media and audiences.

Spoken communication: A clear spoken voice and the patience to listen give me an instant facility to get my message across and digest the views of others. For example, by building a consensus between the diverse range of interested parties during my internship at Notional Rail.

Teamwork/Liaison with colleagues: Strong ability to listen to colleagues and provide support through encouragement, leadership and hard work. For example, at Long Homes, by persuading partners to make better use of our contact database.

IT: Happy to use a wide range of software including Word, Excel, PowerPoint and Access to interpret data and make formal presentations. Demonstrated my ability during my editing work at Notional Rail, my analysis of sales figures at Long Homes and my personal art blog.

Management: Throughout my employment experience I have effectively led people by sharing my enthusiasm and providing consistent support. For example, during my time at Child Volunteers where I was able to inspire new recruits and give them the confidence to succeed.

Adaptability/Initiative/Creativity: Always happy to seek new solutions. For example, at Notional Rail, by widening the use of social media to improve internal communication between regional managers.

Enthusiasm/Hard-working: Clearly demonstrated by my invitation from Notional Rail to complete an internship this year, after my previous successes at the firm.

Referees

Academic: Dr B. E. Learned, Personal Tutor, S. Plymouth University, Plymouth PL1 4TY, 01752 645 3456, learned@splymouth.ac.uk.
Professional: Mr M. Manager, Director, Internal Communications, Long Homes, London, WC1 2YF, 0207 564 6778, m.manager@lhomes.co.uk.

As far as possible, specifically outline **how** you demonstrate each skill

Three or four lines are enough for each skill

Page 2

Example CV5 – a good skills-based CV when you're just starting out

Experience is split into two sections to highlight the more relevant work history

Most students and new graduates put education at the head of their CVs, as their degrees are their main selling points

Use reverse chronological order (put your most recent experiences first)

Include your most relevant social network details (usually LinkedIn)

David Davies

D.davies@email.com
07565 678 6551
www.uk.linkedin/myname
20 Tee Park, Plymouth, PL4 2PY

If your degree isn't obviously relevant, outline what you've done that is

Education

2018–present   **South Plymouth University, BA English**
Written and spoken communication in a
range of modern contexts.

2012–2018   **Childs Hill School, Plymouth**
A Levels: English B, French B, History B
9 GCSEs including A grades at English and maths

Provide more detail for your degree than your school qualifications, as they are now old hat

Work experience
Summer 2018   **John's Toys, Kew, Salesperson/Supervisor**
• Ensuring customer service satisfaction in
a busy inner-city store.
• Supporting customers with complaints.

School
holidays from   **JTE Accountants, London, various roles**
2015–2018   • General office duties such as designing office
templates and directing new customers.
• Marketing the firm via Twitter and
writing the company's blog.

This candidate really makes the most of his experience because he only actually went to work at his dad's firm once or twice

Additional
experience   **University Business Society**
10/2018 –   Liaising with local businesses to improve web-based
present   communication.

2016–2018   **School Entrepreneurship Society**
Learning fundamental business concepts,
marketing and digital bookkeeping.

Make the most of all your experience (paid or unpaid)

Interests
• Making toys for my local school and selling them online (with a
profit, so far this year, of £346).

Page 1

Finding a job

Skills are taken directly from the job advert. Don't be afraid to use the same words and make sure they stand out

Bullet points can make the skills easier to scan

Using the first person ('I') is increasingly okay, and it gives a more personal touch, but avoid it in CVs for more traditional employers

Skills Profile

Customer service/Commercial awareness/Hard work
At John's Toys, I was awarded a sales bonus because I diligently:
- Ensured that product queries led to sales.
- Focused on continually improving my sales techniques to achieve ambitious targets.

Clearly link your previous experience to the specific skills required in each role

Written and spoken communication
- At JTE Accountants, I was universally praised for my excellent promotional tweets and interesting Facebook articles.
- I speak clearly and carefully adjust my message to the situation and audience. For example, I am enthusiastic with customers and calm with colleagues but always happy to listen.

Teamwork/Liaison with colleagues/Enthusiasm
At John's Toys, I motivated my team to achieve record sales by:
- Quickly taking personal responsibility for my own tasks.
- Supporting others and making sure everyone felt positive.

IT
I am happy to use a wide range of software, as demonstrated through my analysis of sales figures at John's Toys and in my eBay buying and selling business.

Management
I lead by listening, encouraging others and providing support. For example, at John's Toys I supervised colleagues in a project to offload old lines, helping us sell more units than any of our other stores.

Adaptability/Initiative/Creativity
I derive great fulfilment from looking at business problems and finding new solutions. For example, I recently turned around disappointing sales for the toys I sell on eBay by promoting them as part of a general educational programme linked to the National Curriculum.

References
Academic: Dr B. E. Learned, personal tutor, S. Plymouth University, Plymouth PL1 4TY, 01752 645 3456, learned@splymouth.ac.uk.
Professional: Mr M. Manager, Store Manager, John's Toys London, WC1 2GE, 0107 554 6778, m.manager@johnstoys.co.uk.

Always include your referees' details unless you have a good reason not to, such as you don't want them to know you're going for another job. In that case, you can just state 'References on request'

Page 2

CV checklist

Finally, before sending off your CV make sure it looks good from the employer's perspective, i.e. that it quickly and clearly proves you have the qualities they need. You want them to scan the document and quickly exclaim, 'Wow – she (or he) is perfect!' Here are ten questions you can ask yourself before buying a stamp or pressing 'Send':

- ☐ Have I targeted my CV at the specific skills and experience required?
- ☐ Have I demonstrated how I've shown each skill (rather than just listed them)?
- ☐ Have I used appropriate headings?
- ☐ Have I used positive action words and keywords from the personal specification?
- ☐ Have I highlighted the main points?
- ☐ Are the dates easy to see?
- ☐ Have I checked the spelling and grammar?
- ☐ Is it attractive and easy to read?
- ☐ Are my CV, and the various sections, short and to the point?
- ☐ Have I whetted the reader's appetite?

Two-minute test

One way to make sure you've targeted your CV appropriately is to ask a friend to look at it for one minute and tell you what skills the organisation requires in that specific role. If they identify the correct skills then you know that you've targeted things appropriately and are on the right track.

Reflecting on your answers: If your CV isn't perfect on your first go, try again, and again … Don't be tempted to just call it a day and send it out anyway; there's no point. This may take a great deal of time at first, but you'll soon get quicker once you've had some practice.

Useful links

Websites
www.cv-library.co.uk – See 'How to write a CV'
www.kent.ac.uk/ces/advice.html – See 'CVs and applications'
www.prospects.ac.uk – See 'CVs and cover letters'

Tip-top application forms

> So – inoculation I have all the experience you require.
> *Extract from a genuine application form! (Watch that spell-check!)*

Graduate Recruiters, Cancer Research UK

There are a variety of competencies that we shortlist candidates against:

- problem-solving
- achieving results
- communicating and influencing
- leadership
- drive and motivation
- building relationships

We recommend that you demonstrate these competencies in your personal achievements in order to reach the interview stage. It is a requirement that every candidate for the graduate scheme has a 2.1 or above in any degree discipline. Candidates also have to complete psychometric tests including numerical and verbal reasoning before being invited to interview.

We do look for candidates who have experiences outside of academia; however, these do not have to be in the charity sector. Many candidates who apply have a personal experience of cancer and therefore the charity is close to their hearts.

Alex Popa, Recent graduate

You should take about 15–20 hours over each application because it's more about quality than quantity. Copy the questions into Word and think about them for a few days before answering them – also, double check your spelling!

Why employers use application forms

Employers started to use application forms because the CVs they were receiving were becoming more and more vague and untargeted. Therefore, they hoped that forms, with specific questions, would be more useful recruitment tools. Unfortunately, however, most completed application forms are also completed poorly and reveal little of what applicants can offer. This chapter shows you how to complete application forms effectively and, therefore, quickly stand out from the crowd.

Questions about you (your personal details)

Make sure you give your home and term-time address (if they are different) plus the dates when you'll be at each, and make sure you have a professional-looking email address.

Questions about what you know (your education/ qualifications)

Highlight the most relevant aspects of your studies. For example, if the recruiter asks you to include the individual units that make up your degree, list the most relevant ones first. If you haven't achieved the UCAS points or degree level required, don't just send the form off and hope for the best, because it will probably be discarded (computer says no). Contact the organisation, give them a good reason why your grades weren't as good as you had hoped and ask them to look at your application anyway. Alternatively, look for jobs in organisations where your grades are not crucial, this includes an increasing number of the larger firms and most of the smaller and medium-sized businesses.

Questions about what you've done (your work history)

This section gives you a great opportunity to demonstrate that your work history is relevant to the role you're seeking. Here are some tips:

- Try to link your previous roles to the new position; be creative but don't lie. For example, if you're going for a job as a trainee accountant you could describe a vaguely relevant previous job as 'Accounts Assistant'.
- Highlight your most relevant tasks and achievements in previous roles, even if they were only a minor part of the job.
- Use positive words (see Chapter 13) and stress your individual responsibilities.

For example, the following work history section of an application form has been targeted at the specific personal specification. The links are circled.

Example personal specification for a job in retail

Job description: Retail Trainee Selection criteria:	
Personal qualities	*Skills*
● Adaptability	● Good customer service
● Initiative	● Communication
● Enthusiasm	● Teamwork and management
● Creativity	● Liaison with colleagues
● Commercial awareness	● Analysis

Relating your work history to the job requirements

Job title	Responsibilities
(Retail) supervisor	● (Managed) new recruits
	● (Liaised) with (customers), colleagues and managers (to analyse) promotions
(In truth, this job actually involved a wide range of mundane tasks in a car plant including the odd supervision of new staff.)	● (Ensured) standards of customer care
	● (Contributed to) 10% increase in sales by introducing (a creative) new stock rotation policy

Questions about your skills

The good news is that there is a well-established process for breaking down skills-based questions and answering them effectively, as follows:

1. Clarify the question

Break each question down into its constituent parts. This will enable you to tackle each section at a time and mirror the structure of the questions in your answers.

Look at the example below and try it yourself in the self-assessment exercise that follows.

Describe a challenging project you have managed. Outline your objective, how you planned for success, what you did, how you overcame any problems and how you measured your success. (200 words)

This question is asking you to:

(a) Describe a challenging project you have managed.
(b) Outline your objective.
(c) Outline how you planned for success.
(d) Outline what you did.
(e) Outline how you overcame any problems.
(f) Outline how you measured your success.

Self-assessment: Dissecting skills-based questions

Break the following question down into its constituent parts. The answers are provided below.

Describe a team situation where you influenced others. Outline the circumstances, how you persuaded your colleagues to adopt your approach, how you overcame any disagreements and what you achieved.

(a)

(b)

(c)

(d)

(e)

Answers: (a) Describe a team situation where you have had to influence others. (b) Outline the circumstance. (c) Outline how you persuaded your colleagues to adopt your approach. (d) Outline how you overcame any disagreements. (e) Outline what you achieved.

Reflecting on your answers: Don't panic if you struggled first time around. Look at a few application forms in the sector you want to enter and you'll soon get the hang of breaking questions down.

2. Ask yourself – Why are they asking me that?

Before answering each question, research the role and try to figure out exactly why the employer has focused on that particular skill – there are usually several clues on the application form and/or your other sources of research (see Chapter 13). For example, you may be able to identify that teamwork has been highlighted because the employer is worried about upsetting the delicate balance in her long-established staff relationships. This will help you target your answers: for example, in the above scenario, you could start your answer with a statement such as 'I quickly settle in to new group situations and build rapport with colleagues.'

3. Answer the question

Address the sub-questions in the same order they are asked. Provide the briefest possible details about the situation/task and focus primarily on how you performed the skill to a high level. At this stage, don't worry too much about your spelling and grammar, or the word limit. Let your creative juices flow; you can edit your work later. Here are some useful guidelines:

❝ Provide the briefest possible details about the situation and task so you can focus on how you performed the skill to a high level. ❞

- Use short, punchy sentences.
- Devote a paragraph to each of the question's sub-sections (if there aren't too many).
- Add keywords from your research into the organisation/role and positive words and phrases.
- Avoid comments that imply uncertainty like 'I think I can ...'/'I believe I am ...'
- Stress your own role, and what you personally achieved, i.e. use the word 'I' not 'we'.
- Use recent and relevant examples from every walk of life.
- Include the key text from the questions in your answers, as shown below:

Describe a team situation where you influenced others. Outline the circumstances, how you persuaded your colleagues to adopt your approach, how you overcame any disagreements and what you achieved.

You could start each paragraph in your answer as follows:

- 'A team situation where ...'
- 'The circumstances were ...'
- 'I persuaded my colleagues by ...'
- 'A disagreement I faced was ...'
- 'I overcame this by ...'
- 'I achieved ...'

4. Edit your answer

Adjust your grammar and spelling, the tone of your answer and its length.

Some good and bad examples of answers

Question 1: *Describe a challenging project you have recently managed. Outline your objective, how you planned for success, what you did, how you overcame any problems and how you measured your success. (200 words)*

Too much focus on the situation and task

Bad spelling/ grammar

Poor answer: While I was In my second year at uni I had to plan how to raise money for a new set of gym eqipment for our Karate club I tried hard with Gill Hunter and Jane Barber and Brian Heddon and James and we tried hard to think of ways to raise cash and we met once a weak in the common broom at the top of the Grounds (bilding) down by the river. We had to figure out who would want to give us some monee and how to get it out of them Brian had a few ideas and so did Jane so we tried it and asked lots of people and came up with a plan and pretty soon we got some (monee) and our parents came through in the end with the rest.

There is not enough focus on personal actions, i.e. what 'I' did, not what 'we' did

This answer doesn't fully answer the question

The full quota of words is not used

There are insufficient paragraphs

Good answer: I recently managed a challenging fund-raising initiative for my university's karate cub. My objective was to raise £2000 for new gym equipment.

Brief, clear outline of situation and task

Positive words create a positive image

I (effectively) planned the task by brainstorming ideas with colleagues, asking for help from experienced contacts and writing a specific proposal including contingency plans.

After (exhaustively) considering all our options, I decided on a dual strategy of chasing corporate sponsorship and launching an eye-catching event involving leading UK athletes and local celebrities.

The answer clearly answers the question

This answer stresses the candidate's personal actions

Unfortunately, a significant problem soon emerged. It became clear that, whereas the corporate sponsorship activities were immediately bearing fruit, the event was taking up far too much time. At first, I just worked harder but, after discussing things with colleagues and professional event managers, I decided to scale things back and focus on the sponsorship side of things. I was careful to share my reasoning with colleagues and earn their full support before moving on.

I measured our success by counting the money we had raised and assessing how I could improve my project management skills. I made £2100 and built good relationships with new commercial partners and decided that, in the future, I would more carefully link activities to the available resources, particularly time!

A positive ending

Question 2: *Describe a team situation where you influenced others. Outline the circumstances, how you persuaded your colleagues to adopt your approach, how you overcame any disagreements and what you achieved.* (200 words)

This answer doesn't answer the question, it just lists various teams the candidate has joined

Poor answer: I love working with other people. I've worked in numerous teams throughout my time at school and university. At school I was in the rugby team and the hockey team. At university I also played rugby and really got involved with social activities on campus. I get on with people easily because I'm quite outgoing and I think I can be fun. In my job at McDonalds it's really busy and teamwork is essential. I helped my dad out last year in his quest to balloon from the east coast of England to the west. We had great fun. In our rugby team we regularly get together to discuss things and improve our play but so far we still haven't won a game! So, in conclusion I am a popular fellow and am welcomed into teams with open arms.

The full quota of words is not used

There is little use of the words 'I', 'my' and 'me', not 'we' and 'us' (they want to assess your skills not the whole team's)

The answer is rambling, for example, rugby is mentioned early on and again in the last section – these comments should be connected

There are insufficient paragraphs

Good answer: I greatly enjoy sharing my ideas with teammates and working collaboratively. For example, I recently influenced colleagues in my Art History Society to develop a new interactive website that would hopefully increase our membership.

The applicant clearly outlines how he persuaded his colleagues and solved the disagreement

I persuaded colleagues to engage with this project by outlining the financial ramifications of decreasing student numbers, sharing good practice from another society and personally building a consensus for change. This involved listening to my colleagues' concerns, making compromises and supporting them with their pet projects.

One key disagreement I faced was over the amount of work required when we all had busy lives. I solved this dilemma by making it clear that I understood that time was short and promised to assiduously look for a solution. I established a twenty-minute brainstorming session to come up with some creative ideas and asked everyone I knew for help. Through my open and positive attitude, I encouraged colleagues to get involved in the problem-solving process and our least enthusiastic member eventually came up with the answer.

Each paragraph systematically addresses a sub-section in the question

Using funds from a university work-experience initiative, we hired an IT student to write the website over the summer holidays. The finished product was amazing and we tripled our membership in the following year. •—— A positive ending

The STAR method of proving your skills

Sometimes, employers allow you to structure your answers as you wish. In this situation, you can promote how and when you have demonstrated the requisite skill using the STAR method outlined below.

S A situation where you have used the skill: Briefly outline the details of where and when you have effectively demonstrated the skill required (use ONLY 10% of the words allowed).

T The task you faced: Briefly paint a picture of what you had to do. Again, use just enough words to establish the context of your example (use ONLY 10% of your allocated word limit).

A The actions you took: This should be the main element of your answer (70% of the word limit) because employers need to quickly identify **how** you demonstrated the requisite skills to a high level. State explicitly how you performed the attributes required using terms that are clearly transferable. For example, to prove your organisation skills in a project you could clearly highlight how you planned ahead, set specific targets, assessed your progress, made changes where required, and measured your success.

The STAR method of proving your skills

Situation – 10%
Task – 10%
Action – 70%
Result – 10%

R A positive result: You will always leave a good impression if you quantify your success. For example, the good answer below states that 'the children's grades rose by 17%'.

Two-minute test

In order to practise reflecting on your skills using the STAR approach, think of some of your greatest achievements in life (personal or professional), identify the key skills you used and consider **how** you demonstrated them so effectively.

Reflecting on your answers: Now you've got used to reflecting in this way, you should be able to use this approach effectively in your applications.

Examples of answers incorporating the STAR approach are shown below.

Question: *Give an example of a time when you have had the opportunity to demonstrate effective problem-solving skills.* (100 words)

Needs more detail about what the problem was and how it was solved

Poor answer: My job as sales coordinator involved making decisions about which of the team was to work in which area, and what to do if appointments were cancelled. As a retail assistant in charge of a department I had constantly to solve problems as they arose. As an English Teacher in Hungary I had to decide on the progress of the pupils and how to stimulate their learning.

Only one example is required, not three!

Good answer using the STAR method: I demonstrated problem-solving skills as an English Teacher in Hungary. My problem was controlling the students and stimulating them to learn.

Brief outline of situation and task

I improved matters by asking students, colleagues and parents for help, researching teaching strategies and designing stimulating activities. I found out that the previous teacher had not followed typical Hungarian protocol; for example, she had given the children unfamiliar freedoms without the necessary discipline. With this knowledge, I set up a far more rigid and firm environment and established a new, interesting curriculum.

Action: Outline how you specifically performed the skill to a high level

The rest of the summer was a wonderful experience and the children's grades rose by 17%.

Result: Short and positive

Questions about your commitment

Application forms also tend to ask questions about your commitment, in particular, what attracts you to the particular career, industry, organisation and/or role. Two such questions are shown below, along with a breakdown of what's required.

- *What attracts you to our firm and this graduate pathway?*
- *Why are you interested in training to become a chartered accountant at our firm?*

Read these questions carefully as it's not always obvious what's required. For example, the second question above actually has two questions wrapped up in one, i.e. Why are you interested in becoming a chartered accountant? AND Why are you interested in training at that specific firm?

In order to answer these questions, you need to show that you know what's involved in the route you've chosen, it conforms to your interests and aspirations and your experience has confirmed your decision (see Chapter 13 for more detail).

Some good and bad examples

Question 1: *What attracts you to our firm and this graduate pathway?* (200 words)

Vague PR speak which doesn't look genuine

Poor answer: I have always wanted to work at your firm because you are a dynamic organisation that is ambitious and dedicated to its customers and committed to the future of engineering. I have always wanted to work for you ever since I was at school.

This answer should outline what attracts you to them, not your skills

I have the degree you require and the skills such as CAD and teamwork, organisation and teamwork. I have gained some useful experience during my holidays at Old England Engineering and Jet3 Design in Sunderland. I also have other work experience and have got involved in many activities at university such as rock climbing and media production. You are the first company I am applying to.

Rambling and irrelevant

Starting your answers using text from the questions makes them easier to follow

Good answer: I am attracted to PWK for two key reasons. Firstly, the extensive training programme, recently acclaimed by www.carindustry.com, will provide me with valuable expertise in my chosen speciality, and secondly, I am keen to learn my trade at a firm renowned for producing popular cars at the cutting edge of technology, such as the Panther 2.1 GS.

My passion for working at PWK was recently confirmed during my placement at Jet3 Design, in Durham, where I contributed to your new Greyhound Brake Force Distribution System. During this project, I was lucky enough to visit your assembly plant and get a first-hand view of your internationally renowned research facility.

Be specific about what attracts you to the role, sector or organisation

I have chosen the Electrical and Electronic Engineering Development Graduate Pathway because I am greatly excited by recent technology advancements in the field of digital motor electronics within the auto industry which lead to enhanced performance and greater safety. For example, as part of my current studies, I have been recently designing application specific integrated circuits that provide intuitive driver information systems such as a GPS chip, which allows motorists to drive more economically in difficult traffic conditions.

Show your knowledge of the organisation and specialisation

Question 2: *Why are you interested in training to become a chartered accountant at our firm?* (150 words)

What?

Poor answer: I want to be a chartered accountant because I love numbers and have studied maths and accounting at school and university. This is a challenging career which I feel I have what it takes because I have always gained good grades and enjoy what I am doing. My father is a chartered accountant. Audit and tax. Sometimes I consider other careers but they are too demanding because I just like numbers. I don't enjoy the more social aspects of some roles but I can be relied upon to get numbers right. My mother is in a different career but she enjoys it. Accountants are meant to be boring but what's wrong with that!

Short and focused

Good answer: I am passionate about becoming a chartered accountant in public practice because I enjoy managing financial systems and budgets; undertaking audits; liaising with clients and providing financial, tax and transaction advice.

Show how your experience confirmed your decision

I confirmed this career interest during my employment experience last year at GWD where I gradually developed the technical skills to assist trainee accountants in every aspect of their role and communicated with a wide range of clients. I greatly enjoyed the busy environment and the excitement of supporting a diverse range of businesses.

The answer clearly addresses each of the two parts of the question

I am interested in training at Coopers because you initially offer a wide range of work opportunities and this will enable me to confidently choose my specialism once I am part qualified. I am also attracted to your expert training because it is carefully integrated into students' monthly schedules so I will always be able to link my studies to my daily activities.

Show you've done your research

Self-assessment: 'I love this vacancy because ...'

To test your genuine interest in a vacancy, complete the following table as follows:

1. Identify a particular vacancy in your chosen sector that you find attractive.
2. List the top three aspects of that role that you find attractive (be specific and show your research).
3. Pretend you're on the phone to your closest friend and outline them clearly in **less than 30 seconds**.

The specific vacancy you're looking at:	
What attracts you to that role	• • •

Reflecting on your answers: Did you identify three key aspects of the role that sounded impressive? Did you show deep thought/that you had researched the role? Were you short and sweet, or did you bore the person on the other end of the line to death?

Personal statements

What's required

Employers often give you the chance to demonstrate your relevant competencies in a single, persuasive account called a personal statement. This is your chance to prove that you are the right person for the job.

> **This is your chance to prove that you are the right person for the job.**

You will usually be asked to outline qualities such as your relevant knowledge, education/ qualifications, skills, commitment and experience, but sometimes you'll just get a vague request such as 'Please provide a statement in support of your application.' Either way, the key to completing these statements is to clearly and systematically demonstrate that you have the specific attributes required. If no specification is provided, it's up to you to research the qualities required and prove you have them – find out how to do this in Chapter 13. If no word limit is provided, then one or two pages will usually suffice.

Structuring your statement

In order to make it easy for employers to follow your statement and identify the key information, follow these guidelines:

- Include an introduction and conclusion. The introduction should outline what you're going to cover in your statement and the conclusion should tie everything together and provide a positive ending.
- Divide the text into short separate paragraphs for each point.
- Use headings if they help you highlight your key attributes, but beware that formatting elements like this may be re-formatted by the computer programme at the other end (so, before sending off your forms, you may want to check with employers that things like headings and bullet points will show up as you wrote them).

Some examples

Example: *Please provide a personal statement to back up your application.* (The personal specification is shown opposite.)

Poor answer

No introduction or conclusion

I have had a burning passion to help youngsters in trouble ever since my parents divorced when I was thirteen and I had to move across the world to a new school without any friends.

The qualifications should be linked to the role

I have a degree in psychology and am currently studying for a Level Two Certificate in Youth Work Practice.

No outline of HOW the applicant's skills were performed to a high level

I also have all the skills you require. I communicate effectively with young people by listening to their needs, encouraging them and setting clear boundaries. I have an enhanced criminal records bureau check and have been working with young people for many years without any issues arising. I have continually maintained high standards

Much of the content is relevant, but it doesn't mirror the structure of the personal specification

by remaining vigilant and always taking careful precautions such as never touching children or meeting them without other people around. I recently demonstrated my capacity to persevere during a residential summer school at Bath University with a group of fifty school students connected to our youth club.

I have extensive experience of helping young people. At school, I volunteered as a play leader for younger children at our local youth club. At university, I provided guidance for young students on our special phone-in service and helped out at Bath Youth where I helped large groups of young people in residential care.

What did the applicant learn from this experience?

Clear introduction of what's coming up, making it obvious the statement has targeted the exact criteria in the personal specification

Good answer

Throughout the following paragraphs, I have systematically addressed the qualifications, experience, skills and special factors required in the role.

Qualifications: A psychology degree has given me an understanding of human behaviour and the interpersonal and facilitation skills needed to provide practical help for young people. I am currently studying for a Level Two Certificate in Youth Work Practice at Bath Youth where I have specialised in building rapport with large groups.

Headings taken directly from the personal specification

Previous experience of leading young people: I have extensive experience of helping young people. At school, I volunteered as a play leader for younger children at our local youth club. At university, I provided guidance for young students on our special phone-in service and helped out at Bath Youth where I supported large groups of young people in residential care. My experience has taught me the

---

Personal Specification Trainee Youth Worker

Qualifications and experience

- Level 2 Qualification in Youth Work (attained/working towards)
- Previous experience of leading young people
- Knowledge of the voluntary sector

Skills and abilities

- Commitment to personal development and learning
- Strong verbal communication skills and ability to build rapport with a large group of young people
- Ability to set professional boundaries
- Ability to persevere

Special factors

- Enthusiasm/ commitment for working with young people

importance of building rapport, setting firm boundaries and working hard!

Relate your experience to the skills required in the post

Knowledge of the voluntary sector: My training and experience have given me a sound understanding of the scope and work of the voluntary sector in modernising public services in our 'Big Society'. On a more personal note, I also appreciate the current funding limitations, increased workload and fundamental need to be ever committed and dedicated.

Bullet points can break up text but you may want to avoid them if you're filling in the form online and you're not sure how they'll appear, at the other end (you may want to contact the employer to see if they'll be okay)

Committed to personal development and learning: I have demonstrated my commitment to personal improvement in three key ways:

- My extensive voluntary employment experience.
- My choice of a relevant degree.
- My decision to start my youth work certificate whilst still at university.

I plan to extend my qualifications once I have started training and look forward to working with colleagues and managers to enhance my skills.

Use examples to prove your skills but also outline how you demonstrate the skills to a high level

Strong verbal communication skills and ability to build a rapport with a large group of young people: I communicate effectively with young people by listening to their needs, encouraging them and setting clear boundaries. For example, I recently managed a successful trip to a local theatre for our youth centre by letting the students choose the play, giving them an incentive if they followed the plot (a trip backstage) and establishing firm but fair procedures for when individuals misbehaved.

Throughout my career, I have built a strong rapport with people from all walks of life and empathy for the objectives of colleagues and young people. I treat people with kindness and respect and therefore receive the same in return.

Ability to set professional boundaries with young people: I fully appreciate the great responsibility we have to ensure the safety of the young people under our care. I have an enhanced criminal records bureau check and have been working with young people for many years without any issues arising. I have continually maintained high standards by remaining vigilant and always taking careful precautions such as never touching children or meeting them without other people around.

Ability to persevere: I recently demonstrated my capacity to persevere during a residential summer school at Bath University with a group of fifty school students connected to our youth club. I was determined to share the great opportunities that university can offer but the young people seemed to be far more interested in each other than the activities on offer. I stuck with my plans and found creative ways to inspire them and was really happy when our feedback showed that 70% of the group expressed an interest in signing up for a degree once they finished school.

A bit of your personal story can balance the formality of the rest of the statement

Enthusiasm/commitment for working with young people: I have been passionate about helping youngsters in trouble ever since my parents divorced when I was thirteen and I had to move across the world to a new school without any friends. My enthusiasm was recently applauded in an article in our local newspaper as follows:

Short quotes can add colour to your statement

"Dave's enthusiasm for working with students always leaves them positive and energised."

I hope this statement convinces you that I can add value to your service and would cherish the opportunity to discuss the role more fully at interview. ———— Positive ending

Your referees

Unless otherwise stated, you will normally have to provide details of an academic and professional referee. Preferably, your referees should be people who supervise you in some way and can therefore attest to your strengths and suitability for the role. Academic referees are usually contacts in your faculty, such as personal tutors or lecturers. Your professional referees should be current or recent managers/supervisors at work. Get permission from your contacts before including them as referees and keep them up to date.

Online applications

Employers often ask candidates to complete their applications online. Sometimes, you will just be asked to complete a word-processed document but, nowadays, you will probably be presented with a bespoke online form, as shown below. Usually, the first thing you need to do is create a username and password so you can save what you've done at any time and come back to it later. You are usually allowed to return to your form as many times as you want and add to your answers or edit what you've already written (but check this). However, you should be careful not to leave your application until the last minute because, sometimes, the company's server will become overloaded and you could be locked out.

A typical welcome page for an online form is shown below. As you can see, in this instance, John Doe has already completed three sections and is returning at some later date.

A typical online application form

Your application

Welcome back, John Doe

Work your way through the sections below. Before the closing date you can adjust the information as many times as you wish. Once you have marked each answer as complete, you will be able to submit your application.

Section	Status	Started	Last updated
Personal details	Completed	11/05/2018 07:36	13/05/2018 09:23
Current employment	Not started		
Education	Not started		
Personal statement	Not started		
Additional information	Not started		
Reference 1	Completed	11/05/2018 08:12	11/05/2018 08:12
Reference 2	Completed	11/05/2018 07:15	11/05/2018 07:15

Update these sections anytime by just clicking on the link

You can usually answer the questions in any order

There are some distinct advantages to online forms:

- You can save your work online and return to it anytime, anywhere.
- If you apply for more than one job at the same organisation, you won't have to repeatedly fill in your personal, employment, education and referee details.
- You can easily read through previous applications.

However, you should look out for the following complications:

- Online text generally contains more errors than the printed word because applicants tend to be less careful.
- The spell-check facility used on the form may not be as robust as the one on your own PC and may not reveal errors.

For these reasons, it usually makes sense to initially write your answers on your own PC, print them out to check and finally, cut and paste them into the online form. However, once you have incorporated your text into the form, make sure your answers are still formatted as they should be and the word/character count is within the permitted limit (different programs count words and characters in different ways). One way to do this is to use TextEdit (on a Mac) or Notepad (on a PC), rather than Word.

Getting your work checked

Once you've been looking at your work for a long time, your incredible brain automatically corrects any errors in your head by substituting what you actually typed with what it was meant to be! Therefore, you often don't notice the most glaring errors. For this reason, you really need someone else to check your work for spelling and grammar mistakes and also to ensure you've actually answered the questions!

ℹ️ Useful links

Websites
www.ed.ac.uk/careers – See 'Application forms'
www.targetjobs.co.uk/careers-advice – See 'Applications and CVs'
www.thestudentroom.co.uk – Look for discussions on application procedures for specific organisations
Google "Application form" and "Name of Organisation"

On YouTube
'Completing Graduate Application Forms' – AHECS Higher Education Careers Services
'Completing Application Forms', The University of Manchester Careers Service

On Twitter/Instagram
Join in with conversations about the application procedures for particular employers

---

CHAPTER 16

Cover letters that open doors

> **❝** I am applying to your firm because you have good benefits, sick leave and early retirement.
> *Extract from a genuine cover letter!* **❞**

What are cover letters?

Cover letters are short introductions to your application that should whet the reader's appetite and encourage them to delve deeper into your CVs and/or application forms.

When to use cover letters

The default position is to include a cover letter with every application form and/or CV unless it is not possible or you have been otherwise advised. If you're applying by email, send it as an attachment.

What to include

Cover letters were, traditionally, your chance to tailor your generic CVs or application forms to the specific skills required in each individual position. However, now employers expect you to target all your application documents, you should use your cover letters to highlight the key points in your CVs/application forms and establish your unique selling points.

> **❝** Highlight the key points in your CVs/application forms and establish your unique selling points. **❞**

You should see them as your elevator pitch, i.e. your chance to promote yourself to the recruitment manager in the time it would take for you to travel with him to his floor in an elevator.

Formatting your letters

Use the following layout as a template for your letter:

Your name and address

Date

The full name of the person being addressed
Their position
Address

Dear Mr/Mrs/Ms ——————,

RE: **Name of position and reference number**

Paragraph 1: Write a positive introduction outlining how you heard about the job, listing the documents you have enclosed.

Paragraph 2: Outline why you are interested in the role. Clearly demonstrate that you have researched what's involved in the job and have reflected on its suitability.

Paragraph 3/4: Highlight your key skills and experiences.

Paragraph 5: End positively, outlining when you will be available for interview.

Yours sincerely

Your signature

Your name

There are a few guidelines to follow in your cover letters:

- Use one page of A4 paper.
- Try to address your letter to a named person. If no name is provided in a job advert, contact the organisation and/or look them up online to find out who deals with recruitment. If you still can't find a name, direct your letter to Dear Sir/Madam and sign off 'Yours faithfully'.
- Use a formal, professional tone.

Speculative letters

Sometimes you may want to write to an organisation out of the blue offering your services; this is usually called a speculative application. These 'fishing' letters may be effective, especially if you have some outstanding qualities or experience, but nowadays they usually fall on deaf ears unless you have already established some form of initial contact and your letter is integral to your wider networking strategy. You can find out more about effective networking in Chapter 8.

Example cover letters

A poor cover letter

The following cover letter is designed to accompany CV3 in Chapter 14. The spelling and grammar are good but the letter is clearly too generic to get the employer excited. The job description and personal specification for the role are provided alongside.

Neil Cochrane
18 Avery Park
Plymouth
PL4 2PY
25/05/2019

John Hughes
Manager – digital production
Demand Publications
12 Huntingdon Lane
London, WC1 2AA

> The contact details have clearly been cut and pasted into a generic template

Dear Mr Hughes

RE: Graduate Media Publishing Assistant, Ref. AT 234/34

Please find attached my CV for the above role which I recently noticed in a professional recruitment website.

I am interested in working for Demand publications because you are a well renowned firm in the sector.

My CV shows that I have all the qualities you require. As you can see, I have good communication, teamwork, organisation, problem-solving and editorial skills as well as in-depth commercial awareness.

I have a relevant degree and extensive experience where I have undertaken all the duties required in this role. I also speak French and Spanish.

I hope my CV convinces you of my suitability for the role and I look forward to discussing my application more fully at interview. Please do not hesitate to contact me if you have any questions.

Yours sincerely

Neil Cochrane

Neil Cochrane

> Skills and experiences are not related to the specific job

Job description (For CV3, Chapter 14)

Graduate Media Publishing Assistant

You will assist with all aspects of content development for books, journals and digital publications.

Key duties:

- Day-to-day development of content, including liaison with authors and editors
- Scheduling, i.e. chasing authors, editors and other contracted services
- Assisting editors in a fast-paced environment
- Supervising interns and volunteers when required

Experience/skills required:

- Experience of managing freelance editorial and production work
- A relevant degree
- An interest in media, especially films
- Quick, accurate and effective editing skills
- Excellent English skills and a second language
- Good communication skills
- An ability to build relationships with a wide range of people
- Good IT skills, including knowledge of Adobe InDesign and Photoshop

A better cover letter

The following cover letter is designed to accompany the same CV and job description as the previous example (the job description is, again, provided alongside).

Neil Cochrane
18 Avery Park
Plymouth
PL4 2PY
25/05/2019

Genuine interest is demonstrated by the reference to Digital World

John Hughes
Manager – digital production
Demand Publications
12 Huntingdon Lane
London
WC1 2AA

Introduction refers to previous contact with the employer – this will get you noticed

Dear Mr Hughes

RE: Graduate Media Publishing Assistant, Ref. AT 234/34

Thank you for discussing the above role last Thursday on the phone. I particularly enjoyed hearing you talk so positively about the exciting opportunities opening up in this sector. Please find attached my CV.

As I explained last week, this vacancy immediately sparked my interest because it represents a stimulating and fulfilling introduction to modern media publication in a firm that is renowned for creating new opportunities, as shown by your recent innovation award from Digital World.

My CV shows that I have all the qualities you require. In particular, I would like to draw your attention to my communication skills, ability to build rapport and capacity to undertake and manage freelance editorial and production work at a large multinational firm. Furthermore, I also speak French and Spanish.

My genuine interest in this sector is demonstrated by choice of a media-related English degree and extensive relevant experience. During my internships, I also mastered all the duties required in this role. For example, I developed and edited a large number of public communication messages using software packages such as InDesign and Photoshop and constructively liaised with authors and colleagues across the organisation.

I hope my CV convinces you of my suitability for the role and I look forward to discussing my application more fully at interview. Please do not hesitate to contact me if you have any questions.

Yours sincerely

Neil Cochrane

Neil Cochrane

Relevant skills and experience are highlighted

Job description (For CV3, Chapter 14)

Graduate Media Publishing Assistant

You will assist with all aspects of content development for books, journals and digital publications.

Key duties:

- Day-to-day development of content, including liaison with authors and editors
- Scheduling, i.e. chasing authors, editors and other contracted services
- Assisting editors in a fast-paced environment
- Supervising interns and volunteers when required

Experience/skills required:

- Experience of managing freelance editorial and production work
- A relevant degree
- An interest in media, especially films
- Quick, accurate and effective editing skills
- Excellent English skills and a second language
- Good communication skills
- An ability to build relationships with a wide range of people
- Good IT skills, including knowledge of Adobe InDesign and Photoshop

Another good cover letter

The following cover letter is designed to accompany the retail-based Example CV4 in Chapter 14. The job description and personal specification for the role are, again, provided alongside.

Job description
(For CV4, Chapter 14)

Graduate Trainee (retail)

We are looking for graduates from any degree discipline with the following attributes:

Skills:
- Good customer service
- Communication (written and spoken)
- Teamwork
- Liaison with colleagues
- Analysis
- IT
- Management
- Commercial awareness

Personal qualities:
- Adaptability
- Initiative
- Enthusiasm
- Creativity
- Hard-working

Neil Cochrane
18 Avery Park
Plymouth
PL4 2PY
25/05/2019

> The candidate demonstrates genuine interest in this specific role by outlining what attracts him to the organisation's training programme

Jenny Jones
Trainee Manager
Johns and Spencers
32 Windmill Lane
London
W1 4YP

Dear Mrs Jones

RE: Graduate Trainee Role (Retail)

Please find attached my CV to support my application for the graduate trainee (retail) roles you recently advertised on plostacs.co.uk.

I am attracted to this vacancy because of the international regard Johns and Spencers has in terms of caring for its workforce and the inclusive and developmental nature of your nine-month training programme which provides practical experience from day one.

My CV shows that I have all the qualities you require. In particular, I would like to draw your attention to the customer service and communication skills I have demonstrated during my various commercial roles. I find it easy to build rapport with customers, colleagues and managers by showing respect, listening carefully and sharing my ideas positively. Furthermore, I will also add value to your organisation through my ability to speak French and Spanish.

> The applicant outlines how he performs the key skills to a high level

My successful customer facing experience and wide interests are testament to my enthusiasm and creativity as well as my ability to work hard and balance my commitments. For example, I expanded my blog last June and brought in increased advertising revenue at exactly the same time as my exams.

> A few examples back up your arguments

I hope my CV convinces you of my suitability for the role and I look forward to discussing my application more fully at interview. Please do not hesitate to contact me if you have any questions.

Yours sincerely

Neil Cochrane

Neil Cochrane

A good speculative letter

The following cover letter is for a speculative application to a local bookshop, which may be successful as part of an overall networking strategy (see Chapter 8).

Jane Ford
34 Lister Street
Highgate
London
N6 2KL
25/05/2019

[Handwritten notes: Tues 10th Nov 08:30 – 12:30 – Cov [10–11] career planning 12:30 onwards 3pm Margate Test • Prep 1 MT webinar • Certificates for CSW + Survey M. results • Chase last 6 w/shops.]

...ussing the opportunities [...] the twenty-first century. [...] ork for you during your [...] fore enclosed my CV. [...] nt consultant in the retail [...] so I will benefit from such

If possible, your speculative applications should be part of a wider networking strategy

As you can see from my CV, I have all the qualities you require. In particular, I would like to draw your attention to the wide reading I have undertaken during my English A level and degree. I also have excellent customer service and communication skills which I developed during my previous retail roles at Shiver Sheds and RV McColl in Archway.

Outline your relevant skills and experience

I am particularly interested in continuing to work at Holford Books because I have greatly enjoyed the way you communicate your longstanding enthusiasm and commitment for your role even though you clearly work so hard.

I hope my CV convinces you of my suitability for the role. Either way, I wish you well over summer. Please do not hesitate to contact me if you have any questions.

Yours sincerely

Jane Ford

Jane Ford

Show your best wishes and genuine thanks for any help already given

Useful links

Websites

www.themuse.com – See 'How to Write a Cover Letter'

www.guardian.com – See' Three excellent cover letter examples'

Find links to advice on changing or improving your career on the companion website.

CHAPTER 17

Impressing at interviews

" I like to do all the talking myself. It saves time and prevents arguments.
Oscar Wilde "

So, you have an interview

If you have secured an interview, then give yourself a big pat on the back. This is a major achievement because:

- Employers just wouldn't go through all the hassle of meeting you if they didn't think you were up to the job!

" If you're chosen for one interview, then you'll probably secure many more. "

- Even if you're unsuccessful in one or two interviews, you'll still come out on top, because all employer interactions are a great opportunity to practise your technique and make valuable contacts.
- If you're chosen for one interview, then you'll probably secure many more.

Each new interview is unique so you can't exhaustively plan for every single question, but there are many common practices and techniques for which you can prepare. This chapter takes you through the whole process from start to finish.

199

Declan Ramsay, Associate Assurance, Grant Thornton

The key to impressing recruiters at interviews is to discuss things confidently and assuredly. By this stage in your application employers will know what you can offer academically and what experience you have. The interview is designed to see if they like you and whether or not you will impress their colleagues and clients (after all – they will be spending a lot of time in your company!).

You can enhance your self-confidence and your interview technique by getting involved in extra-curricular activities, getting help from your careers service and through lots of practice.

Why employers use interviews

As with all transactions, employers like to see what they're buying before handing over the cash. They want to make sure:

● They like what they see.
● You have the potential to quickly build rapport with colleagues, customers and managers.

What's in it for you?

Like employers, you should view interviews as a chance to weigh up what you're getting into and make sure you're happy to go ahead. It's understandable if you're tempted to just listen and accept whatever the interviewers say, but

❝ You should also view interviews as a chance to weigh up what you're getting into and make sure you're happy to go ahead. ❞

you owe it to yourself to ask perceptive and discerning questions. This due diligence will also, in itself, impress employers.

Types of interview

You can expect at least one interview for most jobs, and graduate employers often make you sit through two! The five main types of interview you might face are outlined below. Further advice on body language can be found later in the chapter.

Telephone interviews

Nowadays, many initial one-to-one interviews for graduate roles are conducted on the phone. These interviews are usually quite short and general in what they cover because they're effectively designed just to sift out the least prepared candidates, as quickly as possible.

Prepare for telephone interviews by finding a secure landline in a quiet room where you won't be disturbed. It also often helps to stand up and smile while answering the questions because this communicates your enthusiasm. You may also want to bring in some short, clear notes, but avoid bringing in your full answers in longhand as it will be clear you're reading your answers! One tactic is to bring in brief skills cards as described later in the chapter, in the section 'Preparing for questions on your skills'.

Video interviews

First interviews and those for geographically distant roles are often carried out on Skype or some other video platform. They may be conducted by one person or a panel and the sound and video quality is not usually that good.

Make sure the room is well lit, you're dressed impeccably and you have an attractive but uncluttered backdrop. Also, practise on the software beforehand so you can deal with any problems that may arise on the day. You may want to arrange notes out of view of the interviewer, make sure these are big and clear (don't sit there obviously reading text). Finally, practise with someone you trust and a Careers Adviser.

One-to-one interviews

As the name suggests, this is a meeting where you will discuss your application with just one representative from the organisation. This is the more common type of interaction for casual and voluntary roles, employment experience opportunities and the initial interview for graduate positions (where you will usually meet someone from human resources, or even an outside agency).

Group interviews

This is where you'll be interviewed alongside other applicants and typically asked to join group discussions on specific topics.

If you're being interviewed alongside other interviewees this is probably to save time and see how you work in a group. This can be tricky, as it is probably unfamiliar and you need to find ways to stand out without seeming too brash or quiet. Quite a challenge! As with other interview styles, the best way to perform is to be yourself, but the best self you can be. Therefore, try to identify your top two or three strengths in group situations and make sure you demonstrate these on the day. For example, if you're good at listening to people, encouraging them and suggesting ideas, make sure you cover each of these strengths in the time allotted. See Chapter 19 for more advice.

Panel interviews

In panel interviews, you typically face questions from three or four current employees, managers, clients and/or representatives from human resources (HR). This type of interview is usually undertaken towards the end of the recruitment process for more professional roles. In this scenario, try to memorise everyone's name (or learn them beforehand), directly face interviewers as they ask their questions and look at every member of the panel as you provide your answers.

How questions are structured

Interviewers tend to ask four types of question to test your skills, commitment and knowledge. These are generally labelled as straightforward, behavioural, situational and strength.

The table below provides examples of each of these questions in relation to skills but, of course, the same categories of question may be used to test your commitment and knowledge or a combination of all three. The table outlines:

- How each of this type of question is structured.
- Some examples focused on three skills: keeping workers on track, solving complex problems (transferable skills) and data mining (a technical skill related to a particular type of job).
- How you can make the most of this format.

The different types of question

Types of question	Structure	Some examples	Making the most of the opportunity
Straightforward	Direct enquiries about your attributes	• Why is it important to keep colleagues on track? • How do you solve problems? • What do you know about data mining?	These questions are easy to interpret and you either know, or don't know the answers. However, you should make sure you delve deeply into the specific attribute required and give an example.
Behavioural	How you've demonstrated particular attributes in the past	• Tell us about a time you have struggled to keep colleagues on track. • How have you solved a problem in a previous role? • Did you use data mining strategies recently?	These give you the chance to relate your skills to a past experience and therefore reveal more about what you can offer, but don't babble on about the minutia of the situation – focus on your particular strengths.

Situational	How you think you would demonstrate particular attributes in a hypothetical situation	● If you get this role, how will you keep workers on track? ● How would you deal with a breakdown in our supply chain brought on by Brexit? ● What would you see as a good way to use data to improve our sales?	These give you a great opportunity to link your skills to the particular role; however, don't go off into flights of fancy that have little bearing on the everyday reality of the job.
Strength	What you enjoy and don't enjoy	● What do you like doing in your spare time? ● Have you enjoyed university? ● What didn't you enjoy in your last role?	This is a relatively new type of personal query to see if you enjoy the job and test whether you'll be a good 'fit' and, as such, it links your commitment to your skills and knowledge (see the section on this below). Promote what you have to offer by demonstrating your passion as well as your skill.

What employers want to know

As outlined in Chapter 13, the key attributes sought by employers are your skills, commitment and knowledge. Therefore, almost all the questions will focus on these elements, as portrayed in the Venn diagram below. As you can

❝ The key attributes sought by employers are your skills, commitment and knowledge. Therefore, almost all the questions will focus on these elements. **❞**

What's important in an interview

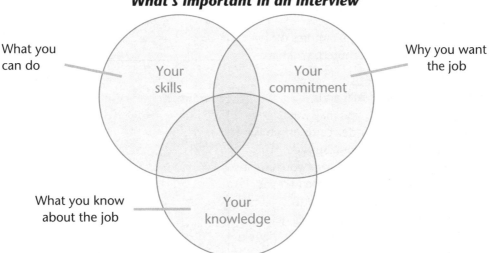

What you can do

Your skills

Your commitment

Why you want the job

What you know about the job

Your knowledge

see from the diagram, some questions will fall into more than one category. For example, a question such as 'Tell us about yourself' actually tests your skills, commitment AND knowledge. More detail on these 'multifaceted questions' is provided later in the chapter.

Preparing for questions on your skills

Questions about your skills form the heart of most graduate interviews. Here's how to prepare.

1. Do your homework

In the days and weeks before the interview:

(a) Use the resources listed in Chapter 6 to research the skills that are required in the industry and the vacancy itself, including both the technical attributes related to the role and your relevant transferable abilities, such as teamwork and organisation.

(b) Identify three ways you demonstrate each of these skills to good effect (for example, your strengths in relation to teamwork could be listening, engaging and working hard).

(c) Identify a focused example to back up each skill (i.e. come up with a specific instance of when you have demonstrated each ability during a particular event or activity, and avoid vague recollections such as 'I did it at university').

(d) Learn your skills and examples off by heart so, when prompted, you have instant recall.

In order to learn your skills and examples off by heart, you may want to briefly list them on index cards, or similar (as shown in the examples alongside). This will allow you to revise whenever you have a spare five minutes. However, don't list your skills and examples in full and try to remember the whole spiel, or you'll get tongue-tied on the day; just describe them in up to three or four words.

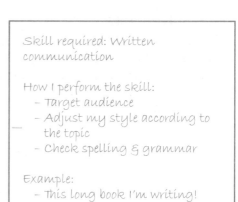

Skill required: Problem-solving

How I perform the skill:
- Identifying the issues
- Researching solutions
- Finding a well-supported resolution

Example:
- Illness last summer at SWPartners

Skill required: Written communication

How I perform the skill:
- Target audience
- Adjust my style according to the topic
- Check spelling & grammar

Example:
- This long book I'm writing!

Skill required: Teamwork

How I perform the skill:
- Listening
- Encouraging
- Working hard on my task

Example:
- Website in last job

2. Practise your answers

Now you have a good idea as to how you carry out each of the skills required, practise fitting your three specific attributes and examples into a vast array of straightforward, behavioural and situational questions targeted on each (and a few more for good measure). You may want friends to come up with the questions, so you have to think on your feet. In that way, for each question you can get used to:

● Identifying the particular skill being tested.
● Designing a response that fits the structure of the question.
● Proving your skill accordingly.

This preparation will mean that, on the day, even though you won't know the questions, you will know the answers!

Some example questions and answers

The examples below show you how to wedge your skills awareness into a range of questions on a technical skill related to a specific role (translation) and a general transferable skill (problem-solving). Read through them and then try it yourself in the following exercise.

> ❝ This preparation will mean that, on the day, even though you won't know the questions, you will know the answers! ❞

Example 1: Questions on your ability to translate technical documents

Although this is a specific technical skill that will be required by few graduates, the following advice clearly shows these sorts of questions, in general.

Your personal reflection on this specific skill:

Skill required: Translating technical documents

How I perform the skill:
- Refer to similar translations
- Use industry-related glossaries
- Consult professionals

Example:
- User manual for German record player

Fitting your skill outline into typical questions:

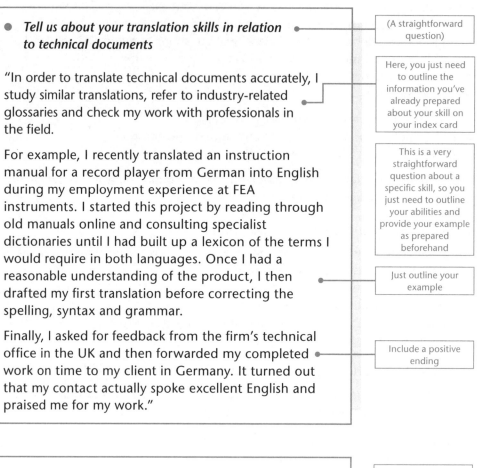

- *Tell us about your translation skills in relation to technical documents* — (A straightforward question)

"In order to translate technical documents accurately, I study similar translations, refer to industry-related glossaries and check my work with professionals in the field. — Here, you just need to outline the information you've already prepared about your skill on your index card

For example, I recently translated an instruction manual for a record player from German into English during my employment experience at FEA instruments. I started this project by reading through old manuals online and consulting specialist dictionaries until I had built up a lexicon of the terms I would require in both languages. Once I had a reasonable understanding of the product, I then drafted my first translation before correcting the spelling, syntax and grammar. — This is a very straightforward question about a specific skill, so you just need to outline your abilities and provide your example as prepared beforehand / Just outline your example

Finally, I asked for feedback from the firm's technical office in the UK and then forwarded my completed work on time to my client in Germany. It turned out that my contact actually spoke excellent English and praised me for my work." — Include a positive ending

- *Give us an example of when you had to translate technical documents* — (A behavioural question)

"In order to translate technical documents accurately I study similar translations, refer to industry-related glossaries and check my work with professionals in the field. — Again – just outline the information you have already prepared about your skill on your index card

For example, I recently translated an instruction manual for a record player from German into English during my employment experience at FEA instruments. I started this project by reading through old manuals online and consulting specialist dictionaries until I had built up a lexicon of the terms I would require in both languages. — This behavioural question again requires no tailoring at all – you can just provide your prepared answer, without any changes

Once I had a reasonable understanding of the product, I then drafted my first translation before correcting the spelling, syntax and grammar. Finally, I asked for feedback from colleagues and practitioners and then forwarded my completed work on time to my client in Germany.

Again – include your positive ending

It turned out that my contact in Germany actually spoke excellent English and praised me for my work."

Again – just outline your example

● ***Imagine I asked you to translate a German document from a totally unfamiliar industry, what would you do?***

(A situational question)

"Firstly, I would like to say that I have translated numerous unfamiliar documents throughout my studies and my employment experience at FEA Instruments where I recently translated an instruction manual for a record player from German into English. Therefore, I would go through the same process I have gone through before.

Link your example to this specific question

Namely, I would start off by studying similar translations and collecting industry-related glossaries. I would then read through old manuals online and consult specialist dictionaries until I had built up a lexicon of the terms I would require in both languages. Once I have a reasonable understanding of the product, I would then put together my first translation before correcting the spelling, syntax and grammar. Finally, I would ask for feedback from practitioners in the field and make sure I forwarded my completed work on time.

This situational question just requires a small adjustment to your introduction

At FEA, it turned out that my contact in Germany actually spoke excellent English and praised me highly for my work."

Once again – provide your positive outcome

- ***What do you enjoy about translating technical documents?***

| (A strength-based question) |

"After studying translation at great depth at university and my internship at FEA Instruments, I have found I really enjoy translating unfamiliar technical documents and that is largely why I've applied for this job.

| Link your example to what you enjoy |

| This strength-based question just requires a small adjustment to your introduction |

I enjoy the challenge of finding the right words by studying similar translations and collecting industry-related glossaries, reading through old manuals online and consulting specialist dictionaries until I have built up a lexicon of the terms I will require in both languages. Then, once I have a reasonable understanding of the product, I find it so rewarding to put together my first translation before correcting the spelling, syntax and grammar. Finally, it's exciting asking for feedback from practitioners in the field and making sure I forward my completed work on time.

| Once again – provide your positive outcome |

At FEA, it turned out that my contact in Germany actually spoke excellent English and praised me highly for my work."

Example 2: Questions on your ability to solve problems

Your personal reflection on this specific skill:

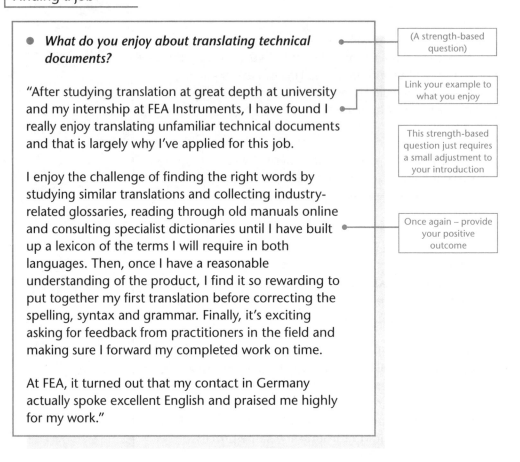

Skill required: Problem-solving

How I perform the skill:
- Identifying the issues
- Researching solutions
- Finding a well-supported resolution

Example:
- Illness last summer at SW Partners

Fitting your skill outline into typical questions:

- *Tell us about your problem-solving skills*

  (A straightforward question)

  "I solve problems by calmly identifying the specific issues involved, widely researching possible solutions with the help from colleagues, and creating a well-supported resolution.

  This question is so basic it's easy to wedge in the information you have already prepared about your skill on your index card (and in your memory)

  For example, during my internship at SW Partners I realised that, due to illness, we would not have enough German speakers to translate two important documents by the agreed date. I immediately looked into the problem and identified exactly how much work was still required and how long this would take. I discussed the problem with my most experienced colleagues and asked them to talk to their teams to see if we could find a solution.

  Following this path, I gained respect and support from colleagues across the business and two extra German translators were temporarily seconded to my department. This approach meant we got the work done on time but I also established a new company protocol for sharing resources."

  Provide an example even if one is not expressly requested

  Include a positive ending

- *Tell us about a time you solved a difficult problem under great time pressure*

  (A behavioural question)

  "I solve problems by calmly identifying the specific issues involved, widely researching possible solutions with the help from colleagues, and creating a well-supported resolution.

  For example, during my internship at SW Partners I realised that, due to illness, we would not have enough German speakers to translate two important documents by the agreed date. This was a crucial contract and we were under a great deal of pressure as we couldn't let standards slip.

  Include the information you have already prepared about your skill as per your index card (and in your memory) but add a few lines to stress the time pressure

I immediately looked into the problem and identified exactly how much work was still required and how long this would take. I immediately discussed the problem with my most experienced colleagues and asked them to talk to their teams to see if we could find a solution, stating I needed an answer within the hour.

> Provide your example but pay more attention to the time pressure

Following this path, I gained respect and support from colleagues across the business and two extra German translators were temporarily seconded to my department, so we could get the work done on time. I also established a new company protocol for sharing resources."

> Include a positive ending

● **Imagine a valued client calls you for urgent help but you don't normally provide this service. What would you do?**

> (A situational question)

"I solve problems by calmly identifying the specific issues involved, widely researching possible solutions with the help from colleagues, and creating a well-supported resolution.

> Sometimes, questions about specific skills don't actually name the attribute involved, so it's up to you to figure out what it is (in this case, problem-solving)

I'm smiling because I had extensive experience of this particular scenario during my work experience at SW Partners, so I can quickly pass on what I would do. I would carefully identify exactly what the client required and the proposed deadline. I would then tell him that I would call him back in half an hour. In the meantime, I would discuss the problem with my most experienced colleagues and ask them to talk to their teams to see what help we could provide. Finally, I would thrash out the best solution we could provide at such short notice.

> Here, you just have to link the way you demonstrate your problem-solving skills (as written on your index card) to the example provided, instead of the one you've prepared

Once we'd found the solution, I would ring the client back at the time stated and positively outline the help we could provide. At a later time, I would also re-contact the client to discuss the issues involved at greater leisure and see how our service level agreement could be adapted to everyone's benefit. In this way, I would not only help the client but also increase our custom."

> Just relate your stated problem-solving skills to this scenario

> Include a positive ending

- *Which do you prefer, the process of finding solutions or sorting things out and moving on?*

(A strength-based question)

"This is tricky to answer because I love both. In terms of solving problems, I enjoy calmly identifying the specific issues involved, widely researching possible solutions with the help from colleagues, and creating a well-supported resolution. As far as 'moving on' goes, I also get a thrill from a job well-done and the prospect of a new challenge.

This question could be designed to test if you enjoy the job AND getting the work done (i.e. the process)

For example, during my internship at SW Partners I realised that, due to illness, we would not have enough German speakers to translate two important documents by the agreed date. I immediately looked into the problem and identified exactly how much work was still required and how long it would take. I discussed the problem with my most experienced colleagues and asked them to talk to their teams to see if we could find a solution.

Link your skills and example to both aspects of the question

Following this path, I gained respect and support from colleagues across the business and two extra German translators were temporarily seconded to my department. This approach meant we got the work done on time but I also gained a great deal of pleasure from getting over the hurdle and establishing a new company protocol for sharing resources which we used in all future projects".

Include a positive ending

Try it yourself

Now you know how to answer these skills-related questions, try it yourself.

Self-reflection: Proving your skills

1 Fill in the index card below about your personal teamwork skills.

Skill required: Teamwork

How I perform the skill:
‒
‒
‒

Your specific example:

2 Think of four questions employers in your sector could ask about your teamwork skills and practise incorporating your personal reflection into your answers (stick to note form – there's no need to write your answers out in full).

Question 1 (a possible straightforward question):

Your answer

Question 2 (a possible behavioural question):

Your answer _____

_____

_____

_____

_____

_____

Question 3 (a possible situational question):

_____

_____

_____

_____

Your answer _____

_____

_____

_____

_____

_____

Question 4 (a possible strength-based question):

_____

_____

_____

_____

Your answer _____

_____

_____

_____

_____

_____

Reflecting on your answers: Hopefully, as you practise tailoring interview answers to your skills in this way, it will become easier and easier – try it over and over again on the bus or the walk home and it will slowly become second nature!

Preparing for questions on your commitment

What they want to know

Employers want to make sure you have the commitment to succeed as well as the skills, i.e. you have diligently researched the vacancy and carefully confirmed that it is suitable. Some typical commitment-based questions are shown below.

- What do you think this job involves?
- Why do you want to work for us?
- What do you see as the main challenges in this role?
- Why have you chosen this career?
- What attracts you to this role?
- Did you enjoy your employment experience?
- How does this job fit in with your personal career plans?
- What are your salary requirements?
- What characteristics will the successful applicant need for this position?
- Why did you choose your specific degree?
- What subjects have you most enjoyed/least enjoyed studying and why?
- What motivates you and stimulates your interest?
- Where do you see your career going in the next five years?
- Can you think of any improvements to our products/ services?
- You don't have much experience – are you sure you want to get into this career?

Self-assessment: Your career path

Link two key events in your life to the vacancy, role, organisation and sector you're targeting.

Your experience/achievement:
_____

How this experience prepared you for the job you're seeking:

_____
_____
_____
_____
_____

Your experience/achievement:
_____

How this experience prepared you for the job you're seeking:

_____
_____
_____
_____
_____

Doing your homework

This may seem like a daunting array of questions, but you will be able to answer them all if you are able to articulate the following aspects of your application:

1 In-depth knowledge of the vacancy, role, organisation and industry.
2 How the vacancy matches your interests and aspirations.
3 The positive steps you've already taken to turn your career dreams into reality.
4 How your experience so far has confirmed your decision.
5 Where you want your career to go in the future.

Try it for yourself in the exercise on p. 214.

Some examples

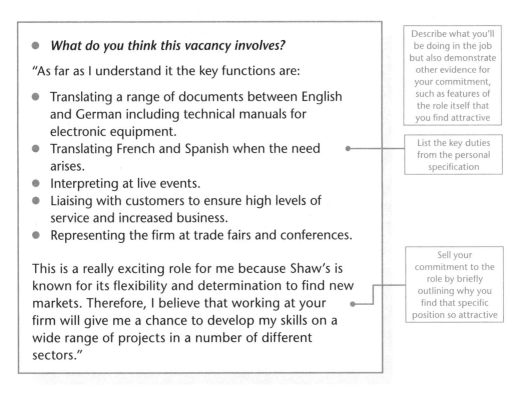

● *What do you think this vacancy involves?*

"As far as I understand it the key functions are:

● Translating a range of documents between English and German including technical manuals for electronic equipment.
● Translating French and Spanish when the need arises.
● Interpreting at live events.
● Liaising with customers to ensure high levels of service and increased business.
● Representing the firm at trade fairs and conferences.

This is a really exciting role for me because Shaw's is known for its flexibility and determination to find new markets. Therefore, I believe that working at your firm will give me a chance to develop my skills on a wide range of projects in a number of different sectors."

Describe what you'll be doing in the job but also demonstrate other evidence for your commitment, such as features of the role itself that you find attractive

List the key duties from the personal specification

Sell your commitment to the role by briefly outlining why you find that specific position so attractive

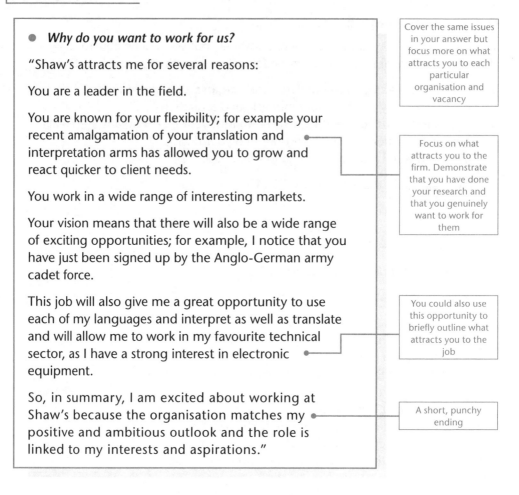

- *Why do you want to work for us?*

"Shaw's attracts me for several reasons:

You are a leader in the field.

You are known for your flexibility; for example your recent amalgamation of your translation and interpretation arms has allowed you to grow and react quicker to client needs.

You work in a wide range of interesting markets.

Your vision means that there will also be a wide range of exciting opportunities; for example, I notice that you have just been signed up by the Anglo-German army cadet force.

This job will also give me a great opportunity to use each of my languages and interpret as well as translate and will allow me to work in my favourite technical sector, as I have a strong interest in electronic equipment.

So, in summary, I am excited about working at Shaw's because the organisation matches my positive and ambitious outlook and the role is linked to my interests and aspirations."

Cover the same issues in your answer but focus more on what attracts you to each particular organisation and vacancy

Focus on what attracts you to the firm. Demonstrate that you have done your research and that you genuinely want to work for them

You could also use this opportunity to briefly outline what attracts you to the job

A short, punchy ending

- *What do you see as the main challenges in this role?*

Define the main challenges you will face but also make it clear how you will overcome them.

- *Why have you chosen this career?*

Outline what attracts you to the career and the steps you've taken to make it happen/what attracts you to that specific vacancy.

- *What attracts you to this role?*

Same answer as above.

- *Did you enjoy your employment experience?*

Outline what you enjoyed about your experience but also show how it informed your career decision and your motivation to go for this particular job.

- *How does this job fit in with your personal career plans?*

Define the career steps you want to pursue now and in the future, and clearly outline how this role fits in with your plans and ambitions.

- *What are your salary requirements?*

Demonstrate that you know the going rate but try to avoid giving a specific figure.

- *What characteristics will the successful applicant need for this position?*

State one or two of the elements listed on the job description and outline how you have overcome them during your previous experience.

- *Why did you choose your specific degree?*

Honestly outline why you chose your particular degree. Don't worry if you initially planned on going into a different career; everyone has a right to change their mind! Either way, you should also relate your degree to your current career plans by outlining the skills you've gained and what you've learned.

Preparing for questions on your knowledge

These are straightforward questions about your technical understanding of specific work-related issues, for example:

- Translate the following sentence for me into German: 'Make sure you disconnect the equipment from the mains before unscrewing the cover.'
- What is thermal oxidation?
- What is a pseudomorph?

In order to prepare for these questions, it's a good idea to develop a general understanding of the more common jargon, concepts and principles related to the job. Look through your old textbooks and scan some relevant professional websites. If you've only got half an hour, a quick look at Wikipedia should do the trick. Don't worry, these questions are less common than you may imagine because employers tend to value your skills and commitment above your knowledge.

Multifaceted questions

As the Venn diagram here shows, many questions are designed to test a combination of your commitment, skills and knowledge. Some examples are provided below along with advice on what you need to consider.

Multifaceted questions can cover aspects of your skills, commitment and knowledge all at once

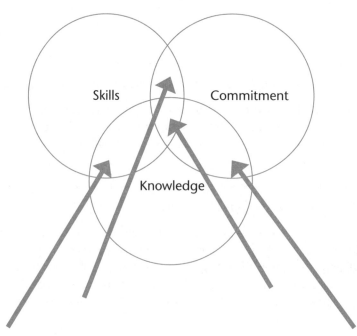

- *Please tell us what you have to offer and why you want to work for us.*

Answer as follows:

1. Start by listing your top two or three relevant skills and briefly illustrating them in a single example. For example, for a role as a Personal Assistant to an MP, you could state:

> This question tests your all-round offering, i.e. your skills, commitment and knowledge

"My main skills in relation to this role are my ability to liaise with a wide range of colleagues, further the Member's agenda and run online campaigns. For example, during my PR role at Withers last year, I was able to build support amongst local politicians and the electorate for a ban on protests at abortion centres."

> These are the key skills required in the role

> Provide an example that demonstrates each of the three skills you have highlighted

2. Outline why you're committed, i.e. why you're interested in the role and that particular vacancy/employer. For example, in the above interview you could follow on by saying:

"In terms of my commitment, I would like to draw your attention to my degree in politics and my work history of supporting people in challenging roles. This role particularly attracts me because I support the Member's agenda, share her passion and believe I can help her move forward in each of her areas of interest."

3. Demonstrate any relevant knowledge. For example, in the above interview you could end by saying:

"Furthermore, I fully appreciate the challenges and opportunities faced by today's political assistants and how political discourse is undertaken."

- *Tell us about your extra-curricular activities*

Don't just list what you do; focus on how your hobbies and interests demonstrate your skills, commitment and knowledge. For example, you could claim that your coaching role at the rugby club demonstrates your commitment to teaching P.E. and that it has developed your all-round teamwork and coaching skills.

> ● *How will your degree help you in this role?*
>
> Outline the skills and knowledge you've gained that are especially relevant to this specific role and career.

> ● *What are your main achievements?*
>
> State your main achievements that are relevant to the role and outline the skills and knowledge you gained.

Some examples

Questions about your weaknesses

Again, these are very common questions because they test each of your attributes. One strategy for answering them is to:

1 Outline a relatively unimportant weakness in relation to a skill that is not so relevant to the specific role.
2 State what you've done to address the skill.
3 Comment on how your actions have actually given you a relative strength in other areas which are relevant to the position.

For example (for someone going for a role as a teacher):

"During my degree, I found that I sometimes had problems analysing complicated legal texts such as deeds of covenant. I addressed this problem by focusing on one section at any one time and taking notes. This technique has solved this problem but it also helps me advise students generally about how to effectively take notes and summarise information."

Off-the-wall questions

Sometimes, employers bowl you a complete googly just to see how you react. These questions typically require you to find an abstract way to demonstrate your relevant attributes. For example:

● If you were an animal/biscuit, which one would you be?
● What was the last film you saw?
● If you were a Premier League footballer, who would you be and why?

It's okay to take your time over these questions – after all, there's no way you could have prepared an answer beforehand! You should endeavour to provide a response that demonstrates you have the skills, commitment and/or knowledge required in the role. If you simply don't know enough about the topic being addressed (e.g. you don't know any footballers in the Premier League), you could structure your answer as follows: "Sorry, I don't know any Premiership footballers, but a sportsperson I would compare myself to is … /this is because …". However, be aware, it is important that you demonstrate your awareness of the culture of the country/area/business as employers will be keen to make sure you fit in. (See more on page 65, 'Your role in context'.) An example is shown below:

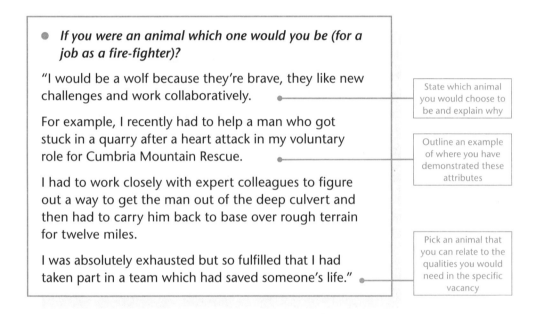

- *If you were an animal which one would you be (for a job as a fire-fighter)?*

"I would be a wolf because they're brave, they like new challenges and work collaboratively.

State which animal you would choose to be and explain why

For example, I recently had to help a man who got stuck in a quarry after a heart attack in my voluntary role for Cumbria Mountain Rescue.

Outline an example of where you have demonstrated these attributes

I had to work closely with expert colleagues to figure out a way to get the man out of the deep culvert and then had to carry him back to base over rough terrain for twelve miles.

I was absolutely exhausted but so fulfilled that I had taken part in a team which had saved someone's life."

Pick an animal that you can relate to the qualities you would need in the specific vacancy

Quick case questions

These questions are usually asked in interviews for management consultancy roles and other similar positions. Four examples are shown below:

- How many red cars are there in Germany?
- If you grew Christmas trees, how would you increase your market share?
- How were Internet sales affected last week by the bad weather?
- How many table tennis balls are there in the UK?

These questions are designed to test your ability to investigate an issue and clearly communicate your thinking. Therefore, your answers aren't as important as the parameters you set and your logical and accurate calculations. The other key to answering quick case questions is to also clearly explain your thinking at each stage of your working and make sure the interviewer is keeping up. If you get the chance, show your assumptions and calculations on paper or a flip chart. Follow this process:

1 **Define the question.** For example, in the first example shown above about red cars in Germany, you could check whether the interviewer just means registered cars or whether you should also include those being manufactured, being stored for export, or rusting away in scrap yards.

2 **Estimate some reasonable parameters.** For example, in order to calculate the number of red cars in Germany you could establish the following numbers (having ascertained that only registered cars are to be counted):

  − The population of Germany is about 75 million.
  − You think most families have roughly 1.5 cars on average.
  − The average single person has about 0.75 of a car (some people don't drive but others have two cars or more).
  − About 50 million people live together as families and 25 million are single.
  − Each family comprises about 2.5 people (including children and one or two adults).
  − Your experience is that about 20% of cars are some shade of red.

3 **Calculate the answer.**

The number of families $= \dfrac{\text{50 million (total number of people in families)}}{\text{2.5 (average number of people in each family)}} = $ 20 million

Number of cars in families = 1.5 x 20 million   = 30 million
Number of cars with single people = 0.75 x 20 million   = 15 million
Total number of cars = 30 million + 15 million   = 45 million

Therefore, the total number of red cars in Germany is roughly $\dfrac{\text{45 million}}{5} =$ **9 million**

Prepare for these quick case questions by working through the three other examples shown above and explaining your working effectively to a friend. You can find out more about this type of question at www.caseinterview.com.

Questions for them

At the end of most interviews you will be given the chance to ask your own questions. This is your opportunity to find out anything you've yet to discover about the role and impress the panel with your research. As a general guide, you should stick to one or two genuine questions you have about the job or the organisation which will clearly affect your specific role.

There's no harm in bringing in four or five questions on a card or a piece of paper, as this clearly shows that you are well prepared, but only ask one or two. In this way, you'll have spare questions if some of your queries have already been addressed.

For example, ask questions like:

(a) I have six hours of lectures each week during the semester; can I get shifts around these times? (For a casual role while you're studying.)

(b) I have noticed that, during my training, I will be given the opportunity to work in a range of sectors of the business. Please could you outline what these are?

(c) Will I have access to a mentor and experienced colleagues when I start working there?

(d) Where do you see my career progressing over the next year or two? (Give them back some of their own medicine.)

You should avoid overly grand questions about the organisation in general, as these will almost certainly not be germane to your application, or queries about insignificant details such as your salary or annual leave.

For example, avoid questions like:

(a) How much will I be paid?

(b) How long will my hours be?

(c) Do you have flexible work hours?

(d) I notice your company is the third biggest on the New York Stock Exchange. What plans do you have for expanding your interests in Europe?

(e) Over the last twenty years, your organisation has expanded massively into North-Eastern Europe. Will you be extending this approach now you have invested in Rotush Energy in Russia?

Another good question could be "Are there any are experiences or skills we've covered during the interview that you would like me to expand upon or clarify?"

Looking good and sounding sharp

So far in this chapter we have focused on your answers to those difficult interview questions, but you should also make sure you speak clearly and use effective body language. In fact, as shown in the pie chart here, the way you look and sound are actually more crucial to your chances of success than what you say! This is because employers will have established your credentials through your application – they want to meet you in the flesh to make sure you're a good fit.

66 The way you look and sound are actually more crucial to your chances of success than what you say! **99**

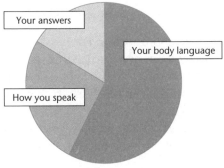

Your body language

The way you present yourself is the most important element of interview success and candidates are usually chosen for jobs within seven seconds of walking through the door!

Obviously, you can't completely change your body language overnight, but there are a number of things you can do to present yourself in a positive light. Many of these are listed below but, before you look, see how many you can identify off the top of your head.

Two-minute test: Your body language

List some elements of good body language.

_____

_____

_____

_____

_____

_____

_____

_____

_____

Reflecting on your answers: Do you really demonstrate these good practices when the pressure's on in professional situations? Ask your friends and family for their thoughts/feedback.

There are a number of strategies you can adopt to improve your image, as follows:

- Dress appropriately. For most graduate roles, this means a well-pressed suit and shiny shoes or a formal dress/skirt and blouse. For some creative roles, alternative attire may be advisable but, if you're not sure, ask the employer. As a general rule, if you can't decide which outfit to wear, choose the one that looks more formal.
- Wash your hair and have your yearly bath, plus don't forget to brush your teeth and put on some deodorant and/or subtle perfume.

- Have a healthy dinner the night before and avoid any alcohol, so you wake up fresh and ready to perform.
- Get to the interview in good time so you are not stressed and hot under the collar.
- Smile and try not to scowl when you're concentrating. This tells the other animals in the room (the interviewers) that you're friendly.
- Be friendly with everyone you meet, as you never know who'll be taking note.

- Walk confidently (upright and purposefully).
- Try to remember the interviewers' names so you can address them personally. First names are usually appropriate nowadays.
- If you shake hands, do it with a bit of gusto – no one likes a limp handshake. You should practise this with your friends and family.
- Sit upright in your chair and don't fold your arms.
- Look at the interviewer when they ask each question and make eye contact with the panel during your answers.
- Show energy and enthusiasm.

Don't worry if you're a bit of a shrinking violet – most students and graduates find it difficult to present themselves confidently under the spotlight. One way to prepare yourself for interviews is to regularly attend events where you have to get all dressed up and speak to powerful people or employers, such as local political meetings or graduate careers fairs. You could also try videoing yourself in practice interviews to see what you look like, or ask your careers service to do it for you.

How you say things

Interviewing people can be boring. Therefore, if you sound like a quiet mouse then the interviewer will be wondering how she's going to stay awake for the rest of the day! Likewise, if you're too loud and abrasive, she may be planning a quick exit! Either way you won't impress. Follow these guidelines:

- Speak slowly and clearly.
- Sound enthusiastic.
- Modulate your voice so that it goes up and down in tone and volume.

Again, if you're not used to public speaking or communicating with professionals it can be very difficult to just magically adopt the right tone when the pressure is on; therefore, you should get some practice. For example, you could join a society where you'll have to appear in public, get involved in presentations at university or find a public-facing job.

A typical interview structure

Interviews often adopt the following format:

(a) **The interviewers will invite you in and say hello:** Be pleasant, walk purposefully, hold your head up high and smile at everyone in the room.

(b) **The interviewer/panel will introduce themselves:** It's a good idea to respond to each interviewer in turn saying something like 'Hello John' (if their name is John). This will help you remember what they're called so you can refer to them by name later in the interview (a good tactic).

(c) **They'll ask a simple warm up question:** They usually ask a 'throw-away' question to help you get warmed up, such as 'Did you find us okay?' This is your opportunity to demonstrate your preparedness by saying something like: 'Yes, I left early so I was sure I would get here on time and looked around the gallery while I waited (for a job in a museum).'

(d) **Question 1:** Some sort of variant of 'Why do you want this role?/Why do you want to work for us?' This is a common initial question. Prove your commitment as advised throughout this chapter.

(e) **Question 2:** Some sort of variant of 'What have you got to offer?/Why should we hire you?' Briefly outline how you perform the top three skills required, as advised throughout this chapter and book.

Make sure you don't mix up your answers to questions one and two, in whatever order they're asked. One refers to why you want the job, the other to what you have to offer (two different things!). Of course, just to confuse matters, they may blend these two questions together, as in the multifaceted example above, so make sure you understand exactly what they're asking and clarify this (if necessary) before firing away.

(f) **Question 3–7:** Various other questions related to the skills, commitment and knowledge required: Take your time to clarify what's being asked and systematically demonstrate your attributes as per your homework. Make sure you give specific examples whether or not they're requested.

(g) **Penultimate question:** 'What are your weaknesses?' Outline a relatively unimportant weakness that's not so relevant to the specific role as per the previous advice in this chapter.

(h) **A typical ultimate question is 'Do you have any questions for us?'** This is your chance to find out anything about the role you've yet to discover and impress the panel with your research.

Planning for the big day

So, you've planned what you're going to say and you look like a million dollars. What else can you do to prepare?

- Double check what's involved and the date, time, venue and so on. Plus, check to see if you need to take anything with you such as a project or a presentation (contact the organisation if the details aren't clear).
- Do your homework so you know as much as possible about the vacancy and what you have to offer.
- Practise answering the questions out loud using your index cards, but don't write the answers out in full, as you will not have access to them on the day!
- Try to find out who's interviewing you and check them out, so you can easily remember their names and refer to their interests.
- Carefully plan your route and itinerary well in advance and leave enough time on the day for unexpected complications.

Dealing with nerves

Don't be surprised if you're really nervous: this happens to us all, to some extent. A good way to deal with your anxiety is to positively use the adrenalin to make sure you're well prepared and 'in the zone'. You can ease your nerves by:

- Arriving at the venue well in advance so you don't have to worry about any delays (and go to a cafe until your turn comes).
- Avoiding coffee and tea (or anything containing caffeine).
- Breathing deeply and slowly.
- Remembering that you have a great deal to offer and they need you as much as you need them.
- Trying to enjoy the opportunity.

After the interview

After you've finished the interview weigh up how you did. How you could improve? Quickly jot down the questions and answers while the interview is still fresh in your mind, so you can go over what you said, when you have more time, perhaps with a Careers Adviser.

If you don't get the job, contact the employer and ask for feedback on how you performed and why you were unsuccessful. However, don't be surprised if they don't tell you much, because there's no onus on them to do so. If you have the courage, why not ask the employer if they could give you some experience to improve your skills – you never know your luck!

Either way, you should stay in touch with interviewers because they could still be useful future contacts.

ⓘ Useful links

Websites

www.guardian.com – See 'Job interview tips: expert advice for graduates'
www.reed.co.uk – See 'Graduate interview questions'
www.thestudentroom.co.uk – Look for discussions on interview procedures for
    specific organisations
Google "Interview" and "Name of Organisation"

On YouTube

'Macmillan Study Skills – How can I perform well in interviews' – Macmillan
    International Higher Education
'How to Ace an Interview: 5 Tips from a Harvard Career Advisor' – Harvard
    Extension School

On Twitter/Instagram

Join in with conversations about the application procedures for particular employers

CHAPTER 18

Psychometric tests

> For so it is, O Lord my God, I measure it! But what it is I measure, I do not know.
>
> *St Augustine*

Contents

What they are
Who uses them, when and why
Verbal reasoning tests
Numeric reasoning tests
Abstract reasoning tests
Verbal/numeric logical reasoning tests
Situational judgement tests
Personality profiles
What's the pass mark?
Common problems and mistakes
Improving your performance
On the day
If you have a disability

What they are

Psychometric tests are examinations of your mental capacities and processes. Specific assessments have been designed to measure all sorts of traits, from your verbal and numeric reasoning ability to your personality type. They usually take about 20–45 minutes to complete.

A number of example questions are shown throughout this chapter. These are broadly representative of the questions you will face, but to get a true indication of your ability you should ask the employer exactly what tests you will be taking and then practise them.

Who uses them, when and why

All sorts of graduate recruiters use some kind of psychometric test during the application process, and you will generally find that the bigger the employer, the greater the chance they will test you in this way. One of the more common types of questionnaire is verbal and numeric reasoning tests. These are usually conducted online very early in the application process, sometimes even before you are asked to complete an application form. This is because it is a cheap and convenient way to sift out large numbers of candidates who don't seem to have the high level of skills required. If you pass these tests at this stage, you will probably face them again at the firm's assessment centre, just to be sure! Other tests may also be conducted at assessment centres, such as personality profiles.

Verbal reasoning tests

These tests appraise your vocabulary, comprehension and ability to identify relationships between words. They can involve a range of questions, but typical graduate tests comprise several passages of text which are each linked to a handful of statements. Your job is to identify whether these statements are 'true', 'false' or you 'cannot say', based solely on what's been written in the text. In other words, **you're not being asked whether you think the statements are true, false or you cannot say, but whether or not the text confirms this**. It's absolutely crucial that you appreciate this distinction. For example, the following passage describes how internal combustion engines work and asks you to identify whether 'Internal combustion engines are used to power most cars'. The correct answer is 'Cannot say' because the text does not confirm or deny this fact (even though it is actually true!).

> **ʺ** Recruiters increasingly set online verbal and numeric reasoning tests very early on in the application process, sometimes even before you are asked to complete an application form. **ʺ**

Example of verbal reasoning question and answer

Passage: The internal combustion engine is an engine in which the combustion of a fuel (normally a fossil fuel) occurs with an oxidiser (usually air) in a combustion chamber that is an integral part of the working fluid flow circuit. The first commercially successful internal combustion engine was created by Étienne Lenoir. The term 'internal combustion engine' usually refers to an engine in which combustion is intermittent, such as the more familiar four-stroke and two-stroke piston engines, along with variants such as the Wankel rotary engine.

Question: Does the passage confirm whether the following statement is true or false, or is it inconclusive?

Statement: Internal combustion engines are used to power most cars.

a.   The passage confirms this statement is true.
b.   The passage confirms it is false.
ⓒ   The passage is inconclusive.

A sample verbal reasoning test

Two passages of text are shown below, each accompanied by four related statements. For each statement, identify whether the accompanying passage confirms it is true, false or inconclusive either way. Give yourself a strict two minutes for each section, and review your answers before moving on.

Answers and short explanations are provided at the end of each section. Two extra questions are provided on the companion website www.macmillanihe.com/rook-gcg-2e. All the passages are adapted from Wikipedia.

Section 1

1. Irish Setter waists are usually smaller than their chests.
   - (a) The passage confirms this statement is true.
   - (b) The passage confirms it is false.
   - (c) The passage is inconclusive.
2. Irish Setters are also called Red Setters.
   - (a) The passage confirms this statement is true.
   - (b) The passage confirms it is false.
   - (c) The passage is inconclusive.
3. The hair on most Irish Setters feathers in places.
   - (a) The passage confirms this statement is true.
   - (b) The passage confirms it is false.
   - (c) The passage is inconclusive.
4. The majority of Irish Setters have white hair on their chests.
   - (a) The passage confirms this statement is true.
   - (b) The passage confirms it is false.
   - (c) The passage is inconclusive.

Irish Setters are a type of gundog. They were bred to trap or 'set' birds for hunters. They are very handsome dogs but tend to be very skittish and require lots of attention. However, they are rarely aggressive and love to live with families who can give them lots of exercise. Unfortunately, they are prone to two disabling and life-threatening conditions: bloat and hip dysplasia.

Males stand from 63 to 69 centimetres and should weigh from 27 to 29 kilograms; females reach a height of 60 to 63 centimetres and should weigh from 24 to 29 kilograms. They have long luxurious red/chestnut coats that usually feather in places such as the tail, ears, chest, legs and body. Therefore, they require frequent brushing. About 40–70% also have small patches of white hair on their chests. They have a peculiar shape with long ears and legs, deep chests, small waists and abundant winter coats.

Answers

Statements	Answers	Explanation
1	c	The text does not categorically state whether or not Irish Setters' waists are smaller than their chests.
2	c	This is true but it is not stated in the text.
3	a	This is clearly stated in the text.
4	c	The text states that 40–70% have white hair on their chests so it could be a minority or a majority.

Section 2

5 Ischaemia can cause infarction of the myocardium.
  (a) The passage confirms this statement is true.
  (b) The passage confirms it is false.
  (c) The passage is inconclusive.

6 Men having a heart attack usually feel sudden chest pain which radiates to the left arm or left side of the neck.
  (a) The passage confirms this statement is true.
  (b) The passage confirms it is false.
  (c) The passage is inconclusive.

7 The main cause of myocardial infarctions is an occlusion of a coronary artery resulting from the rupture of atherosclerotic plaque.
  (a) The passage confirms this statement is true.
  (b) The passage confirms it is false.
  (c) The passage is inconclusive.

8 Silent myocardial infarctions just indicate indigestion.
  (a) The passage confirms this statement is true.
  (b) The passage confirms it is false.
  (c) The passage is inconclusive.

> Heart attacks are also called myocardial infarctions. They are usually caused by an interruption in the blood supply (ischaemia) to the heart caused by a blockage of a coronary artery, called an 'occlusion'. These occlusions are most commonly caused by a rupture of atherosclerotic plaque in artery walls. The resulting oxygen shortage can cause damage or death (*infarction*) of heart muscle tissue (*myocardium*).
>
> During myocardial infarctions, men often feel sudden chest pain and/or pain in the left arm and neck, shortness of breath, nausea, sweating and anxiety. A sizeable proportion of myocardial infarctions are 'silent' that occur without chest pain or other symptoms, and are often confused with indigestion.

Answers

Statements	Answers	Explanation
5	a	This is clearly stated in the text.
6	c	We are told that chest pain is often a side effect of myocardial infarctions but not whether this *usually* happens.
7	a	This is clearly stated in the text.
8	b	The text states that silent myocardial infarctions are often confused with indigestion, not that they indicate it.

Numeric reasoning tests

Numeric tests typically examine your ability to add, subtract, multiply and divide, work with percentages, averages and fractions and interpret graphs, tables and statistics. You are usually allowed a calculator and some paper to calculate the answers.

A sample numeric reasoning test

Take 13 minutes to answer the questions provided below. Answers and explanations are also provided. Another ten-minute test is provided on the companion website.

1 Company A charges £120 per year for each set of the 200 urban traffic lights it cleans for the council, £180 for each of the 400 in the suburbs and £240 for each of the 50 in rural areas. How much cheaper per year would it be to hire company B, which offers to do it for £144 a year for each set of lights wherever they are?
   a. £14,400   b. £93,600   c. £15,400   d. £1200   e. £93,900

Cars sold each year in Bath according to their colour	2007	2008	2009	2010	2011
Red	1500	500	1000	1000	750
Blue	1000	500	250	250	500
White	2000	1500	1500	1750	2500
Other colours	1500	1000	1250	1500	2000

2 In the table above, what percentage of total car sales are red?
   a. 0.2%   b. 25%   c. 20%   d. 2.5%   e. 5%

3 If the number of white cars sold in 2011 had risen since 2010 by the same percentage as blue cars over the same period, how many would have sold?
   a. 1250   b. 3000   c. 2250   d. 3500   e. 250

4 If 20% of the cars with other colours are green, how many cars sold over this period are not blue or green?
   a. 17,950   b. 7250   c. 15,450   d. 18,900   e. 19,800

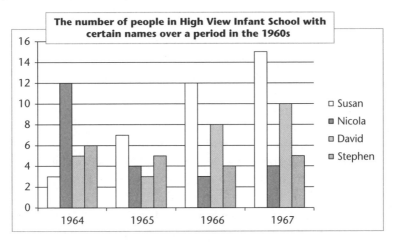

5 Over the period covered by the graph above, how many more children were called Susan than David at High View Infant School?
   a. 11   b. 14   c. 17   d. 37   e. 3

6   If children with these names comprised 20% of the total number of children in High View Infant School in 1964 and 25% in 1967, what is the difference between the total number of children in the school in 1964 and 1967?
    a. 6   b. 32   c. 136   d. 4   e. No difference

7   If there were 120 students at the school in 1965, what percentage were not called Nicola, David or Stephen?
    a. 10%   b. 15%   c. 90%   d. 95%   e. Can't say

Your answers

See how many of these 7 questions you answered correctly.

No.	Answers	Explanation
1	a	The existing cost of cleaning the lights per year = (120 x £200) + (180 x £400) + (240 x £50) = £108,000. The cost of cleaning the lights with the new company equals 12 x (200 + 400 + 50) = 144 x 650 = £93,600. Therefore, the saving = £108,000 – £93,600 = £14,400.
2	c	The total number of cars sold = 23,750 and red cars = 4750. Therefore, the percentage of red cars = $\frac{4750}{23,750}$ x 100 = 20%.
3	d	500 blue cars were sold in 2011 and 250 were sold in 2010. Therefore, the increase in blue cars sold over this period was 100%. 1750 white cars were sold in 2010. Therefore, the number of white cars that would have sold in 2011 if sales had risen at the same rate as blue cars = 1750 + 1750 = 3500.
4	e	Total sales = 23,750 (already ascertained). Blue sales = 2500. Green sales = 20% of other colours = $\frac{20}{100}$ x total number of other sales (7250) = 1450. Therefore, total non-blue or green sales = 23,750 – 2500 – 1450 = 19,800.
5	a	There are 37 Susans and 26 Davids, so the difference is 37 – 26 = 11.
6	a	In 1964, 26 children had these names. If 26 children were 20% of the total number of children at the school then 100% = 5 times this number = 130. In 1967, 34 children had these names. If 34 children were 25% of the total number of children at the school then 100% = 4 times this number = 136. Therefore, the difference is 136 – 130 = 6.
7	c	In 1965, 12 children were called Nicola, David and Stephen and the total number of children in the school was 120. Therefore, the percentage of children called Nicola, David and Stephen was $\frac{120}{12}$ = 10%, so those without these names = 90%. So, the number of children without these names was 90%.

Abstract reasoning tests

These tests assess your diagrammatic reasoning ability without leaning on your language skills and are therefore often used for more technical roles. You are typically asked to look at a series of diagrams and establish relationships and sequences. For example, in the following illustration you are expected to identify which card comes next. Give it a go! The answer is provided below.

Example question

Which figure comes next – a, b, c, d or e?

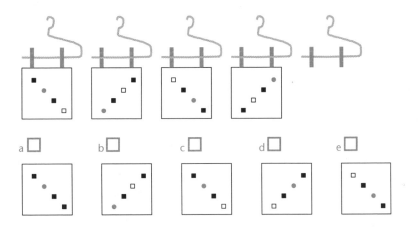

The answer to the problem above is **c**, because the sequence is rotating in a clockwise direction and the blue circle and colourless square change places at each rotation.

Verbal/numeric logical reasoning tests

These tests are less common. They tend to involve written and numeric puzzles much like the puzzle magazines you can pick up at the airport.

Example question

The best player in a team is 5 years older than the youngest. The youngest player in the team is 7 years younger than the oldest. The second oldest is 2 years younger than the oldest and a year older than the third oldest. If the third oldest player is 28, how old is the best player?

    a. 28 b. 30 c. 26 d. 25 e. 29

The answer is **e** (29). This is because:

1 If the third oldest player is 28 and the second oldest is 1 year older than her, then the second oldest is 29.
2 If the second oldest is 29 and 2 years younger than the oldest, then the oldest is 31.

3 If the youngest player is seven years younger than the oldest she is 24.

4 If the best player is five years older than the youngest she is, therefore, 29.

Situational judgement tests

These questionnaires are tailor-made to test your performance in a particular role/task, usually by asking you to identify or rank the most appropriate responses. For example, for a role as a journalist, you may be asked:

You've just finished a long weekend stint on the news desk and your cover calls to say he will be an hour late, but there is an ongoing situation that may become very newsworthy, and you have to get to a very important recital by your brother. Do you:

Rank in order how you'll respond from 1 – 5 (1 = Most appropriate; 5 = Least appropriate)

A. Email your cover to let her know what's going on and leave?

B. Find someone else to take your seat for that hour?

C. Let the editor know you have to depart and leave the alternative arrangements to her?

D. Stay on task for as long as you can but make arrangements for cover in the eventuality that your colleague takes more than half an hour to arrive, plus plan how to get to the recital quicker than you had previously thought possible?

E. Stay and miss some or all of the recital?

Answer: D B E C A

Rationale: With D you're leaving your options open and can stay on top of what's happening; with B, you have a chance to clearly pass on what's going on and the desk is never left empty; E would be hard to do but this is an important role and you should at least get to the venue to see some of the recital; with C, the editor will have enough to do and may not be able to drop everything at a moment's notice, plus this wouldn't be good for team morale as your colleague may assume you're telling on him; A could lead to all sorts of confusion and missed news opportunities.

Personality profiles

These questionnaires look at your preferred way of doing things and how well you'll fit into a role and organisation. Personality profiles are not as reliable as ability tests, so they are generally used just as an indicator of your general personality type along with other pointers such as your behaviour at interview. Of course, there is no single personality profile that suits all graduate jobs because different roles require different traits and teams work best when members have different strengths. However, some characteristics certainly suit corresponding occupations: for example, it would probably be advantageous if all air stewards were outgoing and counsellors were friendly!

Some typical questions are shown below. As you can see, you are usually asked to gauge how strongly a range of statements reflects your personal character, from not at all to 100%. This is certainly very subjective and often quite biased but you shouldn't worry about this – just be honest and trust your instinct, i.e. the first answer that comes into your head is usually the most accurate.

Example questions

I am:

- Confident in group situations   Fully disagree   ☐ ☐ ☐ ☐ ☐   Fully agree

- Good at working independently   Fully disagree   ☐ ☐ ☐ ☐ ☐   Fully agree

- Good at planning ahead   Fully disagree   ☐ ☐ ☐ ☐ ☐   Fully agree

- A worrier   Fully disagree   ☐ ☐ ☐ ☐ ☐   Fully agree

What's the pass mark?

Ability tests are very demanding for two reasons:

- They include numerous questions within a very restrictive time limit.
- They assess your ability in relation to other graduates, not the population in general, so you are usually expected to have better skills than most.

Therefore, don't panic if you struggle. Pass marks vary but you will usually be expected to get a score of at least 70%, i.e. you can make quite a few mistakes and still pass!

Personality profiles are measured according to specific personal traits, typically your **C**onscientiousness, **A**greeableness, **N**euroticism, **O**penness, and **E**xtraversion (CANOE). As shown below, you are typically graded somewhere along a continuum for each of these qualities.

The five personality traits typically measured in a personality profile

Conscientiousness

Efficient/Organised　←————————————→　Carefree/Careless

Agreeableness

Friendly/Compassionate　←————————————→　Cold

Neuroticism

Nervous/Fearful　←————————————→　Confident

Openness

Curious　←————————————→　Cautious

Extraversion

Outgoing　←————————————→　Solitary

Candidates are generally deemed to have failed personal profiles if they are not perceived to be the character type required or if they have provided inconsistent answers (demonstrating either inadvertent mistakes or an attempt to mislead).

Common problems and mistakes

Students and graduates fail ability tests for a wealth of reasons, such as:

- An insufficient ability that leads to mistakes and slow progress.
- Panic.
- A mental block.
- The strict time limits.
- Carelessness.
- Misinterpreting the instructions.
- A loss of concentration/being interrupted.
- Unfamiliarity with the type of test (especially for abstract questionnaires).
- Problems with an Internet connection.
- Problems with resources (e.g. paper/pen/batteries in mouse...).
- Lack of confidence.
- Being too careful (and therefore not finishing on time).

In the exercise on the next page, list the specific problems you had with the personality profile and verbal/numeric questions provided earlier in the chapter and read on to see how you can improve.

Self-assessment: So, what's stopping you?

Identify the main problems you had with the personality and ability questions in this chapter.

Your problems with the verbal reasoning tests:

-
-
-

Your problems with the numerical reasoning tests:

-
-
-

Your problems with the abstract reasoning tests:

-
-
-

Your problems with the verbal/numeric logical reasoning tests:

-
-
-

Your problems with the situational judgement tests:

-
-
-

Your problems with the personal profiles:

-
-
-

Reflecting on your answers: Try to be specific about your weaknesses as this will help you target your areas for improvement. For example, if you struggle with comprehending long sentences, try to isolate exactly why.

Improving your performance

Ability/Reasoning tests

Many students dread this section of the application process because they fear it will expose an inherent weakness that they can't improve. To some extent this is true, but there are a number of things you can do, at the margins, to significantly increase your scores; these are outlined below.

1 **Learn your stuff:** An immediate instinct when it comes to improving performance at ability tests is to get lots of practice, but this is only effective if you know what you're doing in the first place! Therefore, you should start out by fully developing the skills you're being asked to demonstrate – and then rehearse.

Improving your English is a long-term commitment, but it will help in every walk of life. You can indirectly improve your performance by reading widely. You should also get involved in roles, modules and activities that require professional communication. If English is not your first language, you may also want to undertake some further English tuition.

It's relatively easier to improve your numeric ability in a short time frame if you studied the subject to GCSE level. This is because, your maths skills have probably deteriorated since you were 16 and you should be able to quickly re-skill yourself by just digging out your old GCSE maths books and relearning the basics. In particular you should have instant recall of the following:

- Basic number facts including times tables, place value (especially from .0001 to a million), squares and square roots, adding two numbers together to make 100 or 1000, multiplying and dividing by .01, 0.1, 10, 100, 1000 and so on, and doubles (e.g. $25 + 25 = 50$).
- Working out fractions and percentages in your head, on paper and with a calculator.
- Manipulating fractions and percentages in your head, on paper and with a calculator.
- Converting numbers, fractions and percentages in your head, on paper and with a calculator (e.g. $4/5 = 80\% = 0.8$).
- Calculating basic operations in your head, on paper and on a calculator, e.g. long division.
- Interpreting tables, line graphs, pie charts and block graphs.
- Basic probability and chance.

You should also get used to solving problems in different ways – for example, you should be an expert at the following methods:[1]

- Draw a picture/diagram.
- Act it out.
- Make a model.
- Guess, check and improve.

- Make a table.
- Spot a pattern.
- Identify and use a mathematical operation.
- Work backwards.
- Work systematically.
- Try a simpler case or break it up into manageable parts.
- Use logic.

With abstract questionnaires, it's probably a good idea to gain a clear understanding of how most patterns are created; many of these are listed below:

- An increasing number of symbols.
- A decreasing number of symbols.
- Clockwise rotation.
- Anti-clockwise rotation.
- Colours rotating.
- Colours changing places.
- Moving gaps.
- Numbers undergoing basic operations such as adding and subtracting 10.
- Horizontal variations.
- Vertical variations.
- Diagonal variations.
- Symbols which change shape and/or colour in a set way.

2 Develop a strategy: Once you've learned your stuff, there are two advantages to developing a robust strategy for each of the tests you are going to face. Firstly, familiar routines will calm your nerves on the day, and secondly, you'll know what to do when you're stuck. This applies to the tests themselves as well as the individual questions.

In terms of the tests themselves, you should get used to the following:

- Using your equipment (including the computer and calculator).
- The location (if possible).
- Keeping abreast of the remaining time.
- Devoting the appropriate time to each question.
- Speedily checking your answers.
- Knowing in which order you will answer the questions (if you have a choice).
- How you will move on when you get stuck (i.e. how much time you will devote to getting each answer correct).
- Whether you will read the passage first and then the questions, or vice versa.

In verbal reasoning tests, you also need to find a fool proof way of checking that your answers are based on what is actually written in the text, not on your own opinion. Furthermore, for maths and abstract problems, it's also wise to get to know how you will choose the appropriate problem-solving method for each type of question and which techniques you prefer.

3 **Practise:** Now you know what you're doing, and how to do it, it's time to practise under the strict conditions you will face on the day. The recruiter should let you know what specific tests they will use and provide a few practice questions, but contact them if it's not obvious, then look up the websites of the firm that organises each specific test and find more examples. A large number of web-based organisations offer tests for a small fee and many books are available on the subject. Your careers service may well be able to give you access to these guides and may also offer workshops on psychometric tests and practice sessions.

Personality profiles

There's little you can do to prepare for these tests. If you're tempted to cheat and try to present yourself in a more positive light, be aware of the following ramifications:

- The tests may incorporate 'trick questions' to see if you are telling the truth, so any inconsistency could result in rejection. For example, if you are asked 'Are you always honest?', you probably shouldn't fully agree with this statement because we've all told a few untruths from time to time! (4/5 will do!).
- You may get the job by pretending to be someone you're not, but this could easily mean that you won't enjoy it, or indeed perform well.
- Recruiters are looking for a range of different personalities so you may be exactly what they're looking for, even with all your little peccadillos!

A good compromise is to answer the questions as the 'best' you – the one you present to your mum and dad!

> **A good compromise is to answer the questions as the 'best' you – the one you present to your mum and dad!**

Situational judgement tests

You can prepare for these questionnaires by:

- Getting some sort of relevant experience so you can live through some of the scenarios they'll present.
- Researching the role in depth.
- Studying the job description and personal specification.
- Practising this sort of test (just Google 'Example situational judgement tests').
- Getting used to putting yourself in the employer's shoes.
- Looking back at your experience of how people have strongly (and poorly) reacted to events.

On the day

When the big day comes you should relax and enjoy the challenge. Make sure you eat healthily in the days leading up to it, avoid alcohol and get some rest, as your brain works significantly better when it is fresh. If you are attempting the test online, choose the time of day when you're brightest and used to studying – most people do better in the morning, but not everyone.

Check all your equipment is working, powered up and you know how to use it! Get some spare paper and your timepiece in position and kick off!

If you have a disability

There are a number of disabilities which could affect your performance on these tests, such as dyslexia, dyspraxia and autism. The organisations running the assessments should make appropriate adjustments (if you let them know!), but you should also seek help from your university to develop specific strategies to improve your performance.

 Useful links

Websites

www.prospects.ac.uk – See 'Psychometric tests'

Look for example questions at www.shldirect.com, www.assessmentday.co.uk, www.graduatesfirst.com, www.jobtestprep.co.uk and www. practicereasoningtests.com

Google the company that sells the particular tests you're taking to find examples.

CHAPTER 19

Succeeding at assessment centres

" Drawing on my fine command of the English language, I said nothing.
Robert Benchley "

What they are

Assessment centres are the venues where specific job assessments are carried out. Larger organisations often conduct a number of exercises over a few hours or a couple of days; smaller firms may just combine interviews with one or two activities, such as a presentation and/or a group discussion. They are expensive operations and are therefore usually conducted at the latter stages of the recruitment process. As such, they are often the final hurdle on the path to a pay packet! The activities can include:

- Interviews
- Psychometric tests
- Group exercises
- Group discussions
- Presentations
- In-tray exercises
- Social get-togethers
- Case studies.

Interviews and psychometric tests have been covered in previous chapters, so this section focuses on the remaining activities.

Learning the ropes

Once you've received an invitation to attend an assessment centre, carefully organise your trip and your accommodation (if required). You may also need to update your wardrobe and make sure you're well rested, well fed and well ready!

> *Jonathon Field, Managing Consultant, Techsearch*
>
> Students and graduates need to become more savvy about the recruitment process in general and in the need to address organisations' core values when completing applications, you need to separate yourself from the crowd! Therefore, you need to find ways to promote yourself above your competition (other applicants). For example, when attending selection events, such as assessment centres, interviews etc., you need to demonstrate that you are commercially aware by displaying confidence, determination and focus.

Your invitation should outline the timetable and the specific set of activities you will undertake, but contact employers beforehand if you have any questions. Information is power, so any extra details you can find out in advance could give you the edge. For example, you could try to identify who will be interviewing you and what specific type of tests they'll be using (and get in some practice).

You can also chase up various other sources of information on specific assessment centres, as follows:

- Speak to contacts from the organisation or representatives who come to your university/careers fairs.
- Consult the firms' websites.
- Ask your careers service.
- Look up blogs such as those on www.thestudentroom.co.uk.
- Google the name of the firm and the word 'assessment centre'.

Group exercises

Group exercises are one of the more common assessment centre activities because team skills are so crucial and employers want to ensure that their new recruits don't upset the teams they've already established.

What's involved

Candidates are typically split into groups of five to seven members to solve a specific problem within a set time frame. Most group exercises are paper-based but exercises for technical roles may be more hands-on.

Some typical activities are provided below:

- Build a bridge out of straws and paper clips to support a specific object.
- Build a paper airplane that flies the furthest.

- Hire the right person for a fictitious job.
- Pick the 400-metre athletics relay team for the Olympics.

In general, groups are usually given enough information to make a decision but no guidance on how to proceed – this is totally up to them. Just to add a bit of spice, typical scenarios are usually controversial and designed to inspire debate (see the example below).

What they're looking for

On the whole, there are no right or wrong answers as employers are mostly focussing on how effectively you scrutinise the issues involved and engage with the other candidates.

An example

The group exercise shown below is a scenario where you and your team have to choose a new drug (or group of drugs) for the NHS. The key elements in this particular exercise are diverse moral and financial issues, unfamiliar terms and a confusing array of costs.

Your drug of choice

You have 5 minutes to read these instructions and 25 minutes to complete the exercise, after which you will be asked to report your findings.
As a group, you are tasked with choosing a new drug/group of drugs to register for general use in the NHS. Your five options are listed below along with brief information about what each drug treats and what they cost. You have £5 billion (five thousand million) to spend over the next ten years, and must spend it all – which drug or group of drugs do you choose and why?

Flexal (Fibroaximide detrooonium): This is a completely new treatment for acute lymphoblastic leukaemia in children. The treatment is 80% effective, which matches the current medication regimen, and it is cheaper than the

---

existing drug (£100 million over the next five years as opposed to £110 million). However, the tablet has some serious side effects in 1–2% of users which are not present with the existing medication, namely chronic fatigue and migraines.

Gossalder (Elledreinal gysotamine): This new medication is a brand-new treatment for obesity. It alleviates the feeling of hunger and gives more energy to patients, thus encouraging them to do more exercise. The treatment is expected to cost £150 million over the next three years but will reduce obesity by 10%. As obesity costs the NHS an estimated £1 billion a year (one thousand million), this could be a massive saving.

Lassitate (Fibro-stenossum): This can be used to replace up to 20% of the genuine blood used in transfusions. There are no marked side effects and the drug is expected to save £150 million a year, but the set-up costs of incorporating this new treatment are massive because expensive new equipment is required that costs £500 million to install. This equipment lasts for five years and incurs the same running costs as the existing equipment already in place, for which there is already an ongoing budget.

Novelle (Axionmatic indoctrinise): This new drug treats the complications caused by prostate cancer. It does not replace any drugs but is an additional treatment, which will cost £200 million per year. It will lengthen the lives of 10% of the men who get the disease by two years on average, but quality of life is still poor and ongoing treatment for those with the disease costs £50 million per year. This cancer kills roughly 200,000 people a year in the UK and few new treatments have come to the market in the last 20 years.

Dias (Duocturine exhomerate): This is a new statin which has a similar success in reducing cholesterol to that of the medications already on the market. However, it brings significantly fewer side effects to 10% of the population already on statins (ten million) but is twice the cost of the other treatments. A typical patient's statins currently cost £500 a year.

A possible solution

One way to solve this problem would be to audit the costs and savings of each of these drugs over the ten-year period for which you are responsible so that comparisons are easier. Once you do this you'll notice that many of the drugs actually constitute a saving, not an extra expense, and you can even agree to them all if you limit the supply of the final drug, Dias, to patients who have already tried the other options. However, you should probably avoid Flexal, because it makes a relatively small saving and you don't know anything about the costs of treating its side effects.

How to prepare

We all have extensive experience of working with other people in teams. Therefore, you can really enhance your success in group exercises by simply taking a step back and evaluating how you generally perform well in these situations. It can be very challenging to coldly reflect on your own personal skills in this way but it can also be quite revealing. Three steps to success in group exercises are shown below.

1 Identify your favourite roles: The first step to succeeding in group exercises is to identify the team roles you want to follow. This will give you a style and a structured framework which can be used in all situations. Don't worry if you're not a born leader; good teams require a wide range of personalities and people to take on different responsibilities. After all, it would be no good if everyone in a group wanted to be the boss – you'd never get anything done! In the early 1980s Meredith Belbin defined the various team roles as shown below.[1] In the following exercise, identify your favourite roles amongst the nine alternatives displayed.

- Plants: Free-thinking, creative idea generators.
- Shapers: Outgoing, enthusiastic individuals who drive the team to achieve.
- Resource investigators: Outgoing people who explore opportunities and develop contacts.
- Coordinators: Confident leaders who are good at clarifying goals, managing projects and delegating tasks.
- Monitors/Evaluators: Team members who are able to take a step back and objectively, systematically evaluate progress.
- Teamworkers: These diplomatic worker ants go about their roles unnoticed but bring everyone together and keep everyone happy and focused.
- Implementers: Efficient, loyal workers who turn ideas into solutions.
- Completers/Finishers: Independent souls who want to ensure that everything is done correctly and accurately.
- Specialists: Team members who are driven by their interest in a specific subject.

Self-assessment: What are your favourite team roles?

Identify the top two team roles you generally fall into (use Belbin's definitions or your own terms).

My favourite team roles:

1 _____

2 _____

Reflecting on your answers: Are you being objective? – Ask your friends if they agree with your assessment.

2 **Recognise your specific skills:** Once you've reflected on your favourite team roles, the next step is to recognise how you perform them well. Again, don't just rely on your own opinion; ask your friends, family and colleagues to outline your strengths and weaknesses (but don't hit them afterwards!). For example, you may be proficient at some of the following skills:

- Sharing your ideas positively
- Being open to other people's ideas
- Demonstrating reliability
- Listening empathically
- Speaking up for yourself
- Including everyone
- Encouraging others to get involved
- Praising others' contributions
- Staying calm and upbeat
- Showing enthusiasm
- Persuading colleagues
- Compromising

In the exercise below, identify your top three skills in relation to your favourite team roles, and think of practical, obvious ways you could demonstrate each of these skills to invigilators during the group exercise.

For example, if you're a 'Teamworker' (according to Belbin's roles), you could endeavour to undertake the following four tasks:

- Involve colleagues by saying things like 'You and Jenny sound like you've done this before!' and 'Bob – you were saying the same thing as Paul, weren't you?'
- Cheerfully volunteer for unpopular roles. For example, you could offer to keep an eye on the clock or introduce the group's presentation at the end.
- Diligently and noticeably get on with your set tasks, making it clear that you are performing a valuable role.
- Build a good rapport with the leader and proactively offer assistance.

Self-assessment: How do you succeed in teams?

List three obvious ways you could demonstrate your team skills to employers in a group exercise.

Your favoured team role	Three specific skills you demonstrate in this role	Three obvious ways you could show these skills to assessors
	•	•
	•	•
	•	•

Reflecting on your answers: This is no time for false modesty – be honest about your strengths and make sure your techniques for showing them off are obvious and effective.

3 **Practise:** As always, the final step to preparation is plenty of practice. You can do this in two ways:
- Try demonstrating your skills to your friends and colleagues in everyday situations.
- Have a go at some examples at university. An additional group exercise is provided on the companion website and the links at the start of the chapter direct you to many more.

During the exercise

Sit down and introduce yourself to the other candidates – try to remember their names (you may even want to jot them down). Read the instructions carefully and jump in. As time passes, make sure you get involved but remain detached enough to mentally tick off the adoption of each of your strategies. If your chosen role isn't feasible or has already been taken, don't worry – try an alternative role, or just focus on showing off your skills as a teamworker (as defined by Belbin above).

Whatever approach you take, be friendly, enthusiastic and open to your colleagues, but avoid the following pitfalls:

- Speaking over other people
- Speaking too much
- Not speaking clearly
- Not listening
- Being too rigid
- Not speaking at all

- Making too little contribution
- Bullying others
- Not standing up for yourself
- Being overly acquiescent
- Not taking the exercise seriously
- Being too formal

Nicola Snaith, Assistant HR Adviser, Baker Tilly Management Limited

Students need to ask us good questions at fairs which show that they have done their research. It also helps to demonstrate personality and opinions, not just knowledge.

Group discussions

Smaller employers often opt for the softer option of a group discussion rather than an actual exercise. In this situation, you are typically given a topical issue to discuss that's related to the specific industry and/or role. For example, a banking organisation may ask about the recent scandals or the Forestry Commission may instigate a debate about recent proposals to sell off the UK's public forests. Sometimes, you are also encouraged to record your findings and come to a conclusion. Therefore, before you attend a group discussion, try to catch up with the key issues currently being discussed in the industry. Of course, you should do this anyway for your applications and interviews.

These deliberations are usually less formal than group interviews (see Chapter 17) and any number of candidates may be involved. You should engage with the issues just as you would in a group exercise and prepare the same strategies in order to stand out.

At the beginning of the discussions it can be quite hard to get a word in edgeways, but don't worry. Most of what is said at this stage will be haphazard and ill thought out. Listen to the discussion and, when things get a bit quieter and more interesting, jump in with a well-considered point. Mentally tick off your strategies as you would with a group discussion, listen empathically (e.g. nod your head and agree), keep smiling, praise incisive comments and avoid putting other people down.

Presentations

Just the mention of the word 'presentation' sends spasms of fear into half the population, so this is often the most feared of all the assessment exercises. This section outlines what you can expect, and how you can build confidence and perform well on the day.

What's involved

Employers tend to either ask you to prepare an individual presentation in advance to deliver at the assessment centre or develop an individual or group presentation on the day. They typically give you a specific topic and ask you to speak for just five or ten minutes. They also often ask you to provide PowerPoint slides or some other visual aid. The audience often comprises the same people who will be on your interview panel, so the two activities are often conducted consecutively. The topic could be related to almost anything, from the skills you've gained in your degree to a current issue related to the industry.

Big smile

Animated delivery

What they're looking for

Employers ask candidates to deliver presentations because, before they set you free on their clients, they want to make sure you're eloquent, confident and engaging. Therefore, they're not focusing on your ability to impart endless information but to get straight to the heart of the issue and effectively communicate the key points. You should never underestimate how boring it is to assess applicants in this way, so the panel will also greatly appreciate it if you can provide some sort of entertainment (within reason)!

Planning and delivering your talk

In order to develop an excellent presentation, you need to be clear about what you want to say and how you're going to say it.

In terms of what you say, it's always best to narrow down your remit so you only have one or two key points. This method of communication doesn't lend itself to weighty reams of information and data. If necessary, you can provide a handout. As far as your delivery goes, it is crucial to maintain eye contact, show enthusiasm and engage with your audience.

Some important presentations tips are listed below:

- Speak slowly, clearly and energetically. Be careful – your adrenaline will probably be telling you to go at 100 miles an hour.
- Interact with the audience, e.g. through quizzes and questions.
- Use interesting visual displays.
- Present from a comfortable and logical position and don't stand in front of your display.
- Make sure everyone in the room can read your text.
- Use only a few pictures or words on each poster or slide.
- Follow this well-worn guide: 'Outline what you're about to say (the introduction), say it (the main body of your presentation) and then tell them what you've just told them (the summary/conclusion).'
- Face your audience (don't look at your notes or the screen). In fact, try to avoid notes altogether as once you look up and see a sea of faces you'll probably just look down again and read them out loud.
- In group presentations, make sure the handovers are smooth and you maintain

Tiny text

Standing in front
of the slides

pace. Also, if possible, avoid just moving on from one person to another in a sequence – get each member to jump in and out and interact in more interesting ways.

● Keep to the time limit.

Your slides

Facing away from the audience

Posters and PowerPoint slides are often poorly designed. In particular, they can be difficult to read or jam-packed with too much information. You can avoid these common mistakes by using:

✓ A large font size (above size 30 in PowerPoint).
✓ As few words as possible, for example, on PowerPoint, limit each slide to about twenty.
✓ As few slides as possible – six should do for a twenty-minute talk; otherwise they take over and you'll end up just rushing through them without taking the time to properly address any of the issues.
✓ Colour and nice big pictures, but don't get carried away as this can be distracting.
✓ Simple graphs and diagrams.
✓ Elements which require the most basic software. For example, video and websites that look brilliant on your computer at home may not be supported at the venue and you'll look disorganised.

These points are illustrated on the example slide shown below.

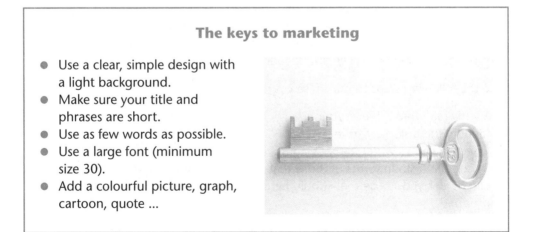

The keys to marketing

● Use a clear, simple design with a light background.
● Make sure your title and phrases are short.
● Use as few words as possible.
● Use a large font (minimum size 30).
● Add a colourful picture, graph, cartoon, quote ...

Have a look at Guy Kawasaki's '10/20/30' video at www.youtube.com for a frank and funny outline of good presentation techniques.

Dealing with nerves

There are a number of strategies you can employ to minimise your nerves:

1 Practise delivering presentations whenever you can.
2 Learn every word and inflexion of your talk off by heart.
3 Repeatedly practise your presentation so you know it fits the time frame.
4 Use simple IT because if it can go wrong, it will!
5 Be totally familiar with your subject.
6 Don't say much – just the key point/s will do. Therefore, you should be able to remember the content of your whole talk off by heart.
7 Avoid too many statistics and difficult technical concepts/definitions.
8 Eat sensibly beforehand.
9 Spend some time in quiet contemplation before you step onto the stage, and control your breathing.
10 Take it easy – if you make light of small mistakes then so will the panel!

In-tray exercises

In-tray exercises put you in a typical work situation to see how you perform under pressure. You are typically given an hour or so to deal with about twenty or so different issues. To help you make your decisions, you will usually be given details about your role, including elements such as the organisation's aims and objectives, its structure, its partners, upcoming events and your specific responsibilities/those of your colleagues. Nowadays, in-tray assessments are often conducted online and are often called e-tray exercises.

You will be tested on how appropriately you deal with each of the items in your in-tray. Speed is the key, but you should also demonstrate accuracy, independence, the ability to prioritise, share problems and delegate appropriately (according to the information you've been given about your role).

Take the following steps to maximise your performance:

1 Swiftly read through everything.
2 Identify the tasks that have arisen.
3 Check the dates when the messages were sent.
4 Divide the tasks in terms of those that are important and urgent, those that can be delayed, those that should be delegated and those that should be dropped.

Obviously, you should spend most time on the important and urgent matters arising but avoid looking into things too deeply as you will run out of time. Just focus on the key details. Sometimes, you are asked to justify your decisions at the end of the test; if this is the case, take notes as you go along. See an example in-tray exercise on the companion website.

Social occasions

All interviews and assessment centres involve important social interaction, but some more than others. Assessment centres often involve a group lunch or dinner where interviewers, managers, partners and clients hope to meet the real you (and like what they see!). In these situations, try to present yourself in the best possible light. You can afford to be a little less formal than at other stages in the recruitment process but don't get carried away. Employers will be looking for engaging applicants who are good communicators.

Obviously, you are at an advantage if you're accustomed to meeting important people in this sort of environment. Novices tend to be too rigid or too lax. Therefore, in order to prepare, you need to find opportunities to meet influential people in similar surroundings. You could do this by joining clubs and societies such as church groups, university or council committees, local resident groups and professional organisations.

And finally, dress appropriately and avoid too much alcohol!

Case studies

These are business scenarios typically run by investment banks, management consultants and corporate law firms to see what you'd be like in the actual job. Recruiters in these fields need to make absolutely sure that you have the ability to make decisions and confidently/persuasively communicate your conclusions.

Applicants are usually given information and data related to a typical business decision and given a fixed time limit to come up with an appropriate course of action. Sometimes, further information is also drip-fed, as the time passes. They are usually conducted in teams. When the time is up, the assessors will usually ask you a set of questions about your proposal and will expect you to clearly and persuasively back up your argument.

According to Job Step Prep (www.jobtestprep.co.uk), the following topics are common:

- Strategic decisions in global or local contexts.
- Expansion of departments, acquisition of new companies or products.
- Entrance into new fields of development and product lines.
- Exploring new markets.
- Reconstructing organisational trees (hierarchies).
- Creating advertising campaigns.

Graduates are not usually required to have specific knowledge and experience but it helps to have a good understanding of the jargon used in the industry you are seeking to enter, so you may want to look at websites such as www.incorp.com/incorp-glossary.aspx.

You can succeed in these activities by:

1 Quickly identifying and focusing on the key issues – much of the information will have little bearing on the case.
2 Analysing the relevant data.
3 Choosing your favourite solution.
4 Preparing positive arguments as to why you have chosen your particular path.
5 Making sure the salient information is at your fingertips.
6 Considering how your analysis addresses common questions.

A major part of the challenge here is dealing with pressure. Therefore, in order to prepare, it can really help to put yourself in this position before the assessment centre and get lots of practice. Your careers service should be able to help out in this regard but you can also find advice and practise case studies on a number of websites, such as the following:

● **Bain & Co:** www.joinbain.com.
● **Boston Consulting:** www.bcg.co.
● **Capital One:** www.capitalone.com.
● **McKinsey:** www.mckinsey.com.
● **Target Jobs:** www.targetjobs.co.uk.

On the big day

Nicola Snaith, Assistant HR Adviser, Baker Tilly Management Limited

Some good tactics for performing well in group exercises are to keep an eye on the time, use open and engaging body language, interact and use the opportunity to demonstrate commercial awareness.

Arrive in plenty of time so you're not in a big panic. Smile as soon as you get through the door and don't stop until you're back on the bus. Warmly greet everyone you meet, try to remember their names and laugh at their jokes. Also, ask intelligent questions and stand out from the crowd without being too overbearing. Finally, establish your passion for the firm and the industry through your questions and body language.

This positive approach will be easy for some people, but others are less demonstrative, especially when they get nervous. If this sounds like you, prepare for the day by envisioning yourself during the assessments and focusing on how you will practically and clearly convey the key messages you want to get across. However, don't try to remember a million strategies, just think of three or four ways you can demonstrate your abilities and impress the employers, hold your head up high and be yourself.

ℹ️ Useful links

Websites

www.thestudentroom.co.uk – Look for discussions on assessment centre exercises for specific organisations

www.ncl.ac.uk – See 'Assessment centres'

www.manchester.ac.uk – See 'Assessment Centres'

On YouTube

'Top 5 Tips … How to ace assessment centres' – Bright Network

On Twitter/Instagram

Join in with conversations about assessment centres for particular employers

CHAPTER 20
Dealing with job offers

" Accept, negotiate, gamble, reject? "

What's in a job offer?

Sooner or later a job offer will land in your mailbox. You'll know it's good news because the envelope will contain more than just a brief rejection – it will be packed with paperwork and information about your new opportunity.

The letter of acceptance will probably include some or all of the following documents:

● A provisional offer, subject to your references and any other requisite documents (see the following section).
● A contract to sign.
● Your proposed pay and conditions.
● Contact details for your new manager/HR.
● An outline of the role.
● Documentation about the organisation and your department.
● Administrative information about things like IT passwords and ID badges.
● A formal acceptance letter for you to return to HR.
● A health questionnaire.

Your response

1 Once you've called all your family and friends and hugged the dog, let the employer know that you've received their offer. Don't be afraid to share your joy but, if possible, avoid formally accepting the offer until you've read through all the small print and made sure it's what you want. If pushed, you could say something like, you are 'happy to accept the offer subject to reading the full terms and conditions'.

2 Carefully read through the documents and highlight anything you don't understand or want to question, plus make sure there are no nasty surprises (such as your start date or salary).

3 Contact the organisation to check any details you need to clarify. It may be tempting to let things slide at this time but don't – you need to start work with a clear understanding of what's involved.

4 Once you're clear about the job offer, decide if it's what you want. Don't be afraid to reject the offer if it's not up to scratch, but, in these difficult times, it's probably better to put up with any awkward aspects in the new role rather than reject it outright. After all, once you start you'll soon have the opportunity to move up into bigger and better things.

If you're badgered to make the decision on the spot, then you have the right to take the time to at least clarify the offer, there and then, before giving your agreement. If you can't pin them down to the exact pay and conditions, then, something fishy may be going on and you may want to request this information before making your final decision. However, play it by ear, stay positive and try not to do anything to make the employer change their mind!

Negotiating the deal

If the job is not up to your expectations but you don't want to reject the offer, this could be a very good time to negotiate terms. You may want to discuss issues such as your start date, pay, hours, holidays, training opportunities or a golden handshake. If you follow this path, make an argument as to why you warrant this extra investment. For example, you could ask for extra relocation expenses and a higher salary as follows:

● 'Unfortunately, as I live in a country town in Derbyshire, my relocation expenses to London will easily dwarf the £500 allowance offered. Can I please ask for an extra £500, which will enable me to move all my possessions in good time (including work-related material) to my new home which is in easy commutable distance to the office.'

● 'Thank you for the wonderful offer of a traineeship in London – I am very excited and cannot wait to start. Unfortunately, however, having looked for a flat-share last weekend, I just cannot see how I can move to the capital city and support myself on the salary offered. Therefore, as I have a relevant degree, exceptional experience and the commitment and ability to quickly add value to your organisation, I would very much appreciate it if you could reconsider my initial pay and conditions.'

Whatever you do, though, make sure you negotiate in a positive, friendly manner.

Balancing multiple offers

If you're lucky you may get more than one job offer at once, or even one job offer and an interview the following week for a much better position. The pros and cons of each of your options in this situation are outlined below:

- Accept the first offer you get but keep looking for better roles. The advantage of this approach is that you will have a job to go to and you might even get a better one before you start. However, you should be aware that employers tend to be very well connected and word may well get around about what you're up to. Not good!
- Delay formally accepting your original offer until you hear if you've been successful with any other applications. This strategy also gives you an opportunity to negotiate while you're waiting, but you won't be able to keep your delaying tactics up for long and, like Aesop's dog, in your bid for the best opportunity, you may lose everything, i.e. the original offer may be withheld because of your delay and your other options may also not come through.
- Take up the original job offer and withdraw from your other applications. The advantage here is that you have been honourable to yourself, the employer and the other candidates with whom you're competing. The disadvantage is that the job you get may not be the job you want.
- Reject the original offer and hope to get a better job in the near future. The big advantage of this strategy is that you can still hope for the job of your dreams. The disadvantage is that you may never get it!

Whichever route you choose, you should remember that this is only the start of your career, so your initial role will probably quickly change and your pay and conditions will improve. With your newfound experience, you could also soon start looking for even better roles. Therefore, any concerns you originally have about a job offer should be balanced against the very real benefit of having a job. A bird in the hand is worth two in the bush!

Preparing for the big day

As soon as you've accepted a job offer you should start preparing for your new lifestyle. This is a major transition so it will really help if you are psychologically, intellectually and practically prepared.

We all have our own unique psychological strategies for dealing with major events and the fact that you've got this far means you're probably doing OK. However, whether you breeze through life or meticulously plan every step, you should take some time to mentally prepare for what's in store. Therefore, before turning up for your first day, reflect on how others see you in the workplace and put steps in place to address any weaknesses. For example, it's never acceptable to be late, so plan on getting to work earlier than anyone else – this will be noticed!

In order to minimise the stress of your first day, you may also want to visit the organisation beforehand and have a chat with your new boss. Feel free to ask.

At first, fitting in a social life can be difficult. Some new workers stop going out altogether and don't get a chance to blow off steam, whilst others continue to stay out all night and can't stay awake at work. Either way, this will not help you get on. Try to fit your social life around your work instead of vice versa and make sure you're having enough fun, but not too much! Remember the following guidelines:

- Your new job isn't just a means to paying the rent; it's a chance to start your quest for a fulfilling and successful future.
- Success is not just about carrying out the tasks you've been given; it centres on taking responsibility and proactively looking for opportunities to develop.
- You need to be professional, i.e. on time, well mannered, well dressed, friendly and cooperative.
- You're still allowed to have fun!

Don't panic about the intellectual challenge presented by your first graduate role – it's rarely as difficult as you may imagine and employers are keen to guide you through. However, you should show your enthusiasm by contacting the organisation beforehand and asking how you can prepare for your first assignments. This may involve reading around a particular topic, researching current trends and/or researching the organisation's policy and practice. This will impress your new employers and take the heat off your first few weeks in the job.

In terms of practical preparation, it can really help to comprehensively sort out your new domestic arrangements before your start. For example, you won't want to be living on a friend's floor and looking for a flat-share whilst embarking on such an important journey. Some of the measures you may need to arrange are as follows:

- A quiet, convenient place to live.
- New clothes.

- Your journey to and from work.
- Cooking arrangements.
- Washing/cleaning arrangements.
- Emotional support.
- Banking facilities and cash.

Day one and induction

On your first day, you'll be very nervous but, amid all the greetings and handshakes, take a moment to congratulate yourself on this auspicious achievement. It's important to retain perspective when the pressure is on at work and maintain your self-esteem. This will give you the confidence and drive to succeed.

Get there in good time and share your joy and excitement with everyone you meet. This will both serve to boost your enthusiasm and build a favourable impression with co-workers.

Induction is a set of activities which employers usually design to introduce new employees to their colleagues and prepare them for their roles. In some organisations, this will involve a quick handshake before lunch, whilst in others there will be extensive meetings and consultations. You can maximise the benefits of this period by clearly defining your tasks and line of management. Good work relationships are fundamental to your success so, during your first few days and weeks, get to know everyone's names and make sure you spend some time with key colleagues and clients.

Part of your induction will probably involve a work plan for your first few months at the firm. Try to engage one hundred per cent with this initiative and endeavour to include your personal aims and objectives along with the organisation's. For example, if you want to learn a new technique or process, but it's not in your schedule, ask your boss to include it. They will respond positively to your proactive approach.

ⓘ Useful links

Websites

www.thebalancecareers.com – See 'How to negotiate, accept, or decline a job offer'

www.social.hays.com – See '6 steps to dealing with multiple job offers'

http://uk.businessinsider.com – See '27 things you should do on your first day of work'

www.reed.co.uk – See 'Starting a new job advice'

On Twitter/Instagram/Facebook/LinkedIn

Follow news, events and people in and around the organisation where you'll be working

PART VI

AN INTRODUCTION TO SELF-EMPLOYMENT

One exciting employment option for students and graduates is to set up your own business and work for yourself. In fact, a recent study by Indeed has found that over 15% choose this option.[1]

This section of the guide is a short introduction to entrepreneurship which will help you:

- Decide whether self-employment is right for you.
- Identify some interesting business ideas.
- Get things going.
- Secure appropriate help.

CHAPTER 21
Becoming an entrepreneur

> God helps those who help themselves.
>
> *Proverb*

Contents

Gig-worker, one-man band or corporate titan?

The phrase 'the gig economy' was not around just a few years ago, but it has quickly gained traction as this sector steadily grows. Put starkly, it just describes organisations that avoid the responsibilities of employing people by taking on workers, not as employees, but as self-employed contractors. If you've been lucky enough (or unlucky enough) to gain a position like this, make sure you clarify your remuneration and properly sort out your taxes and other business essentials such as insurance in case of accidents. This chapter focuses on the needs of the more traditional entrepreneurs.

If you're considering starting your own business, you may be thinking of a mum and dad enterprise that earns just a few extra pounds, a massive blue-chip company that takes over the world, or something half-way between, but the process is largely the same (just on a different scale). Put simply, you need to assess whether this sort of career is for you, come up with an idea, test it, find some investment and get it to market. This section introduces you to the processes involved; if they whet your appetite, speak to an enterprise consultant at your university or in your local area (see links at the end of this chapter) and buy some books on setting up a business, but, most of all, get busy, get out there and start making it happen. The main hurdles to new business success are fear and procrastination.

Steve Rook, author of this guide

I decided to run my own business and came up with an idea when I briefly returned to the UK for a few months in 1999. I had been a supply teacher in London for many years and understood the ins and outs of the industry. I also knew that agencies relied on teachers from countries like South Africa, New Zealand and Australia. Therefore, I figured out that I could procure teachers for them in Western Australia, where none of the existing agencies had offices. I approached a range of organisations and my old employer agreed to work with me. I spent the next two years sitting on the beach in Fremantle finding teachers when I felt like it.

I enjoyed being my own boss but I hated all the paperwork and the worry over not knowing if I could pay the rent each month. I didn't plan this venture in any way and relied on my creativity to face any issues when they arose. After about six months I figured out that my future relied on building a closer relationship with the universities in the area and recruiting new graduates. If I had just thought about things a bit more deeply when I started, I might have worked this out much sooner.

Enterprise and entrepreneurship

The words 'enterprise' and 'entrepreneurship' are often conflated and confused.

In this book, 'enterprise' relates to your ability to proactively solve problems and find opportunities in any walk of life, whereas 'entrepreneurship' strictly refers to the process of launching a risky new venture that could lead either to a profit or a loss. A further glossary of terms, jargon and acronyms used in this sector is provided at the end of the next chapter (Chapter 22).

The pros and cons of entrepreneurship

Pros

The common attractions of entrepreneurship are:

- The potential for great rewards.
- Being able to work around other commitments (e.g. study).
- Getting some experience for your CV.
- Developing necessary skills.
- Using your creativity.
- Being in control of your own destiny.
- Avoiding mundane tasks and miserable managers.
- Working in your chosen area.
- Following your dreams.
- Independence/being your own boss.

> ### Cons
>
> On the other hand, you'll also probably face the following trials, at least until you get things up and running:
>
> - Financial risks.
> - The insecurity of living by your wits and not earning a fixed wage.
> - Never knowing what's around the next corner.
> - Mountains of paperwork.
> - The need to become a business expert.
> - Staying one step ahead of the competition.
> - 24-hour personal responsibility.
> - Long hours.

The skills you'll need

In general, you'll need the following attributes:

- Enterprise and the ability to innovate.
- Enthusiasm and commitment.
- The willingness (and capacity) to work hard.
- The ability to deal with pressure and stress.
- The flexibility and adaptability to deal with a wide range of issues and problems.
- Stamina.
- Self-discipline (will you be able to get out of bed every Monday morning?).
- The capacity to learn from new experiences.
- The ability to communicate and build networks.
- A thick skin – especially the facility to cope with setbacks and rejection.

Is it right for you?

Unfortunately, when you're starting out, it can be quite hard to identify whether you'll enjoy self-employment and whether you'll be any good. This is because you're unique, it's such a novel experience and there are so many potential business models. One way to go about making a decision about whether or not to set up your own business is to compare your favourite business idea with your preferred occupation and see which gives you the biggest buzz. Try this in the exercise below by evaluating each of your options in terms of your personal skills, interests and motivations (as identified in Chapter 3).

Self-assessment: Your career shortlist

List your top six skills, interests and motivations (see Chapter 3) and tick which of them is more closely matched to your favourite occupation or working for yourself.

Your attributes	Which is the closest match?	
	Your favourite occupation	Working for yourself
Your skills		
●		
●		
●		
●		
●		
●		
Your interests		
●		
●		
●		
●		
●		
●		
Your motivations		
●		
●		
●		
●		
●		
●		
TOTAL		

Reflecting on your answers: Go ahead and compare your total scores for each option but, more importantly, ask yourself which option you enjoyed looking into more. Maybe you could do both?

Coming up with ideas

Of course, in order to set up your own business, you'll have to think of something to sell. Don't feel you have to come up with some amazingly creative new idea – you just need to deliver a good or service that some people will buy instead of (or as well as) the main product on the market. For example, you could establish a fancy dress shop or a tablet repair shop for students.

Seven of the more common business idea generators are outlined below. Use these strategies to come up with some possible options in the self-assessment exercise at the end of the chapter.

Focus on your skills, study and experience

Businesses generally stand a much greater chance of success when entrepreneurs know what they're doing and understand the market. For example:

- If you gained good grades at university you could help struggling students with their essays.
- Overseas graduates could share their knowledge and experience with the families of students back at home who are considering coming to the UK.

Research growth markets

There are almost always sectors, businesses and niches that are on the up. Do your research to identify current industries that are strong and successful and consider whether there is an area where you can add value. For example, a selection of the strong sectors in the UK currently includes fintech, digital marketing and advertising, biotechnology and virtual reality (see 'The UK's Fastest Growth Industries' at www.nig.com).

This approach can be especially effective if you look out for markets that are inefficient and outdated and where there is minimal competition in terms of major brands and larger suppliers. For example, services such as bicycle messengering in smaller cities, IT repairs for older people and posh dog-grooming centres (dog ownership is also currently on the up).

Look at common business start-ups

Another way to find business ideas is to see what other new entrepreneurs are doing at the moment. For example, there is currently a plethora of new businesses seeking to address greener energy solutions. Could you turn your hand to this? You can find out about new business initiatives by popping into your university's enterprise centre, contacting professional organisations, noticing who's winning entrepreneurship awards and looking at adverts in local papers/web banners.

Use new technology

Throughout history new technology has led to a wealth of commercial opportunities. Nowadays, most new technologies are connected to IT and communications and numerous opportunities have opened up in these sectors including:

- **Designing apps:** Try to think of apps that would help you at work or during your hobbies. For example, if you like gardening, how about an app that uses a phone's camera facility to identify plants and then provides instructions on how they should be looked after?
- **Designing bespoke websites.**
- **Facilitating search engine optimisation:** Helping small businesses improve their online presence.
- **E-commerce:** Selling your own good or service either on your own website or through a market such as eBay.
- **Blogs:** Constructing blogs and forums that attract advertising revenue.
- **Social media spin-offs:** Come up with a niche new social network such as a lifestyle portal for local people who identify as LGTBQ+ (if you want to share your local knowledge).

Find niche organisations

These are numerous businesses which target small specific markets that major companies or public-sector bodies cannot fully exploit: for example, setting up a corner shop that focuses on the specific needs of local communities, hawking revamped bicycles to students and selling traditional formal clothes to UK Muslims. One good way to identify appropriate niches is to simply identify major goods and services that aren't sufficiently targeted at you, your friends or your family. For example, if you're Jewish, can you get hold of good kosher food in your area? If you're bigger than Kate Moss, can you find any cool clothes that fit? If you're a female who loves hunting and fishing, can you get appropriate gear? The Internet gives you a great opportunity to focus on such niche products and services.

Look overseas

Anyone who's travelled will have seen that there are thousands of business ideas that aren't exploited here in the UK. Why not look for ideas on your next holiday, or transfer a money-making venture from your original country? For example, you could set up a fleet of minibus taxis (prevalent throughout Asia) to transfer groups of students from campus to popular student areas for a pound or two each trip.

Solve your own problems

Simply ask yourself what would make your life easier, more fun or less of a worry and think of how you could create the relevant good or service. After all, if you can find answers to your personal dilemmas, then others in the same situation will probably be prepared to pay. For example, if you find it hard to meet like-minded students on campus, why not set up a dating app? If your dog runs away every time you take him for a walk, how about marketing a cheap GPS collar with its own app? If you can never afford to stay anywhere on your travels, why not set up a business where students can rent out their couches?

Why not?

Self-assessment: Your business ideas

Use the approaches outlined above to come up with three exciting business ideas.

-
-
-

Useful links

Websites

www.entrepreneur.com – See 'So you want to be your own boss'
    Search on Google for "lend genius inspiring people"
www.therisetothetop.com – See '20 unconventional entrepreneurs who will
    inspire you'
www.telegraph.co.uk – See 'The UK's 13 most inspirational rags-to-riches
    entrepreneurs'

On YouTube

'Richard Branson: Advice for Entrepreneurs' – Think big
'How to choose the perfect business Idea' – Daniel Ally
'Need a business Idea? The best way to find one Is to stop looking' – Entrepreneur

On Twitter

www.entrepreneur.com – See 'Fifteen Inspirational Twitter Accounts Every
    Entrepreneur Should Follow'
@Entrepreneur
@StartUpBritain
@BarclaysEntpr
@Newentrefound

On LinkedIn

www.linkedin.com/title/entrepreneur

CHAPTER 22

Getting your business started

> " Don't open a shop unless you like to smile.
> *Chinese proverb* "

Steve Rook, author of this guide

I started a business at the start of the millennium out of desperation for money more than anything else. I had been living in Queensland, Australia, and wanted to move to Perth but needed some funds, so I went back to the UK to teach for a term or two. Everything was going fine until I got pneumonia (the English weather was a bit of a shock) so I had to go back penniless.

However, on my last night in London I had a great idea to recruit Australian teachers from Perth to work in England, where there was a heavy demand. I knew there were agencies performing this function in the big cities in Australia's East (Sydney, Melbourne and Brisbane) but there appeared to be none out West.

So, I got up early and before my flight, wrote a letter to each of the big agencies in London and got on the Tube to deliver them all. It was an exhausting day but, when I landed in Perth, I already had an email expressing interest and I took it from there.

At first, I had difficulty chasing prospective teachers but just kept on trying. I advertised in papers; talked to teachers in schools whilst I undertook supply work; gave out flyers at universities and even contacted Careers Advisers (this was before the Internet took over). Some of these methods failed but the contacts I made bore fruit and they also gave me the idea to move my career into the careers advice field and are therefore responsible for this book!

Defining your customer

Once you've come up with some possible business ventures, it's time to develop your ideas, test them and get going. The first stage in this process is to identify your target customers. This is crucial, because you'll only be able to focus on the specific requirements of your customers when you know who they're likely to be!

It may seem counterproductive to narrow down your planned market before you've even started doing business but this will allow you to design something that's attractive and sellable to a specific audience. You need to consider customer attributes such as age, sex, social class, race and level of education. Try to be selective without being too limited. For example, it may be useful to focus on young male Muslims in Bradford, but not single white females from Brighton called Jane! In the exercise below, define three characteristics of your target customers for one of your own business ideas.

Self-assessment: Picturing your customers

What are your customers like?

Your business idea:
Characteristics of your target customers:
●
●
●

Reflecting on your answers: If you're struggling, close your eyes and imagine someone using your product – What do they look like? Who are they?

Finding your market

Once you've classified your target customers you need to develop and market your business with them in mind. Marketing involves everything you need to do to get your product or service to market and make some sales. Therefore, the process is traditionally outlined in terms of the following four elements: product (an exact description of what you're selling); promotion (publicising and advertising what you have to offer); price (what people will pay); and place (where the product is made and how it's distributed). You need to ensure that each of these 'four Ps' is appropriately developed with your specific customers in mind. The following sections outline how you can do this.

Product

The product or service you're developing should fit the exact needs of your planned customers, not your own or, indeed, those of the technology you're using! It can be very difficult to put yourself in other people's shoes in this way, but it needs to be done if you want to make any sales. For example, you could tailor two of the products and services outlined in the previous chapter as follows:

- **Student minibuses:** If you decide to cater for clubbers, you could have colourful, loud buses that pick customers up from the Student Union and local pubs/clubs. For international students, you could have multi-lingual drivers. If you want to focus on a regular clientele, you could sell discounted passes, allow seat bookings and pick customers up from home.
- **GPS pet collars/implants:** If you cater for owners of professional animals, such as police dogs and racehorses, you'll need to develop an extremely safe, well-engineered product. For wealthy customers, you could design expensive collars that are shiny and attractive but, for everyday people, a cheap, reliable, alternative will probably suffice.

Now it's your turn: Consider how you could tailor the business idea you outlined in the previous exercise to the customer characteristics you've defined.

Self-assessment: Targeting your product

List three ways you could target your customers' needs in your product or service.

Your business idea:
How you could target your product or service at your specific customers:
●
●
●

Reflecting on your answers: Ask people in your market segment (your target customers) what they would like your proposed product to deliver/how it should be sold, etc. and alter your plans accordingly.

Promotion

Another benefit of focusing on the needs of your specific customers is that you can develop a targeted publicity and advertising campaign. Publicity is all about raising your profile; you can do this in a number of ways, such as:

- Entering enterprise awards.
- Attracting media attention.
- Networking.
- Finding partners who will actively raise your profile (if you will reciprocate).

- Maintaining a high web and social media profile.
- After-sales service (e.g. look at how organisations like Amazon target previous customers with targeted product suggestions).

You should also find creative ways to promote your ideas that are linked to your specific product or service, for example:

- If you're opening a student fancy dress shop, why not organise a fancy dress party during fresher's week?
- If you plan to help people mend their phones and tablets, maybe you could offer your technical skills free to a Student Union society.

Advertising also needs to be targeted. For example, local services such as student cafés and academic support would probably benefit from initiatives such as flyers, sponsorship of student societies, promotions in the local media and dynamic activities such as free product placement at major university events. However, campaigns like this will be largely useless if you're running some sort of e-commerce activity and all your potential customers are in Brazil! In this case, you should probably focus on web banners, blogs, forums, social networking and search engine optimisation.

Price

The equation for working out how to price your product is quite complicated. You need to consider factors such as:

- Your costs.
- Your personal salary and profits.
- What your customers can pay, and what they're prepared to pay.
- Incentives for repeat trade.
- How much your competitors are charging.
- The price sensitivity and elasticity of your product/service (search for 'price elasticity' at www.economicsonline.co.uk to find out more).

Place

Of course, all the above is just theory if you haven't figured out:

- Where you're going to get your raw materials.
- How you're going to transport them to your site.
- Where you're going to be based.
- How you're going to put together your product or service.
- How you're going to get it into your customers' hands.
- How you're going to be paid.

These logistical issues can be very expensive but, at each stage, you can minimise your costs. For example, if you're providing a free, hard-copy magazine for black and Asian students at your university you could build a partnership with a local printer to keep costs down, store them in your garage and deliver them yourself to local shops and societies.

Testing your market

Good market research can give you a clear perspective on how to market your product. It isn't just about finding out if your idea is popular; it should also focus on the commercial viability of your particular product or service and how it should be designed to deliver maximum impact. You can start by investigating the market size (the money spent on similar products by your target group), the share of the market you're likely to win and recent trends in that sector. Then, you can look for effective ways to differentiate your product or service from those of your competition. For example, you could look into what customers are seeking in terms of appearance, delivery time, performance and quality.

Test your business ideas in the exercise below.

Self-assessment: Testing your market

List some specific resources you could use to assess your intended business.

Outline:

Your business idea: _____

_____

How you could measure...

(a) Your market size: _____

_____

(b) Your possible market share: _____

_____

(c) The buying habits of your market segment: _____

_____

(d) What your customers think of your business idea: _____

_____

Reflecting on your answers: Make sure you look deeply and listen to advice, even if you disagree (especially if you disagree), and remember, the customer is always right!

Market research

Market research usually involves web research, direct contact and pilot studies.

Web research: You can research business sectors and market trends on the following websites …

- Prospects: www.prospects.ac.uk – Look up the job sectors section.
- Relevant professional organisations (see the companion website www. macmillanihe.com/rook-gcg-2e).
- The Office for National Statistics: www.ons.gov.uk.
- Business Link: www.gov.uk.
- The Confederation of British Industry: www.cbi.org.uk.
- Media related to your field, e.g. What Car? magazine (www.whatcar.com/), The Taoist Tai Chi Society of Great Britain at www.taoist.org/uk.
- Your competitors.
- Your local Chamber of Commerce (see www.britishchambers.org.uk).
- Business directories such as www.yell.co.uk and those available from your local Chamber of Commerce.

You can find out statistical information about people (demographics) and their habits and values (psychographics) on these sites:

- Zoopla: www.zoopla.co.uk – See the information on 'Area Stats'.
- Caci: www.caci.co.uk/acorn-classification.aspx – See the ACORN classifications, which are geographically focused demographic segments of the UK's population.
- Index Mundi: www.indexmundi.com – International demographics.
- Experian: www.experian.co.uk – Look up 'Location Analyst'.
- The Office for National Statistics: www.ons.gov.uk.
- UK National Statistics: www.statistics.gov.uk.

Alternatively, you can Google your business idea or something like 'Demographics of the … sector'. You should also get involved with other online tools such as relevant forums and discussion boards.

Talking to real people: Start by getting in touch with agencies that help small businesses in your area. Your university's enterprise centre should be your first port of call but there are numerous other bodies that can help. You could also speak to:

- People in your market segment.
- Distributers and retailers.
- Customers at trade fairs.
- Sales representatives of organisations in your chosen sector (why not pretend to be a customer and ask really tricky questions?).

Pilot studies: Try to sell your product in a small trial to test your ideas. This will also give you a chance to correct any problems before you hit the market at full speed. For example, if you decide to sell bicycles to students, you could advertise them at fresher's week and offer free personal delivery.

Test your business ideas in the exercise below.

Choosing a business structure

Once you've adapted your product appropriately and tested your market it's time to get out there and turn your dreams into reality. You can do this by choosing a business structure and signing up. New entrepreneurs in the UK are often attracted to the business types shown in the table below.

Some popular business structures for new entrepreneurs

Business structures	Advantages	Disadvantages	How to register
Sole traders: One-person businesses where the owner receives all the profits and has unlimited liability for losses and debts.	● Relatively few regulations ● Complete control ● Option to raise funds publicly or privately	● Lack of confidence from investors ● Increasing personal liability as the business grows	Just register that you're self-employed with HMRC. Profits are classed as income.
Ordinary partnerships: Organisations of two or more people (or businesses) in which each partner is fully liable for the full overall debts.	● Simple and flexible	● Each partner may be liable for all the debts ● Larger organisations may not deal with you	One of the partners registers with HMRC for self-assessment. You should draw up a partnership agreement.
Private limited companies: Companies with only a few shareholders and shares are privately transacted (not through a stock market).	● Shareholders are not responsible for debts ● Access to finance through shares ● More favourable tax regime than for sole traders	● The need to file accounts annually with Companies House ● All profits must be shared	Register at Companies House (www. companieshouse. gov.uk). File company tax returns to HMRC.

Public limited companies: Companies where shares are sold on the public market and shareholders have limited liability for debts.	• All members have limited liability • Great potential to raise funds	• Little control over who buys or sells shares • Costly to set up • Inbuilt resistance to change	Register at Companies House and file company tax returns to HMRC.
Community interest companies (CIC): A new business structure for social enterprises where founders are given a legal identity separate from their limited companies.	• Assets and profits can only be distributed if allowed by law – giving confidence to ethical investors	• More difficult to set up • Must publish an annual community interest company report	Same as limited companies but regulator has the power to make sure you are helping the community.

Numerous other business types are available such as private unlimited companies, limited partnerships, cooperatives, offshore companies and limited liability partnerships. Find out more on www.startups.co.uk. You may also want to consult a solicitor or accountant to make sure you're doing everything by the book.

Legal/tax issues

Once you've set up your business there are various other legal and tax issues you will need to consider. These are summarised below.

Intellectual property

Make sure you're not copying and using any unique creative products/industrial secrets that are owned by others (without their express permission). This includes endeavours such as design features, text, artwork, logos, trademarks and patents. You should also make sure that your ideas are protected. Find out more at the Intellectual Property Office (www.ipo.gov.uk).

Tax

Sign up for the appropriate tax regime for your type of business (including VAT) and keep your records in order. You may also want to employ an accountant to make sure you're following the correct procedures and minimise your liability. If you're employing anyone, you'll also need to sort out their tax through PAYE and National Insurance. You can find out which taxes you should be paying, and how to register, on Her Majesty's Revenue and Customs (HMRC) website at www.hmrc.gov.uk. In the meantime, keep hold of all your receipts!

Licences

Depending on what you're selling you may also require a licence – these are usually provided by your local council. Business Link has an excellent tool to help you identify any licence you may need at www.businesslink.org.uk. Of course, you may also be required to come up with extra licensing fees for relevant software and services, such as Sky if you want to put a telly in your café.

Insurance

Your business will also need various forms of insurance, such as public liability and business equipment cover. Business Link also has useful resources on risk management at www.businesslink.org.uk.

Financial planning and forecasts

Obviously, finances are a major concern for most people starting a new business. This section shows you how to forecast your costs, income, profits and losses and accurately keep track of them so that you can make sound decisions about the future and enhance your chances of success.

Set-up costs

Your first task is to carefully work out how much money you'll need to set up shop and start trading. Depending on the nature of your business this could involve paying out for things such as:

- Product development.
- Machinery and equipment.
- Staff.
- Training.
- Designing a website.
- An office/warehouse/retail outlet.
- Paying bills and wages until the receipts come rolling in.

These costs can be astronomical if you just jump in with your chequebook and start buying the best products and services on offer but, with a little thought, you can make substantial savings, at least until you start earning enough money to reinvest. For example, you could:

- Set up your office in the free facilities that may be available from your university's enterprise centre or other local agencies (often called incubators).

- Trade from your own bedroom and store things in the garage.
- Rent the equipment you need or buy it second-hand.
- Hire interns over the summer from your local university (including someone to set up your IT and sales strategy).
- Learn how to sell your goods or services effectively on the Internet.
- Distribute your own goods from the back of your car.
- Promote and advertise your goods and services yourself.
- Shop around!

In the exercise below, list the key resources you'll need to set up your business, and work out how you can get them as cheaply as possible. This will help you calculate the funds you'll need just to get going.

Self-assessment: Minimising your set-up costs

List the costs you will incur in setting up your business and outline how you can minimise your outlay.

Your business idea:		
The resources you'll need	How you can get them cheaply	What they will cost
		£
		£
		£
		£
		£
	TOTAL	£

Ongoing costs

Once you commence trading, you'll immediately start incurring extra, ongoing expenditure. These flexible costs will rise according to how much you sell, but the marginal costs of producing and selling each extra unit will gradually fall because of the economies of scale. In other words, the more you sell, the lower your average expense. For example, if you make music, it will probably cost hundreds of pounds to produce your first compact disc (including equipment, studio time, production etc.), but your second one will probably only cost 50p! Therefore, your average costs depend heavily on the number of units you sell.

Some of the major marginal costs faced by most new businesses are listed below:

- Payments to suppliers: Raw materials/wholesale products.
- Promotion and advertising.
- Purchases: Everything from raincoats to networking lunches.
- Wages/professional fees: Pay for your staff and accountants, lawyers etc.
- Tax: Including PAYE and NI for your staff, VAT and your income/business taxes.
- Rent and rates.
- Electricity/gas.
- Car costs/travel.
- Telephone: Office and mobile.
- Stationery.
- Logistics/postage.
- Repairs: Especially important if everything is old and rusty!
- General expenses.
- Capital: Better machinery, equipment and IT.
- Bank interest and charges.

Forecasts

Once you've calculated your potential costs, sales and income you can produce monthly financial forecasts for your first year or two of trading. These will help you gauge the success of your business as you proceed and they can be carefully assessed by interested investors. You can see example cash flow, profit and loss, and balance sheet forecasts on the companion website.

Finding the funds

Of course, starting a new business can be expensive and risky but intrepid entrepreneurs, with impressive business plans, can still access a number of sources of funding, many of which are listed below:

- Your own savings.
- Your mum, dad and uncle Eric.
- Keeping your 'day job' (i.e. set things up while you're still working).
- Business 'angels': wealthy individuals who invest in new businesses for a percentage of the returns. Find out more on the websites of the UK Business Angels Association at www.ukbusinessangelsassociation.org.uk and the Angel Investment Network at www.angelinvestmentnetwork.co.uk.
- Bank loans.
- Bank overdrafts.
- Local, national and European government grants: See the Business Link website at www.businesslink.org.uk, Sage Advice at www.sage.com and www.gov.uk/business-finance-support.
- Soft loans: Loans with favourable terms, often available from local authorities and professional organisations (see www.startuploans.co.uk).

- Charities (such as the Prince's Trust at www.princes-trust.org.uk and www. charitybank.org/charity-loans).
- Community Development Finance Institutions (see www.cdfa.org.uk).
- Crowdfunding: Securing funds from a multitude of investors – usually arranged through websites such as www.kickstarter.com, www.fundingcircle.com, www. pleasefund.us and www.crowdfunder.co.uk.

Lenders will expect you to demonstrate your CAMPARI, i.e. your **C**haracter and **A**bility, the **M**argin you will earn, the **P**urpose for the loan, grant or gift, the **A**mount you need, how you will **R**epay what you owe and the **I**nsurance or collateral you are able to provide.

Business plans

Once you've identified your market and set up an appropriate business structure, it's time to formally draw up your plans for the coming years. This will give you confidence that you can achieve your aims, help you avoid getting bogged down with day-to-day problems, monitor your progress, impress investors and find the funds you'll need to get up and running.

Because business plans are so important, you should put a great deal of time and energy into making sure yours is positive, comprehensive (but concise), engaging and realistic. You can find out more about what you need to incorporate through the resources listed at the beginning of the chapter and get help from Business Link (www.businesslink.org.uk), accountants and/or financial advisers.

What you should include

There is no universal business structure since no two businesses are the same, but you should include the following elements:

1 **A cover page:** Show your business's name, contact details and the date the plan was prepared.
2 **An executive summary:** A persuasive one-page summary of your venture.
3 **A table of contents.**
4 **An outline of your business and product/service:** More details including an outline of your business structure, what your product does, how it will benefit customers, why it's distinct from similar merchandise already on the market, how it will be developed and updated and how the business has performed so far.
5 **Details of your management and staffing:** Summarise your personal, academic and business achievements, relating them to your business, and do the same for your colleagues and staff. Include specific information relating to staff training and any services you may outsource.
6 **Market intelligence:** Include details of the size of your market and the share you are planning on gaining, your likely customers (including demographics

and psychographics), your competitors (and how they will react to your entry), how the market has performed in the past, current trends and future potential.

7   **Your sales strategy:**
   ● Outline how, where and who will sell your product or service. For example, will you use the Internet, direct mail, telephone, third parties or your own retail outlet?
   ● Your pricing structure.

8   **How you will use the Internet (e-commerce):** Provide technical details of how you will use the world wide web and social media to support your business, including everything from ordering raw materials, selling your merchandise and after-sales service.

9   **Your operational details:** Provide information on where you'll be based, your suppliers and the equipment and machinery you'll be using, including any information technology.

10 **An analysis of your finances:** Provide forecasts of costs, earnings and profits for your first trading year and use them to justify any extra funds you are after. Include specific details about what you will do with any cash injections.

11 **A risk assessment:** Describe any potential problems you may face and how they will be overcome. You may want to do this through a SWOT matrix where you analyse the following aspects of your product or service:
   ● Its strengths (how it's superior to those of your competitors).
   ● Its weaknesses (its limitations compared with your competitors).
   ● Your opportunities (positive external factors in the sector/market).
   ● Your threats (negative external factors).
   You can find details on conducting a SWOT matrix at www.businessballs.com.

12 **A picture of your long-term prospects:** End your business plan on a positive note by describing your plan for the next five years and how this will be achieved. Focus on anticipated returns and whet investors' appetites by indicating what they will earn if the business is floated or sold.

A one-page business plan

If you're not quite ready to put together a full business objective at this stage then a shorter, more concise plan can be a good stepping stone. Construct your sleek strategy in the exercise below.

Self-assessment: A one-page business plan

Answer the following questions to develop a short, focused business plan.

Your business name: _____

What is your product/service? _____

What resources will you need to put it together? _____

_____

Where will you be based? _____

_____

Who's going to buy it? _____

_____

How will they find it useful? _____

_____

What will you sell it for? _____

How will you organise payment? _____

_____

What other sources of income does it enable? _____

_____

How will you attract customers? _____

What do you still need to find out? _____

_____

Reflecting on your answers: You may want to use this short business plan to help you come up with your next moves.

Glossary of terms used in the sector

If you're going to start a new business or do any further research, you should get a handle on the terms and phrases that are used in the sector, such as:

Accounting year end: Each 12-month anniversary of when a company is incorporated, at which time all entries must be adjusted in order to prepare financial statements.

Affiliate: A partner organisation or a business that links to your website for their own marketing benefit.

Application programming interface (API):   Software that allows you to feed continually updated data linked to your own sites.

Artificial Intelligence (AI):   Machines that can learn and take decisions based on environmental cues.

Assets: Any valuable tangible or intangible economic resources that can be bought or sold.

Balance sheet: A brief summary of a company's assets, liabilities and equity on a specific date (often the end of the financial year).

Banner: A web advert that acts as a gateway to your site.

Biometric signature: Verification through biological means such as a scan of the retina or fingerprint.

Brand: Either a unique variation of a good/service (for example, Nike is a brand of sportswear) or the specific symbol that identifies a unique variety of a good/service (for example, the Nike 'tick' shown on the company's apparel).

Brand advocate: Someone who promotes a brand.

Business angels: Private investors in small businesses.

Business plan: A formal outline of a business's goals and how these are going to be achieved.

Business start-up: Newly established enterprises still in a state of development (particularly in the digital field).

Business strategy: A statement outlining how a business intends to succeed, including what's being offered, the needs of customers, how it will beat the competition and remain profitable in the long term.

Cash flow: The amount of money that has moved into or out of a business, usually over a fixed period.

Channels: Your social platforms.

Click-through: Clicking on an online advert.

Cloud: Big grey things all over the north of England/A shared pool of resources on remote servers.

Companies House: UK body responsible for forming and dissolving public companies.

Content marketing: Content designed to influence views/generate sales (usually on the web or social networks).

Conversion rate: The proportion of people who click on a particular link, as requested in a post.

Digital marketing: Online advertising.

Direct marketing: Advertising delivered directly to the customer, e.g. texting, emails, fliers, catalogues and promotional letters.

Domain registration: Claiming ownership of a specific website address.

Earned media: User generated content outside your influence.

E-commerce: Business transactions over electronic systems such as the Internet.

E-commerce platform: Commercial programs that comprise all the elements required for selling online.

Economies of scale: The tendency to incur lower average costs when you produce more (to an optimum point when they start to rise again).

Engagement rate: The extent to which users are interacting with your channels.

Enterprise Zone: Regions in the UK where taxes and regulations are relaxed to encourage entrepreneurs.

Fintech: Businesses involved in using technology to enhance financial activity.

Fixed costs: Basic business costs that are accrued whatever the level of sales.

Flexible costs: Business costs that vary according to how much you produce.

Franchising: Piggybacking on another organisation's business model whereby an owner of a business grants a licence to another person (or business) to use their idea.

Google analytics: Google's free service that analyses your web traffic.

Gross: Before deductions (such as tax).

Handle: Your Twitter username.

Hits: The number of times a server is asked to upload particular web pages and their associated elements such as images, JavaScript and Cascading Style Sheets. Therefore, a single view of one web page will create a variable amount of hits.

Impressions: The number of times a web advert is displayed.

Incorporation: Setting up a company.

Incubator (in this context):   Space and resources such as IT and phone lines provided for free, or at low cost, to business start-ups, especially within universities.

Influencer: Someone on social networks who has the power to promote your brand.

Intellectual property: Any creative endeavour that's considered to be the property of its creator.

Klout: A score of your social media influence that allows you to be ranked against competitors.

Lifestyle business: Businesses designed to fit around your existing life.

Logistics: The process of getting your product or service to the customer including production, packaging and transportation.

Marginal costs: The costs of producing one more unit.

Market research: Information gathering about markets and customers.

Market segmentation: Targeting the needs of specific groups of customers.

Marketing: Everything involved in creating and selling a product or service that attracts and keeps customers, such as product design, advertising, and how and where it's sold.

Marketing mix: The factors that make up a good marketing strategy, traditionally comprising the four Ps: product, promotion, price and place.

Meta tags: Information contained in the coding of web pages which describes issues such as who wrote them, what they're about, and targeted keywords to describe their content. These keywords have a crucial role in the prominence of individual sites in web searches.

National Insurance (NI):   Contributions paid by workers, employers and the self-employed towards the costs of state benefits.

Net: After deductions (such as tax).

Niche market: A market subset at which a particular product or service is targeted.

Owned media: Content posted on your channels.

Page views: The number of times a server is asked to upload particular web pages but not their associated files (*see* **hits**).

Paid media: Social advertising.

Patents: New, useful and non-obvious processes, machines or articles that have been registered with the state. They typically convey exclusivity in making, using and selling the product or service for a fixed period.

Pay-per-click: A method of payment whereby online advertisers pay the owners of a host website a fixed amount each time their advert is clicked.

Point of sale: Where goods and services are transacted – for example, cash registers, credit/debit card machines, computers and mobile phones.

Reach: How far your posts have gained traction in terms of the views they have received (not counting repeated viewings).

Search engine marketing (SEM):   The process of increasing your website's visibility and use.

Search Engine Optimisation (SEO):   Gaining as much traffic to your website as possible through search engines.

Seed funding: Early funding for a new business to sustain it until it grows and can support itself.

Small business: These are businesses (usually sole traders, privately owned companies, or partnerships) with fewer than 50 employees.

Social enterprise: A profit or non-profit organisation devoted to enhancing environmental and human wellbeing.

Social media analytics: Analysis of how your social media channels manage and enhance sales.

Social ROI: The effectiveness of your investment in social media.

Social selling: The process of selling online.

Trademark: Unique symbols which indicate the source of particular products and services (*see* **brand**).

User generated content (UGC):   Feedback/input from online punters.

Variable costs: The costs incurred by an organisation that rise or fall according to how much they produce.

Venture capital: Financial capital provided to businesses in return for a share in equity.

Web analytics: Analysis of how your website manages and enhances sales.

Web traffic: The total data sent and received by websites as determined by the number of visitors and pages viewed.

Initialisms and acronyms

B2B	Business-to-business (commercial transactions between businesses)
B2C	Business-to-customer (commercial transactions between businesses and customers)
CRM	Customer Relations Management (a system for managing customer relations/sales)
HMRC	Her Majesty's Revenue and Customs
NI	National Insurance
P2P/F2F	A personal interaction
P&L	Profit and loss
PAYE	Pay As You Earn tax contributions paid by most employees
PO	Purchase order
QTD	Quarter to date
SME	Small and medium-sized enterprises (organisations with fewer than 250 employees)
S_t	Sales (during time period t)
SWOT analysis	A formal assessment of a project's strengths, weaknesses, opportunities and threats
VAT	Value added tax
YOY	Year on year
YTD	Year to date

ⓘ Useful links

Websites

www.entrepreneurhandbook.co.uk – See '15 Steps to start a business from scratch with (almost) no money'

www.guardian.com – See 'How to start a business in 30 days', '5 tips for starting a small business', 'Eight dos and don'ts for launching a successful business'

www.gov.uk – See 'Set up a business'

https://blog.hubspot.com – Search in blogs for 'How to become an entrepreneur with no money or experience'

On YouTube

'How to Start a Business' – The School of Life

'How to Start a Business with No Money' – Trent Dyrsmid

On LinkedIn

www.businessnewsdaily.com – See '20 LinkedIn groups every entrepreneur should belong to'

PART VII

DOWN THE LINE

So, you're ready to head off into the big blue yonder – and the best of luck!

But, remember, careers are for life, not just for Christmas! So, make sure you don't get bogged down, and keep looking for new opportunities to move forward.

This part outlines how you can keep your eyes open at every stage.

CHAPTER 23
Moving your career forward

" If it's your job to eat a frog, it's best to do it first thing in the morning. And, if it's your job to eat two frogs, it's best to eat the biggest one first.
Mark Twain "

Succeeding

You can't guarantee success but good things come to those who work hard, get on with colleagues and show enough enterprise. Some useful guidelines are as follows:[1]

- Ask questions and keep asking until you understand the answers.
- Be reliable in your timekeeping and attendance (many graduates only learn the importance of this requirement once their contracts have not been renewed).
- Contribute to the team effort in all tasks, including the menial ones.
- Meet objectives set, including the timescales, and, if in difficulty, raise issues well before deadlines.
- Be respectful but not subservient.
- Recognise knowledge and experience in others and don't be a know-it-all.
- Dress for the job you want, not the one you have (unless you want to be a deep-sea diver).
- Keep your own counsel and don't be too trusting – you are now entering a political, business world, where people have their own agendas.
- Avoid becoming entrapped in office politics.
- Be good-humoured and ready for any 'leg pulling'.
- Treat people at face value unless they demonstrate that they are not sincere.
- Be principled: have the courage of your convictions but be ready to learn the art of compromise.

- Always act honestly.
- Own up to your own mistakes and don't compromise others.
- Learn from your mistakes – you will make them, but try not to make the same ones twice (especially in front of your boss).
- Avoid any form of harassment or discrimination.
- Ask your mentor for help when you're not sure what to do (if one is offered).
- Treat people with respect and consideration (remember, you're always networking); you may need their help or support in the future.
- Where constructive criticism is given, accept it with good grace and use it in your personal development.

Moving on up

Human nature is such that we're never satisfied with what we have, so as soon as you find a job, you'll probably want one that's better. There's nothing wrong with this ambition as long as you can maintain a balance, whereby you work hard in your current position but continually strive for more. Here are some strategies:

> 66 Work hard in your current position but continually strive for more. 99

- Build a reputation for hard work and reliability.
- Consciously develop your skills and maintain your commitment.
- Proactively look for better ways to benefit your employers.
- Find ways to get more involved in the tasks you enjoy, and those of a higher level.
- Energetically engage in your personal development and strive for promotion.

Self-assessment: How are you looking?

Take a selfie at work and look at it later with the following questions in mind:

1 Are you happy?
2 Are you giving it your all?
3 Is there more you can do to make the most of your position in terms of a promotion/networks?

Reflecting on your answers: Hopefully, things are going well, but don't just sit back and enjoy the ride – there are always ways to make things better.

Moving on?

Sometimes it's a good idea to leave your job altogether and move into a new organisation and/or role. This could give you greater fulfilment, a higher salary, more opportunities and a fresh start. On the downside, the new job/role may not turn out to be as rosy as you thought; you'll have to relearn the ropes and build new contacts. Therefore, if you feel the need to move on, be open to the idea, but don't rush headlong into the first new job you see. Objectively compare what's on offer at your existing workplace with available opportunities at other organisations; don't jump ship just because you feel bored.

If it's not the job but the role or sector that's the problem, don't panic; it's usually quite easy to make a sideways move. Take the following steps:

1 Identify what you don't like about your current role.
2 See if there are opportunities to eradicate these aspects of your job at your current workplace or with a new employer.
3 Examine similar jobs in your sector that could be more fulfilling. For example, if you're a medical researcher, maybe you would prefer to be a medical writer; if you're a teacher, you could consider home tutoring or going into academia.
4 Re-explore all your options (see Chapter 4). Your degree, experience and skills will make you very attractive to employers in numerous fields, whether or not they are connected to the work you're doing.
5 Speak to people about your options including your mentor at work.
6 Make a decision.
7 Plan your next moves so you can, hopefully, make a smooth transition. For example, you could stay in your existing role while you develop specific skills, apply for jobs and go for interviews (if you're moving on).

Keeping your eyes open

In his song 'Beautiful Boy', John Lennon wrote: 'Life is what happens to you when you're busy making other plans.' You should remember these lyrics as you plan your career. In other words, as long as you're busy and focused on getting to the next stage in life, other interesting avenues will inevitably present themselves. You need to keep your eyes open to take advantage of these opportunities. For example, if you've always wanted to be a navy diver but you really enjoyed diving in Thailand over the summer, why not reconsider your naval career and set up your own dive school on some exotic beach?

Some specific moments when you should especially be open to new stimuli are:

- When you have to think of a career and all the books have little to offer.
- When you can't figure out your next steps.
- When you have no idea about what you want to do but feel too overwhelmed to look into it.
- When you're depressed.
- When you're travelling and you don't ever want to go back.
- When you think all this talk of skills, and commitment is a load of b... .
- When you're scared.
- When you think you've found a path, but it's not as much fun as you thought.
- When you're ready to make your career a marvellous adventure.

Getting back in the game

Graduates often leave the rat-race for any number of reasons such as travel, caring for someone, raising a family or just languishing in unfulfilling roles, wondering whether a degree was even worth their while.

In this situation, you can understandably lose your nerve, self-esteem, drive and ambition. Graduates still earn more than non-graduates, so you just need to develop your strategy, get back in the game and hope for a little luck.

Take some time to reflect on the skills you have gained in the meantime (for example, parenting helps you organise your time and solve problems, whilst working in a bar gives you excellent communication skills) and sort out any issues that are holding you back. Then, when you're ready, you can restart your journey, one step at a time. For example, you could start by looking for any opportunities where you currently work or sign up for some further training.

No one is pretending the journey will be easy, but you'll soon start overtaking graduates who've yet to experience the 'university of life'. Also, don't hesitate to talk to people such as friends, family and Careers Advisers at your old university (even if they're younger than you!).

> **❝** You'll soon start overtaking graduates who've yet to experience the 'university of life'. **❞**

Penny Maynard, Economics Graduate

I graduated with a BA Honours in Economics in the early 1990s, which was in a time of recession, so graduate jobs were difficult to find. I found myself unemployed for several months, and therefore I had to settle for any job I could get. I started my working life in the stockroom of a well-known record store. I remained with this company for twelve years, progressing to supervisor level, and then to a role within Accounts Payables at Head Office. This was a job I thoroughly enjoyed even though the salary was never on a par with some of my graduate friends.

Unfortunately, I had to leave this company to relocate to my home town as a result of divorce, so I could look after my young daughter. At this stage I accepted job roles for which I was overqualified because I lacked confidence. Over time, however, I have gained extra vocational qualifications in accounting which have been funded by my current company. I have also tried to develop in my current role and take on new tasks that will gain me new skills. This will hopefully enable me to pursue my career in the very near future.

Looking back, my degree has not added any value to my working life. In hindsight, it might have proved more worthwhile if I had gone on to an apprentice role straight after school, which would have provided me with valuable skills to compete in the job market. I cannot remember being offered any useful advice from the Careers Office at the university, but maybe I didn't make full use of the service either. The main problem was when I had completed my degree; I had no real sense of what I wanted to do, and did not investigate all possible avenues.

My main advice would therefore be to firstly identify what career you would like to pursue and then view all options on how to achieve this.

Simon Reevell, Former MP

Sometimes careers just ebb and flow. All I ever wanted to be was an Army Officer. I applied for and received an Army Scholarship when I was 16. With that came a career in the army to age 55. By the time I was 22 I was injured and my career in the army looked to be over. I decided to qualify as a barrister as an alternative and by the time I was 25 I was practising in the courts. This was now to be my chosen career. Because I knew something of the military, I often found myself in the Military Courts dealing with Courts Martial. In one of those I found myself representing a soldier charged with manslaughter. The incident happened in Iraq but he had been sent there without proper training and it wasn't his fault. He was acquitted despite an attempt to cover up his lack of training. I was furious; I could have been that soldier. So I decided to stand for Parliament. Someone who was to have fought a Yorkshire seat – just the sort of seat I wanted – decided to stand down and so a new candidate was needed. Dewsbury is the only seat I have ever applied for and the 2010 election is the only election of any kind that I have fought. I am now an MP! I have no idea what the future holds but I am sure it holds something!

ℹ️ Useful links

Websites
www.telegraph.co.uk – See 'Take charge of your career progress'
www.myworldofwork.co.uk – See 'Career progression'
www.inc.com – See '10 Guaranteed ways to move up in your career'

On YouTube
'How to Change Careers when You're Lost' – Felicia Ricci/TEDxYale

CHAPTER 24
Frequently asked questions

" Successful people do not lack problems, they just learn how to solve them.

Proverb "

Some common concerns

Some of the more common problems faced by students and graduates are outlined below with advice on what you can do in each situation. You should always remember that you're not alone and, if you're struggling, reach out for help and contact your careers centre and/or the author of this guide at steventhomasrook@ yahoo.co.uk.

I still don't have a clue what to do next because everything's got on top of me!

Like any project, career planning can be daunting and, sometimes, overwhelming. This is quite natural because there are just so many factors to consider and you're bound to get snowed under from time to time. Therefore, you need to take the pressure off yourself, stand back from your problems and systematically plan your way forward one step at a time. Review Part II and take your time over the activities.

How can I have more fun in life?

The answer to this question could go on forever but, in terms of careers ...

Because jobs are so linked to success, people often forget that they're also meant to be fun. In fact, you'll only probably succeed if they are! Therefore, if you're procrastinating because you want to delay your inevitable progress into some boring career, then you're not thinking straight. If the career options you're contemplating are boring then why on earth are you considering them? Throw any uninspiring roles into the bin and look for positions that make you excited. Someone has to be an advertising copywriter, a Premiership football coach or Prime Minister. Why shouldn't it be you?

Nonetheless, whatever role you choose you will almost certainly have to undertake any number of unfulfilling positions to get to your destinations, but it won't be so bad if you make constant progress and always have a view of the sunny uplands ahead! See Part II.

Help! I lack direction

This could be down to a number of factors from a lack of aspiration to just not being interested in any of the jobs you've seen. Students and new graduates commonly face this dilema if they've forgotten how to dream. You need to fight this and find something inspirational. There are hundreds of thousands of roles out there, so there must be something for you! Genuine passion will also help you force your way into a fulfilling role, so start dreaming! See Part III.

Why can't I find any fulfilling occupations?

Three of the more common factors restricting a successful job search are listed below – which ones are holding you back?

- **You're not looking widely enough:** The majority of graduates don't look further than the obvious options such as teaching, accountancy and the various graduate training programmes. In fact, these popular careers constitute only a tiny fraction of graduate destinations in full and there are numerous less obvious roles such as flying planes, managing national parks and designing dresses.
- **You're looking for jobs not a career:** Most of the time, you'll have to gradually work your way into your chosen role via activities such as voluntary work, alternative roles and postgraduate study.
- **You're not taking things seriously enough:** Knuckle down, you've only got one life – live it!

Whatever's holding you back, don't put yourself down. In fact, it's important to do exactly the opposite. Take time over the exercises in Part II and allow yourself to dream. There are probably millions of wonderful roles out there that will suit you down to the ground – you just need the confidence to look, and turn your dreams into reality.

What if I haven't got a 2.1?

An ever-increasing number of graduate employers require a 2.1. You have various options if you don't fall into this lucky group:

- Apply before you graduate and state an expectation of a 2.1 – you may be lucky and still get in with lower grades.
- Contact the organisations and ask if you can still apply as you have a good reason for your failure to achieve the grades you expected. Don't just enter your lower degree classification into the normal application forms because they will probably be immediately rejected, often by a computer!
- Look for employers in your chosen sector who aren't so grade sensitive (usually the smaller ones who don't advertise their positions so aggressively).
- Get so much experience that you can't be refused.
- Look for any old job in the sector you want to enter and work your way up into the job you want.
- Try a different role for a while.

See Part I.

Help, I don't have the skills I need!

Careers are a continuous lifelong process of skill development, so don't panic if you've still got some way to go! If you're struggling, establish a few more basic steps at the start of your journey, such as a voluntary position and/or a part-time job, and steadiy develop your skills so you can make steady progress. See Part III.

How can I find a job in my chosen field?

The number of graduates has increased tenfold since the early 1960s, but so has the number of graduate jobs. Therefore, there are still plenty of opportunities.

However, the route into graduate careers has changed markedly. A far smaller percentage of students go directly into traditional graduate training programmes and graduates often have to tread long and circuitous paths to get to their career destinations.

Therefore, if you can't find any jobs, there are probably still paths into your chosen career that are just less direct and obvious, so you'll have to be more creative. For example, if you can't find roles as a dietician, maybe you could undertake some specialised training, look abroad or develop your skills in a related field (such as counselling) until the job market recovers. See Parts I and II.

I apply for loads of jobs but no one wants me!

This could be down to any or all of the reasons outlined below:

- **Your applications aren't up to scratch:** The vast majority of application forms and CVs are rushed, untargeted and full of spelling/grammar mistakes – what about yours? If you can see room for improvement, look at Part V and take it from there. Remember: it is not a numbers game – you should be spending 20 hours or so on each CV and/or application form.
- **You don't have the attributes required:** If you are missing some of the crucial skills required in your chosen occupation, you might want to take some time to develop them in a voluntary position, a postgraduate course or in a less competitive position.
- **You've just been unlucky:** Employers often have to sieve through hundreds of applications and can dismiss them for the most unlikely reasons – so persevere.
- **The employers don't know you:** You'll probably stand a much greater chance of getting an interview if you know the employer, so start networking and trying to get to know some key people in the sector – see Chapter 8.

Help, I've had a break and have nothing on my CV!

Your degree will always indicate that you are a skilled and committed person, but it's only the start, because you also need experience. However, it's never too late to start your journey. Therefore, you should take stock of where you are, where you want to be and how you plan to get there. Also, don't dismiss your existing experience, as it will be invaluable to employers. For example, if you've been a homemaker for a few years, you will be able to demonstrate your ability to manage and organise your time and deal with pressure. Your next steps could include further training, more experience, voluntary positions or anything else that will help you move on. See the first half of this book.

What if I don't know anyone who can help?

Everyone has the opportunity to make good connections. Firstly, your friends and family will have useful links (e.g. your mum's dog-walker may have a brother in your chosen industry). Secondly, your employer and work colleagues will know people (e.g. if you work at a restaurant and want to get into marketing, who does their advertising?). Finally, link your online networking strategy to local employer events and maximise your profile. See Chapter 8. If you just need advice, speak to a Careers Adviser or email the author at steventhomasrook@ yahoo.co.uk.

I think I need to take up some further study but what should I do?

Further education will give you extra skills, contacts and experience and therefore can be very beneficial in your career journey. However, many employers ascribe much more importance to employment experience. For example, the average graduate development programme at a blue-chip employer will look favourably on internships but often give less credit for a Masters, or even a PhD.

Therefore, if you are considering a Masters, or any form of further study, make sure it's part of a focused strategy to get into a specific career (not the other way around). Take more time over Chapter 10 and see what careers are linked to your favourite courses.

I've been doing nothing for a few years; does this mean I'm on the scrap heap forever?

No, it certainly doesn't! Your degree will always indicate that you are a skilled and committed person, but it's only the start – you also need experience. Therefore, you should take stock of where you are, where you want to be and how you can get there.

Don't dismiss your existing experience so readily as it will be valuable to employers even if you haven't had a typical graduate role. For example, if you've been a homemaker for a few years, you will be able to demonstrate your ability to manage and organise your time.

Your next steps could include further training, more experience, voluntary positions or anything else that will help you move on. See Part IV for more help.

All that's left to say is good luck, so … good luck!

References

1 Graduate employment and recruitment

1   Facts and Stats, Universities UK. Available at: www.universitiesuk.ac.uk/facts-and-stats/Pages/higher-education-data.aspx.
2   Elias, P. and Purcell, K. (2013), 'Classifying graduate occupations for the knowledge society'. Futuretrack Working Paper No. 5. Warwick Institute for Employment Research. Available at: http://www2.warwick.ac.uk/fac/soc/ier/futuretrack/findings/elias_purcell_soche_final.pdf.
3   HECSU: What Do Graduates Do? 2017/18. Available at: www.hecsu.ac.uk/assets/assets/documents/What_do_graduates_do_2017(1).pdf.
4   Engineering Degree Occupational Profile. Available at: www.prospects.ac.uk/careers-advice/what-can-i-do-with-my-degree/electrical-and-electronic-engineering.
5   HECSU: What Do Graduates Do? 2017/18. Available at: www.hecsu.ac.uk/assets/assets/documents/What_do_graduates_do_2017(1).pdf.
    HECSU: What Do Graduates Do? 2014. Available at: www.hecsu.ac.uk/assets/assets/documents/wdgd_september_2014.pdf.
6   The Graduate Market in 2017, Annual review of graduate vacancies & starting salaries at Britain's leading employers, High Fliers Research Limited. Available at: www.highfliers.co.uk/download/2017/graduate_market/GMReport17.pdf.
7   Annual Graduate Survey, 2016, AGR. Available at: www.justoncampus.co.uk/wp-content/uploads/2016-AGR-Annual-Survey-2.pdf.
8   Office for National Statistics, Graduates in the UK labour market: 2017. Available at: www.ons.gov.uk/employmentandlabourmarket/peopleinwork/employmentandemployeetypes/articles/graduatesintheuklabourmarket/2017#graduate-and-non-graduate-earnings.

2 Career planning

1   See: www.careerkey.org.
2   See: www.careers.gov.nz.
3   Krumboltz, J. D. (1996), 'A learning theory of career counseling', in M. L. Savickas and W. B. Walsh (eds), Handbook of Career Counseling Theory and Practice. Palo Alto, CA: Davies-Black Publishing, pp. 55–80.
4   Look up 'Mark Savickas and Life Design' – Theories Every Careers Adviser Should Know, at: www.runninginaforest.wordpress.com.
5   Look up 'The chaos theory of careers' – Theories Every Careers Adviser Should Know, at: www.runninginaforest.wordpress.com.
6   Pryor, R. and Bright, J. (2011), *The Chaos Theory of Careers: A New Perspective on Working in the Twenty-First Century.* Abingdon: Routledge.
7   See: www.graduate-careers.org/2016/03/21/dots-model.

4 Identifying your options

1 Tieger, P. D. and Barron, B. (2007), *Do What You Are: Discover the Perfect Career for You Through the Secrets of Personality Type*, 4th edn. New York: Little Brown.

2 Dunning, D. (2010), *What's Your Type of Career? Find Your Perfect Career by Using Your Personality Type*. London: Nicholas Brealey Publishing.

6 Boosting your employability

1 As quoted by Goldman, R. and Papson, S. (1999), *Nike Culture: The Sign of the Swoosh*. London and Thousand Oaks, CA: Sage.

2 Knight, P. and Yorke, M. (2004), *Learning, Curriculum and Employability in Higher Education*. London: Routledge Falmer.

8 Managing your networks and social media

1 Kelly, M. (2016), *Social Media for Your Student and Graduate Job Search*. London: Red Globe Press.

11 Taking time out

1 Catchphrase from the 1960s, developed by Timothy Leary.

13 Promoting yourself effectively

1 HESA, 'What are HE students' progression rates and qualifications?' See: www.hesa.ac.uk/data-and-analysis/students/outcomes

18 Psychometric tests

1 Taken from the Australian maths curriculum.

19 Succeeding at assessment centres

1 Meredith Belbin, R. (1981), *Management Teams: Why They Succeed or Fail*. London and New York: Butterworth-Heinemann.

Part VI

1 See: www.thersa.org.

23 Down the line

1 This list is loosely based on one in Littleford, D., Halstead, J. and Mulraine, C. (2004), *Career Skills: Opening Doors into the Job Market*. London: Red Globe Press.

Index

Note: Some page numbers are emboldened to indicate their particular relevance to the topic in question.